ROSS ECKLER

MAKING THE ALPHABET DANCE

ROSS ECKLER

MAKING THE ALPHABET DANCE

RECREATIONAL WORDPLAY

MACMILLAN

First published 1997 by St Martin's Griffin, New York

First published in Great Britain 2001 by Macmillan
an imprint of Macmillan Publishers Ltd
25 Eccleston Place, London SW1W 9NF
Basingstoke and Oxford
Associated companies throughout the world
www.macmillan.com

ISBN 0333 90334 X

1 3 5 7 9 8 6 4 2

A CIP catalogue record for this book is available from
the British Library.

Printed and bound in Great Britain by
Mackays of Chatham plc, Chatham, Kent

To

ON TRIMMING BRAD

The barber's a BANDIT. GRIM NORM,
Whenever he runs true to form,
  Charges Brad fifty bucks at the door.
When it comes down to BIRD-NAMING, "MORT"
Is Norm's name for his raven, whose forte
  Is to croak from his perch "Nevermore."
Norm'll frequently BRING ARM TO MIND—
Brad hears him complain "Life's unkind!
  From fingers to shoulder I'm sore!"
What Brad gets every MORNING: BAD TRIM
(The light in Norm's shop is too dim).
  Bad hair days are hard to ignore!

—Ross Eckler

CONTENTS

AUTHOR'S PREFACE

In the Introduction to *Language on Vacation* (Scribner's, 1965), Dmitri Borgmann bemoaned the low state to which recreational linguistics had fallen since the advent of the crossword puzzle in 1914. In contrast with its sister discipline, recreational mathematics, few word recreations of a genuinely intellectual nature were then to be found in print. Borgmann's purpose in writing *Language on Vacation* was to reverse this trend, to sensitize the reader to the beauty of such words as *subbookkeeper* (four doubled letters in a row) or *aftercataracts* (a word typed with the left hand only), and to teach methods for generating similar word specimens that dictionaries failed to list.

In the past thirty years there has been a renaissance of interest in recreational linguistics. Many books on the popular level have been written by such authors as Willard Espy, Gyles Brandreth, Tony Augarde, Paul Dickson, Harry Eiss, Richard Lederer, and Don Hauptman. In 1968, Greenwood Periodicals founded *Word Ways,* a quarterly journal addressed to the more recondite aspects of wordplay, with Dmitri Borgmann as its first editor. Since 1970, *Word Ways* has been privately edited and published by the author. The National Puzzlers' League, a group founded in New York City in 1883 to promote rhymed word puzzles and forms (word squares, word diamonds, etc.) popular in the nineteenth century, declined from four hundred to one hundred members between 1930 and 1970, but since then has regained its erstwhile size and vigor. National tournaments offering substantial prizes to the most proficient Scrabble players or crossword solvers have appeared in the last decade, and there is a renewed interest in word etymology, word usage, and modern jargon, as exemplified by the journal *Verbatim* and the newspaper column and books of William Safire. There seems little doubt that Dmitri Borgmann's 1965 objective has been realized.

It has become increasingly evident that the branch of recreational linguistics that views words as collections of letters to be manipulated is far richer and more subtle than anyone suspected. It is time to collect widely dispersed results, mostly published in *Word Ways,* and to show how they relate to each other. This book is not a history of wordplay (such a book remains to be written) but instead is an up-to-date picture of what has been accomplished in the field of letter-play. (This neologism is introduced to focus on the properties of words-as-letters, in distinction to words-as-phonemes or words-as-carriers-of-meaning.)

Following the structure of Hugo Battus's seminal work on Dutch wordplay, *Opperlandse taal- & letterkunde* (Querido, 1981), this book is arranged in parallel: expository text defining and describing the state of the art of a given letterplay topic, accompanied by figures: word lists, tables, and literary examples amplifying the basic text. Although it is not necessary to read these—the basic information is self-contained in the main text—the reader can gain considerable insight by a careful study of these figures. (In *Opperlandse* this provides the non-Dutch reader's only access to the text.) Each figure is identified by the two-digit number of the section in which it is found, with a lowercase letter (*a,b,c...*) appended.

One of the great joys of recreational linguistics is the chance to do original work, to discover new techniques or better examples illustrating old ones. Such contributions can even be made by the diligent newcomer to the field; it is not always necessary to serve a long apprenticeship mastering past results, as is the case in mathematics and the sciences.

The computer is having an increasing impact on the field of recreational linguistics in general and letterplay in particular. As dictionaries and other word-sources such as the national telephone directory by Phonedisc and the Social Security death records become available in computer-readable form, it no longer makes sense to laboriously search by eye for examples of words having certain properties. Already computers have taken over such sophisticated linguistic manipulations as the construction of large word squares (and the estimation of the wordstock needed to assure success), the calculation of the span of a word network, and the assignment of numbers to letters to maximize the number of self-referential cardinals. It should be relatively easy to program computers for other tasks as yet undone, such as the search for short pangrammatic windows (consecutive letter-sequences containing all letters of the alphabet) in running text.

There are two opposing views concerning the advent of the computer in recreational linguistics. Some feel that it takes all the fun out of activities like dictionary-searching, and cheapens the words thus found; others welcome it as a tool that can be used in partnership with human ingenuity to define and solve previously unattainable linguistic problems. Since it will be a long time, if ever, before every dictionary and literary text is placed in a computer file, there is room in recreational linguistics for either viewpoint.

Words are the raw material of any book on letterplay, and therefore one must decide at the outset what a word is. A necessary, but by no means sufficient, definition of a word is one used by computer scientists to process running text: a sequence of consecutive letters (plus certain symbols such as the hyphen and apostrophe) bounded on the right and left by spaces. Even this can be ambiguous; is a sequence of numbers a word? What about a mixture of letters and numbers?

One can say that a word exists if it is found in a dictionary. But dictionaries, to save space, do not always include inferred forms of words, such as plurals of nouns, past tenses of verbs, or participles. Obviously these must be allowed as well. But here, too, fuzz appears around the edges; what about comparative and superlative forms of adjectives? Dictionaries for years have formulated a variety of rules for deciding when -er or -est is to be preferred to more or most, but rigid rules often lead to examples which look and sound unnatural: *priestliest, beggarliest, gentlier.* The *Century Dictionary* flatly states that the prefix *re-* can be placed before any verb to form a new verb implying a repeated action; can one similarly treat other prefixes like *de-, un-,* and *non-*?

Dmitri Borgmann has eloquently argued that the dictionary is man's creation, not his master; there is no need to let it dictate the words he can use. If a hypothetical word can be formed from English-language elements (prefixes, suffixes, other words) in a manner analogous to that used in forming words already in dictionaries, then it is all right to do so. There exists a universe of words yet to be born, many of whose members we can deduce by logical argument. Alluring as this concept is, there is great potential for its abuse in the hands of less skilled or less scrupulous individuals, who may need a "word" to complete some linguistic structure and who may be tempted to bend, or even ignore, the rules of logic to obtain it. This is the reason for man-made laws and regulations in general; some men could behave admirably without them, but not all can be trusted to do so.

If dictionary appearance is to determine the admissibility of a word, which dictionaries should be allowed? Three reputable unabridged dictionaries, the Third Edition of the Merriam-Webster, the Funk & Wagnalls, and the Random House, are currently in print. There are also Webster's unabridged dictionaries offered for sale by discount bookstores or mail-order firms for as little as twenty dollars. More to the point, the *Oxford English Dictionary* Second

Edition (available both in book form and on CD-ROM) offers a rich trove of historical English, including variant spellings last used in Chaucer's time. Medical, technical, and scientific dictionaries provide additional thousands of words that, although hardly ever seen in newspapers, magazines, or general-interest books, are found in technical journals and understood by specialists.

Many recreational linguists are willing to admit proper names—either geographical placenames or personal given names and surnames—as legitimate objects of letterplay study. Placenames are generally available in gazetteers, but comprehensive lists of surnames have until recently been hard to obtain. In 1974 there were about 240 million surnames in Social Security files, representing nearly 1.3 million different surnames. Ninety percent of these are borne by one hundred or fewer registrants; thus, most names are unlikely to appear in the typical *Who's Who* or analogous biographical reference. In 1993 CSRA, a small firm in Irvine, California, placed on CD-ROM some 47 million recipients of Social Security who had died by then; the surnames alone can be downloaded to the hard disk of a computer for further analysis and manipulation. ProCD, a small firm in Marblehead, Massachusetts, has similarly provided on CD-ROM the names, addresses, and telephone numbers of all people listed in the white pages of U.S. telephone directories, but the surnames cannot be similarly downloaded. Unlike dictionaries and gazetteers, these have a considerable number of keypunch errors, and it may be prudent to independently verify the existence of some of the stranger-looking ones, particularly if borne by only one or two individuals.

If one decides to use placenames and personal names, further decisions must be made. Is the name of a small Albanian village found in a comprehensive English-language gazetteer admissible in English wordplay? If not, where does one draw a line between it and the largest city, such as Jakarta or Moscow? Are foreign surnames legitimate, if one can point to at least one bearer in a U.S. telephone directory? The boundary between English and other languages becomes especially fuzzy when applied to proper names.

Dmitri Borgmann's call for linguistic creativity took a new form with respect to personal names: he argued that any given name can be combined with any surname, since it is possible that such a person could exist, either now or in the future.

Even when one has satisfactorily decided all these issues, the job is not done, for one often encounters nondictionary neologisms in print. The most eye-catching examples are the "words" used in comic strips to denote various sounds or mental states. Less dramatic, but more prevalent, are hyphenated compounds of two or more dictionary words, like *Chicago-style* or *gallus-snapping*. And should one accept as words pronounceable acronyms like *VP* (veep) or also the ones spelled letter-by-letter like *TV*? One solution is to admit only those acronyms labeled with parts of speech in dictionaries.

The point is simple: each person must draw his own line between words and nonwords and, once having done so, communicate carefully to others what stockpile of words he is using. There is no right answer, and the purpose of the preceding paragraphs has been to sensitize the reader to the many choices that must be made.

In this book, many studies are restricted to the unhyphenated boldface entries in the Pocket Merriam-Webster, plus -*s* plurals, -*ed* past tenses, and -*ing* participles inferrable from these entries. If more words are wanted, the next step is to allow all the words in the *Official Scrabble Players Dictionary,* or, if words of eight letters or more are wanted, the unhyphenated boldface entries in either the second or third editions of the unabridged Merriam-Webster. Occasionally other dictionaries such as the *Oxford English Dictionary* are cited. Gazetteers and telephone directories are used principally to finish type collections of words not completable using standard dictionaries.

—ROSS ECKLER
May 1995

ACKNOWLEDGMENTS

I am most of all indebted to the late Dmitri Borgmann for demon-strating, in *Language on Vaction,* that the field of letterplay is not merely a collection of isolated curious results, but a connected body of knowledge. Perhaps more important, he founded the journal *Word Ways,* which enabled previously isolated logologists to share results and inspire each other to make new discoveries. I am mindful of the sympathetic support given by such established authors as Martin Gardner, Willard Espy, and Richard Lederer, who generous-ly (and frequently) mentioned *Word Ways* in their books, and by Scot Morris and Will Shortz in *Omni* and *Games* magazines. Without their help the logological community would be impover-ished. Among the scores of *Word Ways* contributors who have shaped my thoughts (and often pointed out new logological direc-tions), I salute Darryl Francis, Ralph Beaman, Philip Cohen, Jeff Grant, Ed Wolpow, Sir Jeremy Morse, Kyle Corbin, Tom Pulliam, Susan Thorpe, Peter Newby, Christopher McManus, Lee Sallows, and Leonard Gordon. The last three have been of particular help in bringing logology into the computer era, a development Borgmann would have deplored. And one cannot ignore the contributions of the artists and poets who view logology with a fresh eye: John McClellan, James A. Lindon, Howard Bergerson, Harry Partridge, and David Morice.

INTRODUCTION

Recreational linguistics and recreational number theory are forms of amusement as old as speech and counting. The ancient Chinese were delighted to discover that the digits 1 through 9 could be arranged in only one way to form a magic square with the sum of 15 for each row, column, and main diagonal. The Romans surely were similarly pleased to find that letters could be placed in square arrays so every row and column was a Latin word. Number play explores curious combinations of elements in the formal system of arithmetic. Wordplay explores curious combinations of elements in the informal system of a natural language.

Anagrams have strong analogies with number play. Multiply 142857 by any digit from 1 through 6 and the products are all cyclic anagrams of the original number. Pangrams resemble endless puzzles with numbers that contain all nine digits. Divide 987654312 by 8 and you get 123456789. A book could be written about theorems involving palindromic numbers. Lipograms are like problems concerning numbers and sequences that omit a given digit. Word ladders have their analog in binary gray codes. And so on.

With such strong similarities between number amusements and recreational logology, it is not surprising that so many mathematicians relish wordplay. One thinks at once of Lewis Carroll, who taught mathematics at Oxford University, and who injected so much entertaining wordplay into his writings and letters. Vladimir Nabokov was not a professional mathematician, but there is a close connection between his ubiqitous wordplay and his fondness for chess, a combinatorial game based on the formal system of chess rules. Nor is it surprising that Ross Eckler obtained his doctorate in mathematics at Princeton University in 1954, specializing in statistics. Throughout the next thirty years he advised Bell Laboratories engineers on statistical experiments and on probability models applied to missile defense and telephony. For more than a decade of that period he headed a small department of statisticians and mathematicians engaged in similar work.

Word Ways, the first journal ever devoted solely to recreational linguistics, started in 1968 with Dmitri Borgmann as editor. He was followed by Howard Bergerson in 1969, who in turn was replaced by Eckler in 1970. Today the quarterly is both published and edited by Eckler and his wife, Faith, from their home in Morristown, New Jersey.

Borgmann's two books, *Language on Vacation* and *Beyond Language,* were pioneering efforts to pull together what had been done in the field since Charles C. Bombaugh's classic *Gleanings for the Curious in the Harvest Fields of Literature* was published in 1874. Bergerson's *Palindromes and Anagrams* became another basic reference, along with several delightful books on wordplay by Willard R. Espy, Eckler's *Word Recreations* and *Names and Games,* and Tony Augarde's recent *Oxford Guide to Word Games.*

The volume you now hold, based mainly on contributions to *Word Ways,* takes up where the books cited above leave off. The new achievements are truly mind-boggling. No one knows the field more thoroughly than Ross, and his and his wife's own contributions are of the highest order.

Many discoveries reported in Eckler's survey could not have been made without the help of computers. All English words are now available on software that can be cleverly manipulated to obtain results about which precomputer logologists could only dream. There are programs that instantly generate all possible anagrams of a word, and can even create anagram sentences. Donald Knuth, Stanford University's eminent computer scientist, developed a program that cranks out minimal-length word ladders joining any two five-letter words, or proves that a ladder does not exist. Another Knuth program produces giant word squares. Computers now serve as aids in creating crossword puzzles, solving cryptograms, and cracking sophisticated codes.

I must not give the impression that computers are required for making new discoveries. Wordplay research is open to anyone who loves his native language, and who likes to explore unusual ways of putting together letters and words. Even if this fantastic book does not turn you into a wordplay addict, I cannot imagine a reader not enjoying and finding awesome what the field's experts have achieved.

—MARTIN GARDNER

ROSS ECKLER
MAKING THE ALPHABET DANCE

ONE
FORBIDDEN LETTERS, OBLIGATORY LETTERS

THE ALPHABET HAS twenty-six letters which can be used to form hundreds of thousands of dictionary words. Logologists delight in classifying and arranging these words in far more ingenious ways than the prosaic alphabetization of the lexicographer. This book explores many of these ways in detail.

This chapter considers restrictions based on the letters of the alphabet contained in the words. Historically, the oldest version of this type of wordplay is the lipogram, a literary piece in which a letter is forbidden to appear. Conversely, one can insist that a certain letter appear in every word of a text. In acrostical writing, the obligatory letter is placed at the beginning of the word (or line, in poetry). Alternatively, the obligatory or forbidden letter in a word may be determined by letters appearing in other words in the text.

Letter restrictions can be considerably more complex than mere prohibition or inclusion; for example, certain pairs of letters may not be allowed in the same word. This restriction sometimes is presented in mechanical form: think of the letters of the alphabet inscribed on a set of dice. Or, the alphabet is replaced with a reduced alphabet in which each new letter represents not merely itself but also one or more old ones, creating potential ambiguity; the most well-known example of this is spelling out words on the telephone dial.

11 LIPOGRAMS

The writing of prose or poetry in which one or more letters have been deliberately suppressed is a very ancient pastime. According to Georges Perec's "History of the Lipogram" translated in *Oulipo: A Primer of Potential Literature* (University of Nebraska Press, 1986) by Warren Motte, the first lipogrammatist was Lasus of Hermione, who lived in the sixth century B.C.; he excluded sigma from an "Ode to the Centaurs" and a "Hymn to Demeter." Other ancients indulging in lipogrammetry were Pindar, Nestor of Laranda, and Tryphiodorus of Sicily. The first lipogram that has survived to the present day is *De Aetatibus Mundi & Hominis* by Fabius Planciades Fulgentius, a sixth-century treatise of which fourteen of twenty-three chapters, each omitting a different letter, survive.

In English, the most ambitious lipogrammatic work ever published was the *E*-less novel *Gadsby* (Wetzel Press, 1939), written by Ernest Vincent Wright in the late 1930s. It is unlikely that more than a few hundred copies were printed, and the book is exceedingly rare. Despite the lack of the letter *E,* the prose seems quite ordinary, coherent, and grammatical:

> Gadsby was walking back from a visit down in Branton Hills' manufacturing district on a Saturday night. A busy day's traffic had had its noisy run; and with not many folks in sight, His Honor got along without having to stop to grasp a hand, or talk; for a Mayor out of City Hall is a shining mark for any politician. And so, coming to Broadway, a booming bass drum and sounds of singing, told of a small Salvation Army unit carrying on amidst Broadway's night

shopping crowds. Gadsby, walking toward that group, saw a young girl, back toward him, just finishing a long, soulful oration....

The book was written as a protest against the "dissipated hopes and energies" that F. Scott Fitzgerald's novel *The Great Gatsby* expresses; apparently Wright wished to counterbalance its negative picture of contemporary American life by showing how Mayor Gadsby, helped by the youth of Branton Hills, rejuvenated that moribund community. In the Preface, Wright explicitly states that his novel, dedicated to Youth, gives the reader

> a great deal of information about what <u>Youth</u> can do, if given a chance; and though it starts out in somewhat of an impersonal vein, there is plenty of thrill, rollicking comedy, love, courtship, marriage, patriotism, sudden tragedy and a <u>determined stand against liquor</u>, and some amusing political aspirations in a small town.

As a novel, *Gadsby* is dreadful, with cardboard characters routinely overcoming adversity in the manner of Horatio Alger heroes. In a penetrating analysis of the novel, Robert Ian Scott suggests that at least part of Wright's narrative difficulties were caused by language restrictions imposed by the lack of *E,* and speculates on the effect upon novelists of other types of exclusions.

One other modern novel has been written without the letter *E:* Georges Perec's *La Disparation* (DeNoel, 1969). Unlike *Gadsby,* this attained a wide circulation, and was so well written that at least some reviewers never realized the existence of a letter constraint. Gilbert Adair translated Perec's novel into English, and it was published under the title *A Void* (HarperCollins, 1995), still excluding the letter *E.* (The review in *Time* magazine also eschewed this letter.)

In general, writing literary works without a common letter is not difficult. Figure 11a shows what can be accomplished with the simple children's poem "Mary Had a Little Lamb," preserving both sense and meter when *S, H, T, E,* and *A* are in turn omitted. The final rewrite, far more challenging, omits half the letters of the alphabet.

Figure 11a   Mary Had a Lipogram (Word Ways [hereafter, *WW*], Aug. 1969)

Mary had a little lamb with fleece a pale white hue,
And everywhere that Mary went the lamb kept her in view.
To academe he went with her (illegal, and quite rare);
It made the children laugh and play to view a lamb in there. (S)

Mary owned a little lamb; its fleece was pale as snow,
And every place its mistress went it certainly would go.
It followed Mary to class one day (it broke a rigid law).
It made the students giggle aloud; a lamb in class all saw. (H)

Mary had a pygmy lamb, his fleece was pale as snow,
And every place where Mary walked, her lamb did also go.
He came inside her classroom once (which broke a rigid rule);
How children all did laugh and play on seeing a lamb in school.
(T)

Mary had a tiny lamb, its wool was pallid as snow,
And any spot that Mary did walk this lamb would always go;
This lamb did follow Mary to school (although against a law).
How girls and boys did laugh and play; that lamb in class all saw.
(E)

Polly owned one little sheep, its fleece shone white like snow,
Every region where Polly went the sheep did surely go;
He followed her to school one day (which broke the rigid rule);
The children frolicked in their room to see the sheep in school.
(A)

Maria had a little sheep, as pale as rime its hair,
And all the places Maria came the sheep did tail her there;
In Maria's class it came at last (a sheep can't enter there).
It made the children clap their hands; a sheep in class, that's rare!

The effect of excluding *E* causes about as much havoc as that of excluding *BCFJKPQUVXZ*. If these eleven letters are not allowed, the probability that a randomly chosen four-letter word in running English text can be used is 0.65, quite similar to the 0.58 probability that such a word does not contain *E*. For five-letter words, the corresponding probabilities are 0.47 and 0.43; for six-letter ones, 0.32 and 0.35.

One can write text with multiple letters forbidden. Howard Bergerson created a press conference with "Ronald Wilson Reagan" using only the eleven different letters of his name in his replies; Figure 11b presents excerpts from this which, remarkably, preserve the presidential philosophy. Bergerson had available only 75 of the commonest 500 words in the English language, in contrast to Wright, who had 250.

Figure 11b Interviewing "Ronald Wilson Reagan" (*WW*, Aug. 1982)

What is your reaction to critics of your Presidency? How does a former actor feel about the awesome responsibilities of the Presidency, with all the world his stage?

Derision or a dressing-down is as degrading as dredging sewage alongside a noose on a gallows ladder. I ignore; no one sees a lone leader's real sorrows.

Do you not agree that the burden of unemployment is disproportionately borne by minorities and youth?

Nonsense! A winnowing is needed! No wages, salaries down or nil, and dwindling dollars and earnings will signal a dire ordeal. Raw rigors will anneal and season all idlers' sinews, all dawdlers' soles. Gnawing rigors will also derail all sorrier losers, loners, ragged ne'er-do-wells, groggier winos, deadwood, illegal aliens, doddering nonagenarian New Dealers, addled ding-dongs, deranged weirdos, renegade swine and insane assassins, redressing gross wrongs, lowdown swindles and worse. Ergo, no dole is all well and good.

How would you sum up your foreign policy?

I'll now answer as an old agrarian landed granger. We are sworn nonaggressors; we need law and order, we disallow war as lawless and senseless, and in a larger sense we also regard war as, now and again, needed. A needed war is no dead-end or swan song, nor need we ride in war as no-good sinners on genderless geldings! We need androgens and derring-do! We need Old Glories, and seasoned soldiers garrisoned world-wide, generals in golden regalia, and raised dander! We need all-seeing world-girdling radar, sea-going sonar and liaison ensigns, newer DEW lines and earlier NORAD warnings, larger arsenals and deadlier arrows in silos, R-and-D on lasers, and goodlier anger! We need no

ring-a-ding dissensions and wild-goose rallies, nor do
we need addled ding-a-ling diagnoses on wielding
dread winged swords and daggers—or on wielding
God's own grenades! Ordained grenadiers alone assess,
and ordained godlings alone will wield God's sidereal
grenades riding on Odin's arrows. Godless Leningrad
warlords and roodless, religionless Red warriors sold on
Red-engendered Warsaw agreeings are as sidling
sidewinders in loose sand! In nine innings (I disdain
gridiron analogies) we will win—no one is dawdling!
We are leaning on oars! We and God will engage all
Red raiders, and, God willing, we will win odds-on!
No one dragoons or goads God!

The pinnacle of the lipogrammatic art is achieved by writing a
dialogue in which one person uses one half of the alphabet, and his
colleague the other half, as demonstrated in Figure 11c by Cynthia
Knight.

Figure 11c   Adelaide and Tony (*WW*, Aug. 1983)

Adelaide McCabe, a feeble hag, addle-headed dame
Tony Russo, worn-out New York tout, snoop

TONY: I'm back, Adelaide!
ADELAIDE: Ooo…your worn sporty soup-to-nuts tux!
TONY: Lambie, I came back…
ADELAIDE: Sorry, Tony. Not now. You run out on us. You
    run out on your own vows! Now you turn up.
TONY: A…kid?
ADELAIDE: Yup. Otto Norton Russo. Your son—Pops!
TONY: Age? He'd be…half a decade?
ADELAIDE: Two, now.
TONY: Aha. I'd 'a called him Jack. He'll call me Dad. I'll like
    him.
ADELAIDE: No you won't, sourpuss.
TONY: Adelaide, I am bad. I led a high, idle life. I fled…
ADELAIDE: Unwort'y!
TONY: I imbibed, I gambled, I blackmailed…I'm a cad.
ADELAIDE: Trust you now? Not to worry. Stop! Out!
    Won't put you up. Worst rott'n…
TONY: Adelaide, I became ill. I'm like a dead flame.
ADELAIDE: Poor Tony!
TONY: Blame me! Kick me!
ADELAIDE: Nuts to you!

TONY: Be calm, Babe. A Camel?
ADELAIDE: No. Port? Or...
TONY: Milk? Limeade?
ADELAIDE: O, wow. Run out now, out o' town!
TONY: I'll be back, Babe.

How best to split the alphabet? Philip Cohen discovered that the split that placed *senselessness* in one group and *chromophotography* in the other maximized the collective length of the separated words (thirty letters). It is better to maximize the availability of short words, weighted according to usage. Typically, one expects that one-half of two-letter words, one-fourth of three-letter words, one-eighth of four-letter words, and so on, can be used. These fractions might be raised slightly by grouping together letters commonly found with each other.

12 VOWEL LANGUAGE

In contrast with lipograms, other authors have written texts in which only one vowel is used. Some examples of univocalics are given in Figure 12a; *E* is easy, *I* and *U* the hardest to do.

Figure 12a Univocalics (*WW*, Aug. 1973, Aug. 1978)

I'm living nigh grim civic blight;
I find its victims, sick with fright.
In Mississippi, kids will nip
Illicit pills, think this is hip.
Insipid drips with dimwit minds
Mix trifling thrills with sickish kinds.

—MARY J. HAZARD

Three speckled eggs held eggs were men enshelled.
Egg-terms the three eschewed ('cheep,' 'peck,' 'peep,' 'nest').
Hens were the helpmeets meeker eggs felt best;
Yet these three pestered Eve herself; these yelled
"We'll get thee...pet thee...wed thee...bed thee...meld—
Beget! We'll gender speckled men, shell-dressed—
Men egg-descended, egg-redeemed, egg-blessed!
Eve let her sheen be seen...
        The eggs beheld

Her tender flesh, dewed cheeks, her tresses scented,
These excellences left the eggs demented...
Defenseless...heedless when she peeled the shells.
Eve well knew eggs were eggs, e'en ere she met them.
She let them wheedle, squeeze her. Then she et them.

—WILLARD ESPY

Most people can cite words containing the vowels once each in order. The commonest answers are *abstemious* and *facetious,* but other unabridged Merriam-Webster words are *arsenious, parecious, bacterious, arterious, caesious, affectious, abstentious, majestious, acheilous, fracedinous, acherious, acleistous,* and *annelidous.* All known Merriam-Webster examples end in -*ous; Dorland's Medical Dictionary* yields *catechicorum, arsenicosum,* and *arteriosum.*

Figure 12b is a type-collection of words with different arrangements of the vowels *AEIOU.* Of the 120 possible, 113 are found in the Merriam-Webster (*opaqueing* an inferred form).

Figure 12b   A Type-Collection of *AEIOU* Words (WW, Nov. 1969, Feb. 1970, Nov. 1993, Feb. 1994)

AEIOU facetious	AUEIO aculeiform
AEIUO Laeviturbo*	AUEOI aureomycin
AEOIU pandemonium	AUIEO marquisedom*
AEOUI haemofuscin	AUIOE cauliflower
AEUIO maleruption	AUOEI autosexing
AEUOI aneuploid	AUOIE authorize
AIEOU ambidextrous	EAIOU precarious
AIEUO antineutron	EAIUO sea-liquor*
AIOEU carillonneur	EAOIU crematorium
AIOUE grandiloquent	EAOUI reavouching
AIUEO antinucleon	EAUIO exhaustion
AIUOE radiculose	EAUOI tentaculoid
AOEIU apothecium	EIAOU pedimanous
AOEUI allotelluric	EIAUO semiauto
AOIEU amortisseur	EIOAU plesiosaur
AOIUE laryngofissure	EIOUA ventriloqual
AOUEI accoutering	EIUAO gesticulatory
AOUIE tambourine	EIUOA semicupola

EOAIU endocardium
EOAUI seroalbumin
EOIAU neostriatum
EOIUA dentolingual
EOUAI encouraging
EOUIA dentosurgical
EUAIO education
EUAOI euharmonic
EUIAO denunciatory
EUIOA equivocal
EUOAI neuropathic
EUOIA sequoia
IAEOU intravenous
IAEUO village burrow*
IAOEU citharoedus
IAOUE dialogue
IAUEO Lillabullero*
IAUOE disaccustomed
IEAOU tricephalous
IEAUO ierfaulcon*
IEOAU Dipterocarpus
IEOUA intercolumnar
IEUAO fieulamort
IEUOA interpulmonary
IOAEU lithofracteur
IOAUE violature
IOEAU micrometallurgy
IOEUA incommensurably
IOUAE discourage
IOUEA isonuclear
IUAEO linguaeform
IUEAO vituperator
IUAOE fistulatome
IUEOA Milquetoast
IUOAE insupportable
IUOEA immunotherapy
OAEIU hypotrachelium
OAEUI pyrocatechuic
OAIEU hoazineus*
OAIUE odalisque
OAUEI opaqueing
OAUIE novaculite

OEAIU overpainful
OEAUI overhauling
OEIAU oeciacus
OEIUA proventricular
OEUAI postneuralgic
OEUIA obsequial
OIAEU poplitaeus
OIAUE foliature
OIEAU moineau
OIEUA ovicellular
OIUAE continuable
OIUEA solifugean
OUAEI outcapering
OUAIE tourmaline
OUEAI housemaid
OUEIA volumetrically
OUIAE communicate
OUIEA bountihead
UAEIO quaternion
UAEOI quatrefoil
UAIEO unpraiseworthy
UAIOE ultraviolet
UAOEI ultramodernism
UAOIE ultraconfident
UEAIO numeration
UEAOI unreasoning
UEIAO pulverizator
UEIOA questionably
UEOAI undemocratic
UEOIA unmethodical
UIAEO Cuitlateco
UIAOE multiramose
UIEAO quindecagon
UIEOA unipersonal
UIOAE unimportance
UIOEA undiscoverably
UOAEI sulphophthaleins
UOAIE unorganized
UOEAI suboceanic
UOEIA uncongenial
UOIAE subordinate
UOIEA unoriental

*village burrow, marquisedom (1706 quote under marquisdom), Lillabullero (1759
quote under Lillibullero) and ierfaulcon (1590 quote under gyrfalcon) are in the OED;
hoazineus and Laeviturbo are in Nomenclator Zoologicus; sea-liquor is in the Century
Dictionary.

It is possible to assemble a complete type-collection of all two-vowel and three-vowel words (*AEIOUY* vowels); this is given in Figure 12c. A similar type-collection of four-vowel words (*AEIOU* only) contains Merriam-Webster examples for all but *IUUO, UUAU,* and *UUUO.*

Figure 12c   A Type-Collection of the Commonest Two-Vowel Words
(*WW,* Aug. 1987)

AA-AY	dAtA, ArE, sAId, AlsO, cAUght, mAY
EA-EY	EAch, wErE, thEIr, sEcOnd, rEsUlt, thEY
IA-IY	fInAl, tImE, wIthIn, IntO, InpUt, cItY
OA-OY	prOgrAm, OnE, nOthIng, tOO, wOUld, OnlY
UA-UY	hUmAn, UndEr, dUrIng, UpOn, UptUrn, stUdY
YA-YY	YArd, YEt, trYIng, YOrk, sYrUp, gYpsY

A Type-Collection of the Commonest Three-Vowel Words (*WW,* Aug. 1987)

AAA-AAY	AtlAntA, chArActEr, AgAInst, mAtAdOr, AbAcUs, AlwAYs
AEA-AEY	ArEA, hAppEnEd, AthlEtIc, cAmEO, cArEfUl, vAllEY
AIA-AIY	cApItAl, cArrIEd, trAInIng, ActIOn, mAxImUm, fAmIlY
AOA-AOY	ApprOAch, AnOthEr, AccOrdIng, bAthrOOm, ArOUnd, hArmOnY
AUA-AUY	nAtUrAl, vAlUE, AcqUIt, AUthOr, AUgUst, fAcUltY
AYA-AYY	mArYlAnd, mAYbE, AnYthIng, mAYOr, plAYfUl, gAYlY
EAA-EAY	brEAkfAst, ExAmplE, cErtAIn, rEAsOn, drEAdfUl, EArlY
EEA-EEY	gEnErAl, bEtwEEn, fEElIng, frEEdOm, chEErfUl, mErElY
EIA-EIY	spEcIAl, prEsIdEnt, bEgInnIng, pErIOd, mEdIUm, dEItY
EOA-EOY	pErsOnAl, bEfOrE, bEcOmIng, bEdrOOm, EnOUgh, thEOrY
EUA-EUY	EqUAl, prEssUrE, rEpUblIc, nEUrOn, pEndUlUm, cEntUrY
EYA-EYY	clErgYmAn, EYE, jEllYfIsh, bEYOnd, bEllYfUl, grEYlY

IAA-IAY	dIAgrAm, prIvAtE, brItAIn, chIcAgO, hIAtUs, fInAllY
IEA-IEY	IdEA, IntErEst, ImpErIl, dIrEctOr, lIEU, lIkElY
IIA-IIY	sImIlAr, InsIdE, crItIcIsm, mIllIOn, dIffIcUlt, dIgnItY
IOA-IOY	ImpOrtAnt, InvOlvEd, InvOlvIng, chIldhOOd, wIthOUt, hIstOrY
IUA-IUY	vIsUAl, fIgUrE, InclUdIng, InstrUctOr, stImUlUs, IndUstrY
IYA-IYY	shIpYArd, bIcYclE, IdYllIc, thIrtYfOld, cItYfUl, IIIYfY
OAA-OAY	sOnAtA, lOcAtEd, ObtAIn, pOtAtO, bOAstfUl, cOmpAnY
OEA-OEY	sOmEwhAt, hOwEvEr, sOmEthIng, gOvErnOr, pOwErfUl, mOnEY
OIA-OIY	sOcIAl, pOssIblE, pOlItIcs, pOrtIOn, sOdIUm, pOlIcY
OOA-OOY	prOpOsAl, lOOkEd, fOllOwIng, OrthOdOx, sOrrOwfUl, nObOdY
OUA-OUY	pOpUlAr, hOUsE, cOUncIl, hOUstOn, OUtpUt, cOUntY
OYA-OYY	rOYAl, OxYgEn, bOYIsh, bOYcOtt, jOYfUl, cOYlY
UAA-UAY	sUmAtrA, sUrfAcE, cUrtAIn, bUffAlO, qUAntUm, sUndAY
UEA-UEY	UndErstAnd, sUggEstEd, sUffErIng, lUnchEOn, sUccEssfUl, sUddEnlY
UIA-UIY	mUsIcAl, UnItEd, bUIldIng, UnIOn, frUItfUl, qUIcklY
UOA-UOY	qUOtA, pUrpOsE, sUppOrtIng, mUshrOOm, fUrlOUgh, trUstwOrthY
UUA-UUY	UsUAl, fUtUrE, pUrsUIt, UnbUttOn, cUmUlUs, lUxUrY
UYA-UYY	pUssYcAt, bUYEr, stUdYIng, bUsYwOrk, sUbphYlUm, UnshYlY
YAA-YAY	YAltA, YAlE, dYnAmIc, dYnAmO, sYllAbUs, sYmpAthY
YEA-YEY	YEAr, YEllEd, sYnthEsIs, YEllOw, lYcEUm, mYstErY
YIA-YIY	phYsIcAl, YIEld, lYrIcIst, lYrIchOrd, YttrIUm, tYpIfY
YOA-YOY	YOgA, hYdrOgEn, thYrOId, plYwOOd, YOU, sYmphOnY
YUA-YUY	YUccA, YUlE, dYsUrIc, YUpOn, YUzlUk, sYrUpY
YYA-YYY	sYmphYlAn, sYstYlE, pYgmYIsm, gYpsYdOm, sYmphYtUm, sYzYgY

13　CONSONANTAL CHARACTERIZATION

It is conventional knowledge that a word must contain at least one vowel; therefore, searching for no-vowel words should be a profitless exercise. However, this is not quite so. To begin with, there are many all-capitalized nouns based on abbreviations and pronounced letter by letter. Pocket Merriam-Webster examples are *TV, TNT, DDT,* and *TB.* If these are ruled out, the pocket dictionary still contains *nth,* as well as plurals of consonants, used in sentences such as "There are four *T*s in this sentence."

Moving on to the unabridged Merriam-Webster, consonantal possibilities widen. Interjections and onomatopoeic sounds are an important source: *grr* (sound of a dog), *hm* or *h'm* (expression of assent), *hsh* (hush), *pst* (to attract attention or enjoin silence), *sh* (hush), *st* (silence, quiet), *tch* (vexation or disgust), *tck* (surprise or displeasure), and *tst* (hissed sound enjoining silence). Other dictionaries augment these: *tprw* (sound of a horn) and *brrr* (shivering) appear in the *Oxford English Dictionary. Shh, tsk,* and *zzz* (snoring) appear in the Random House unabridged. The *Official Scrabble Players Dictionary* has many of these, plus *psst, pht, phpht,* and *tsktsk.*

A second important class of all-consonant words is provided by contractions such as *ch* (pronoun, an aphetic form of *ich*), *'ld* (contraction of *would* or *should*), *'ll* (contraction of *will*), *n't* or *nt* (contraction of *not*), *'rt* (contraction of *art*), *sh'* (elision of *she*), *'st* (contraction of *hast*), and *th* or *th'* (contraction of *the*).

There are a number of words in the unabridged Merriam-Webster that can be called pseudoconsonantal; they employ the letters *W* or *V* to represent vowel sounds. The use of *W* as a vowel has survived in Welsh and is reflected in borrowings such as *cwm* or *crwth.* Other words of this type are invariably obsolete spellings that were last used centuries ago but are preserved in the *Oxford English Dictionary: brwk* (brook), *bwrgh* (burg), *dwr* (door), and so on.

All-consonant words can be found in nondictionary sources such as foreign placenames in gazetteers (*Krk* in the former Yugoslavia and *Llwchwr* in Wales both appear in the unabridged

Merriam-Webster gazetteer). There are all-consonant surnames (*Ng* is probably the most common one), and many coinages found in comic strips (*mrmf, rrrr, sknx, ggg,* etc.). Bowdlerization in older literature produces constructions like *h—l* and *d—m;* these are regarded as contractions.

14 ACROSTICS

If the first letter of a word is the obligatory one, one is dealing with an acrostic. Acrostics have been around for many centuries in various forms: (1) Poems for which the initial letters of each successive line spell out a name, such as that of the person to whom it is addressed, (2) Poems or prose consisting of words beginning with the same letter, (3) Poems or prose in which successive lines or words begin with *A, B,...* on through to Z. Examples are given in Figures 14a, 14b, and 14c, the first by Hector Monro and the last by Emily Schlesinger.

Figure 14a Anathema Alphabetica (*WW*, Aug. 1978)

Advertisers artfully agitate, alarm,
Browbeat, bluster, bombinate,
Coo, coax, caress, captivate, charm,
Delicately, doucely deprecate
(Denigrate? Desecrate?)
Examples eloquently explicate:
   "Elephantine endomorphs! Emancipate! Escape,
   Free from fatness, fell, foul, fateful:
   Great girth Gargantuan (gaze, girls, gape!)
   Huge hulking hams (Heavens, how hateful!)
   I invite inspection: I introduce
   (Justly jaunty) Juvenating Juice!
   Kissably kempt keeps Kitchen Kate,
   Lately lachrymosely lumpish,
   Languishing lads lasciviate
   (Miserably, morosely mumpish)
   Madcap maidens merrily mismate
   (Novice now nurses neonate)
   Over overcoming odious overweight!
   (Others offer only opiates,
   Ours obesity obliterates!)"

Pious purple prose proliferates,
Quakerish questionings quietly quelling,
(Religion's rentable—reasonable rates—)
Sermonized saccharine sanctifies selling.
Televised treacle triples takings,
Urging uglier undertakings:
Uncouth, ululating urchins,
Vacuous, vain, voluptuous virgins!
Violent vulgarity's vapid void's
What we weakly, wearily witness,
Watching Waspish, wog-whipping, witless
Xenophobic xanthocroids!
Yeastier yet your youngster's yen:
Zoolatry's zany zenith—Zen.

Figure 14b   A Calendar Acrostic (WW, Feb. 1969)

JANet was quite ill one day.
FEBrile troubles came her way.
MARtyr-like, she lay in bed;
APRoned nurses softly sped.
MAYbe, said the leech judicial,
JUNket would be beneficial.
JULeps, too, though freely tried,
AUGured ill, for Janet died.
SEPulchre was sadly made.
OCTaves pealed and prayers were said.
NOVices with many a tear
DECorated Janet's bier.

Figure 14c   An Allegory (WW, Nov. 1981)

Adam and alert associate, agreeably accommodated, aptly achieved accord and amiability—ample ambrosias available, and arbors alone adequate against ambient airs. Ah, auspicious artlessness! Adversity and affliction attacked appallingly, as avowed antagonists, Adonai, almighty Author, announced, and Apollyon, archangel-adder, asserted. "Avoid apples and abide amid abundance," admonished Adonai. "Admire apples and acquire acumen," advised Apollyon. Alas! Apollyon attained ascendancy. Ancestor Adam's attractive associate ate, arch and alluring against an antinomian apple-tree. Adam ate also, amoral although aware. Abruptly, arteries and arterioles achingly awash, an ashamed and amorous Adam advanced and *****.

Awesomely aggravated, acerb and acidic Adonai arbitrarily abrogated all advantages, and archetypal adults, abased, abashed, and abandoned, absconded amid acacias, avid after asylum (although austere) and apparel (altogether attenuate). Away, accomplished adder! Audacious, ambiguous adjunct and augur, adroitly amalgamating appetite and agony! Adam, antique addlepate, accumulated arguments, and afterward appraised adders as abominations, apples as aphrodisiacs, and ardor as artful ambush. Adam's attentive associate aye adored Adam.

In recent years, there has been some interest in searching literary texts for naturally occurring (accidental) acrostics. *Games* magazine in 1980–81 ran a contest in which readers were asked to look for acrostics formed from the initial letters of successive paragraphs. The longest word found was *synonyms,* on page 10 of Elizabeth Graham's *Heart of the Eagle* (1978).

If one knows what word-lengths to expect in naturally occurring acrostics in a literary passage, one has a way of deciding whether a long acrostic is accidental or was purposefully inserted by the author. The most celebrated example of this nature occurs in Shakespeare's *A Midsummer Night's Dream*, in which the following passage spoken by Titania spells out her name in its initial letters:

Thou shalt remain here, whether thou wilt or no.
I am a spirit of no common rate,
The summer still doth tend upon my state;
ANd I do love thee. Therefore go with me.
I'll give thee fairies to attend on thee;
And they shall fetch thee jewels from the deep....

From studies of text, it appears that the average number of words of length i in a passage of n consecutive letters is given by the formula $2.2nS/26^i$. S is the number of words of that length in the allowed dictionary. There are approximately 100,000 lines in Shakespeare's plays. Applying this formula to the Shakespeare canon, the average number of seven-letter words in the Pocket Merriam-Webster dictionary spelled out by successive initial letters of lines in Shakespeare is $2.2(100,000)(4591)/26^7 = 0.13$.

Shakespeare allowed two letters of the acrostic to appear at the start of one line, which increases the likelihood of success by a factor of seven. However, the real coincidence is that the acrostic names the character speaking the lines, which reduces the 4,591 seven-letter words to one. It seems most unlikely that a speech by Titania would acrostically generate *titania* by chance!

15   TEXT-DETERMINED OBLIGATORY OR FORBIDDEN LETTERS

In the preceding sections, rules for including or omitting certain letters from words are objectively stated, and do not change from one word to the next (except when running through the alphabet in an acrostic). Howard Bergerson proposed that acrostics be made self-replicating. In the passage "Exquisite, Xavier! Quite unparalleled, I'd say, in textured esprit" the initial letters of successive words recapitulate the message. In Figure 15a Howard Bergerson gives a literary example of the automynorcagram ("mynorca" is a reversal of acronym).

Figure 15a   The Automynorcagrammatical Raven (*WW*, Nov. 1975)

Midnight intombed December's naked icebound gulf.
Haggard, tired, I nodded, toiling over my books.
Eldritch daguerreotyped dank editions cluttered even my bed;
Exhaustion reigned.
Suddenly, now, a knocking, echoing door I cognized:
"Eminent Boreas, open up no door!
Go, uninvited lonely frigid haunt!
Avaunt, grim guest—and roar!"
Distinctly, too, I remember
Embers dwindling into numinous orange death.
Delving elaborately, desiring tomorrow overmuch,
I labored—ineffectually numbing grief.
Outre volumes eloquently retrogressed my yearning—
Brooding on olden knowledge sorrowfully evoked Lenore!
Death's Regent, inscrutable, tragically called her—
Damsel a Godhead Unspeakable elected, rare radiant, evermore!

J. A. Lindon proposed an even more intricate literary construction, the reciprocal automynorcagram, in which two different passages acrostically refer to each other: "Some thoughtful and really intelligent new guests of Vera's entered, reading magazines, yet enduring my presence..." versus "Staring over my empty top hat, Olga's uncle grimaced, his thin features ugly like a nauseating draught...." Largely unsuccessful efforts have been made to generate automynorcagrams by computer.

Homoliteral and heteroliteral texts provide another example of text-determined letter inclusions. In the former, each word must have at least one letter in common with the preceding word; in the latter, no two consecutive words can have a letter in common. Examples of each are given in Figure 15b. Figure 15c, by Eric Albert, is a doubly homoliteral text.

Figure 15b   The Homoliteral Raven (WW, May 1976)

On one midnight, cold and dreary, while I, fainting, weak and
  weary,
Pondered many a quaint and ancient volume of forgotten lore,
While I studied, nearly napping, suddenly there came a tapping,
Noise of some one gently rapping, rapping at the chamber door.
"Oh, some visitor," I whispered, "tapping at the chamber door,
  Only one, and nothing more."

Oh, this night I, tired, remember, during winter's bleak
  December,
When each separate burning ember wrought its ghost on oaken
  floor.
Longing oft for bright tomorrow, grimly did I strive to borrow
From my tomes relief of sorrow—sorrow for one lost Lenore,
For one rare and radiant maiden whom the angels name Lenore—
  Nameless here for evermore.

The Heteroliteral Raven (WW, Nov 1976)

On a midnight, cool and foggy, as I pondered, light and groggy,
Ancient books and musty ledgers, not remembered any more,
As I nodded, all but napping, there I sensed a muffled tapping,

Very much a hushful rapping, just behind my attic door.
" 'Tis a guest, mayhap," I muttered, "knocking at my attic door—
    I can't judge it's any more."
Ah, so well I can remember, it was in the wan December,
As I saw the dying ember flash red light upon the floor;
Wishing for a sunny morrow, in my writings could I borrow
Any surcease of my sorrow?—pain so keen for my Lenore?
Ah, so fair, so cheerful vision, called to heaven, my Lenore,
    Away from us forevermore.

Figure 15c   A Double Homoliteral (*WW*, May 1983)

> When Herschel Chalutz, the pediatrician, started dating
> Sandra Greenblatt, Rachel (her mother) crowed "How won-
> derful! We wanted an attorney or doctor for our daughter's
> husband. Also, Herschel has such charming parents. They're
> quite wealthy, at least that's what Shuska always says."
> Sandra asked Herschel over for Friday's dinner. Conversa-
> tion centered around doctors' salaries. Rachel restrained her-
> self from mentioning marriage more often than necessary
> (seven times). Eventually Herschel screamed "Please, stop
> this intolerable meddling!" and departed. Rachel learned an
> important lesson: Don't count your boychicks before they're
> hitched.

A special type of homoliteral text results if one writes sentences
in which the last letter of one word is the same as the first one of the
next: "Old Doc came even nearer, revealing gold dentures, smiling
grimly. 'You understand, Delbert, that the extra assistance each hour
requires seven, not two, operators,' said Doc. 'Can't this stop perma-
nently?'" A literary example of such word chaining is given in Figure
15d. The only words that cannot be used in a word chain are *a* and
an.

Figure 15d   Winter Reigns (*WW*, Feb. 1971)

Shimmering, gleaming, glistening glow—
Winter reigns, splendiferous snow!
Won't this sight, this stainless scene,
Endlessly yield days supreme?
Eyeing ground, deep piled, delights
Skiers scaling garish heights.
Still like eagles soaring, glide

Eager racers; show-offs slide.
Ecstatic children, noses scarved—
Dancing gnomes, seem magic carved—
Doing graceful leaps. Snowballs,
Swishing globules, sail low walls.
Surely year-end's special lure
Eases sorrow we endure,
Every year renews shared dream,
Memories sweet, that timeless stream.

—MARY J. HAZARD

In October 1994, Will Shortz asked listeners of his Sunday program on National Public Radio to construct chain-link sentences, ones in which the last two letters of one word are echoed in the first two letters of its successor. Some of the results are exhibited in Figure 15e.

Figure 15e Chain-Link Sentences (*WW*, Nov. 1995)

The helicopter Ernest stole leaves escape perilous
Can an anteater erase several almost stonelike Kenyan anthills?
Rush showed editorial alarmism, smeared educational alliance
Broadcast station, once certified, educates estimable legions
The head administrator organized education on online networks
Those sensitive Verdi divas assail illiterate tenors
One neophyte teaches Esperanto to Tonkinese servant
Martha has aspirin in industrial allotments
Sage George Gershwin intones especially lyrical albums
Lineman Angelo loves escargot other erudite teammates eschew
First Stanley eyed Edith; then enraptured Edwin intervened
Frankenstein intimidated Edith through ghoulish shenanigans
Active vermin inhabit Italian antiques establishment
Madonna—naked!—edifies Estonia's asexual aldermen
The hearse sealed Edwin inside; death thus ushered Edwin into
    tomorrow
Staccato tones establish sharper, eruptive velocity
Two women enter erotic icehouse, seduce celibate teacher
The helium umbrella lacked edging
Wine never erases essential aloneness
Tina's Aswan anagram amazed Eddie
Demure Rebecca called Eduardo's ostensive verbosity tyrannical
Gauche hero romanced edgy gymnast

16   TELEPHONE WORDS AND POLYPHONIC CIPHERS

A polyphonic substitution cipher is one in which several different plaintext letters are enciphered into a single cipher letter or symbol. Perhaps the most well-known example of a polyphonic cipher is the telephone dial, in which the letters *ABC* are encoded by the number 2, *DEF* by 3, *GHI* by 4, *JKL* by 5, *MNO* by 6, *PRS* by 7, *TUV* by 8, and *WXY* by 9 (*Q* and *Z* have no numerical correlates). This is quite different from the well-known (monophonic) substitution cipher in which each plaintext letter is associated with a unique cipher letter; if *A* is encoded by *T*, then no other letter is also encoded by *T*.

Superficially, polyphonic ciphers resemble lipograms. In both cases, the reader is confronted with a message that contains fewer different letters than the normal twenty-six-letter alphabet. However, a lipogram is restricted to those words which contain the allowable letters, whereas a polyphonic cipher allows any word to be encoded. In lipograms, all the words look normal but thoughts must be expressed in circuitous ways; in polyphonic ciphers, the thoughts are normal enough but the words are not easily recognizable.

Polyphonic ciphers inevitably lead to ambiguity; two or more different words are encoded in the same way, and there is no way (outside of context) to tell which word is intended. For this reason, they have played only a minor role in cryptography. This section examines the following question: How should letters be assigned in a polyphonic cipher to maximize the chances of comprehension?

The degree of comprehension achievable depends strongly upon the number of different letters allowed in the cipher. One allowing fifteen or more different letters should be easily readable, whereas one with only five is bound to sound like an idiot mumbling Sanskrit in his sleep. Ten appears to be a reasonable compromise, and offers the chance to encode letters into digits.

The allocation of letters to digits was decided by a bigram argument: the letters were chosen so that the commonest bigrams found in English-language text are not confused with each other. For example, to avoid having the bigram *EA* confused with *SA*, one should not assign *E* and *S* to the same digit. By trial and error, it was possible to devise a cipher that distinguished the thirty commonest bigrams, and fifty-seven of the commonest seventy. The assignment arrived at was 1 for *E*, 2 for *TXZ*, 3 for *ACQ*, 4 for *ILB*, 5 for *OGJ*, 6 for *NPKV*, 7 for *RYW*, 8 for *SFM*, 9 for *HDU*, and 0 for the space.

Suppose that a message is written in this cipher; how does one decode it? Perhaps the simplest technique is to place the alternative letters in a vertical column, with the commonest letter at the top, and look for patterns of letters that form words. For example:

```
IN  SHORT  I  AS  AONNINAEH  IOTH  IR  SAITH....
LP  FDGYX  L  CF  CGPPLPC    D LGXD LY  FCLXD
BK  MUJWZ  B  QM  QJKKBKQ    U BJZU BW  MQBZU
    V                          VV  V
```

Reading along the top, the words IN SHORT I leap out at once. AS does not seem too likely a follow-on to I, but AM is a legal alternative. The next word is almost certainly a verb, but the top line is gibberish, and the next three words are equally unclear.

An improvement in the method of presentation is needed. Given two successive symbols, what is the most plausible bigram? For example, in the fourth word of the message above, AO is a very unlikely bigram, and CO the most plausible one. Presenting the most plausible bigrams at each stage, the message becomes

```
IN  SH    L  AS  A                D  I   MAL D AND...
    DORT  I      CONNINCED  IOTH   LY  S   ITH
```

This is far easier to read; the full message, in fact, is

> In short, I am convinced, both by faith and experience, that to maintain one's self on this earth is not a hardship but a pastime, if we will live simply and wisely.
>
> [*Walden*, by Thoreau]

Of the 128 letters in the message, the commonest-bigram scheme identified all but 11 to within two alternatives; even one really rare letter, *X*, was spotted.

Is there any practical use for a polyphonic cipher? Suppose that a telephone subscriber, instead of calling an information operator, was able to use the dial to query a computer for an unknown telephone number. With the surname alone, many ambiguities arise (for example, 22766 dials Aaron, Barno, Baron, Bason, Capon, Caron, and Cason) but these can be reduced or eliminated if additional information (first name, street address) is dialed in as well. Assume that eight numbers on the dial are allowed for the twenty-six letters. Surname garbling can be reduced by one half if variable-length sequences of the alphabet are used (AB/CD/EFG/HIJK/LM/NOP/QRS/TUVWXYZ) and by nineteen twentieths if any ordering is allowed (ADPY/BENZ/CMX/FKTW/GS/HU/ILV/JOQR). In fact, in a list of U.S. surnames, the commonest ambiguities are Garner-Garber, Kinney-Finney, Beal-Neal, Keller-Weller, Moon-Coon, Mooney-Cooney, Mullen-Cullen, Fay-Kay-Way, Dickens-Pickens, Tilley-Willey, and Finn-Winn.

If one is willing to work a bit harder deciphering a message, the number of symbols can be reduced from ten to seven, again using one symbol to represent the space between words. The decoding of this polyphonic cipher works on the principle that one should always select the commonest English word corresponding to a given sequence of symbols; the goal of cipher construction is then to assign groups of letters to symbols so that two relatively common words do not have the same sequence. It is possible to assign letters to six symbols in such a way that the twenty-four common two-letter words all have different sequences; however, it turns out to be necessary to confuse *AT* and *AM* in order to avoid some bad three-letter word ambiguities: 1 for *AKMT,* 2 for *IJLSZ,* 3 for *NPW,* 4 for *BDEQ,* 5 for *CORVX,* and 6 for *FGHUY.* For three-letter words it is useful to compile a 216-entry table listing the two or three most common three-letter words in each, as an aid in decoding a message. Some typical garbles are 151 *act-art-arm-Tom,* 621 *him-hit-fit,* 241 *set-let-sea,* 216 *say-lay-sky,* 254 *job-Joe-ice,* 513 *can-ran-raw,* 416 *day-bay-bag,* and 244 *see-led-Lee.* Four-letter words, distributed into 1,296 different boxes, produce far fewer ambiguities; the worst one is, probably, 6154 *have-face-gave-hard.* The probability that a randomly chosen word in English text is dominated by a commoner one (and, therefore, not used in the most likely decipherment of the polyphonic cipher) is 0.004 for two-letter words, 0.027 for three-letter words, and 0.046 for 84 percent of four-letter words. To test this cipher, the first sentence of W. Allen Wallis and Harry V. Robert's *Statistics: A New Approach* (The Free Press, 1956) was enciphered and subsequently deciphered as: "Statistics is a body of methods for making WILD decisions in the HAVE of uncertainty." The correct choices for the capitalized words were WISE and FACE, the second most common words with that encoding.

A dictionary of commonest words using this cipher has not been prepared for words of four letters or more; however, this could be readily prepared by computer using the Kucera and Francis sample of a million English-language words as a guide to commonness. It would probably be sufficient to compile such a lexicon for four-, five-, and six-letter words, inferring longer ones by letter-juggling.

Polyphonic ciphers have been proposed by other authors. Will Shortz introduced a game at the 1977 National Puzzlers' League convention that sorted letters into four groups according to vowels versus consonants and the presence versus absence of ascenders and descenders: *aeiou-cmnrsvwxz-gjpqy-bdfhklt*. Similarly, Donald Knuth suggested sorting the alphabet into eight groups according to letter width: *m-w-bdhknpquvxy-ago-cez-rst-fj-il*. Either method can be used to decode unknown messages with a moderate amount of trial and error. Both rely upon the shape of letters to aid in word identification, and might be mimicked by a very smudgy Xerox copy of the original message.

17   WORD DICE

Games involving the throwing of dice have captured the fancy of mankind for millennia; the *Encyclopedia Americana* states flatly that there is no period in history, and no nation, in which some form of dice has not been used. The mathematical theory of probability was founded in the seventeenth century by Pascal and Fermat, when they solved a dicing problem brought to their attention by the Chevalier de la Mere.

Word-game inventors have capitalized on this long-standing enthusiasm for gambling by replacing the numbers on the dice with letters; the game of Boggle is perhaps the most popular, but the games of Scrabble Cubes, Perquackey, Tuf-Abet, and Agony also employ dice.

This section describes various logological problems based on letter cubes and their generalizations. Little work has been done, and it is likely that these results can be substantially improved with the aid of a computer.

Suppose, to begin with, that one places twenty-four different letters of the alphabet on four dice. How should these be selected and allocated in order to maximize the chance that a word can be formed out of any four upturned faces? This is a very difficult problem to solve, even with a word list as small as the one in the Pocket Merriam-Webster. Allocating letters to dice according to *AIOUXZ, ECHKWY, BLPRTU,* and *CDFMNS,* one can form 277 out of a possible 1,296 words. If the same letter can be placed on more than one die, rare letters can be replaced with commoner ones. The allocation *AEIOTU, AEGHKO, BLPRST,* and *CDMNRS* generated 420 words.

It is more interesting to turn the question around and ask for that arrangement of twenty-four different letters on four dice for which the fewest Pocket Merriam-Webster words can be formed. David Silverman conjectured that it is impossible to exclude all words, and he is probably correct; the best allocation thus far found, *FJVQXZ, ELORTU, CHMPSW,* and *BDGKNY,* allows the words *cozy, sexy,* and *john.* (A fourth word is provided by the archetypical four-letter word for sexual intercourse.)

Dice can be generalized to contain any number of faces; further, different dice in a set can have different numbers of faces. This leads to many interesting but little-investigated word dice problems. For example, what is the largest number of different letters, each used exactly once, that can be placed on three dice so that a Pocket Merriam-Webster word can be formed no matter which faces turn up? It may well be ten, with faces labeled *CHMRS, AO,* and *PTW.* If repeated letters are allowed, then eleven letters are possible, and the dice are labeled *CHMRST, AO,* and *PTW.* The thirteen letters on four dice *CDFMPTW, LNR, AI,* and *E* yield forty-two four-letter words; the corresponding four-letter dice problem with repeated letters is unsolved.

Going to the opposite extreme, how many different arrangements of upturned faces can form words if all the letters of the alphabet are placed on three dice? For *AEIOUY, BDFKMPTWX,* and *CGHJLNRSVZ,* 194 out of 216 words are possible. *Q* has been omitted from the allocation because no words would be gained even if it were added.

Thus far, it has been sufficient to find a single rearrangement of upturned faces to form a word. A new and equally difficult class of word dice problems is revealed if one asks that, for every arrangement of three dice in a line, the faces can be turned until a valid word is formed. For three-letter Pocket Merriam-Webster words, the smallest number of letters that makes this possible is five: *NE, A,* and *TR* yield the six permutations *ear, era, are, ant, tan,* and *tea.* For four-letter Pocket Merriam-Webster words, *EOR, PAE, TLY,* and *SI* yield the twenty-four permutations *eats, east, eyes, else, rial, rite, pets, pest, ales, also, airy, pile, tops, lose, tars, lair, tire, liar, seat, iota, spot, sale, stop,* and *star.*

If one is allowed to both turn over and rearrange the dice to form words, other recreational linguistic problems can be formulated. For example, Martin Gardner asked readers of his December 1977 "Mathematical Games" column in *Scientific American* how one could place eighteen letters on three dice so that the months *JAN, FEB,... DEC* could all be spelled out. This problem is impossible to solve since there are nineteen different letters in the month abbreviations; however, W. Bol of the Netherlands solved it by using lowercase letters and inverting *p* to form *d,* and *u* to form *n,* as necessary. His solution to the problem: *jfm(p,d)go, (n,u)brysc, aeultv.* Using similar strategies, one can spell out all dates such as *sat 10 dec* with only eight cubes.

18 IS Q ALWAYS FOLLOWED BY U?

In English orthography, it is nearly always obligatory that *U* appear in a word immediately after *Q.* Perhaps the commonest counterexample is *Iraq;* the trade-names *Qantas,* an Australian airline, and *Qiana,* a synthetic fabric, also violate the rule.

In Figure 18a, a list of *Q*-not-followed-by-*U* words taken from six American dictionaries is presented. To avoid an unduly long list, capitalized words have been omitted, as have obsolete words in use in England or Scotland more than five centuries ago. Most of these last substitute *W* for *U,* as *sqware,* or *QW* for *WH,* as *qwere.* A handful of such words are listed in the first edition of the unabridged Merriam-Webster, and at least one, *acqwyte,* even appears in the second.

Figure 18a Must You Join the Queue? (WW, May 1976)

BATHQOL var. of *bathkol,* a divine revelation in Hebrew tradition

BUQSHA monetary unit of Yemen

BURQA var. of *burka,* a veiled garment worn by Moslem women

CINQ var. of *cinque,* the number five in dice or cards

CINQ-CENTS a card game similar to bezique

CINQFOIL var. of *cinquefoil,* a plant of the genus Potentilla

COQ a trimming of cock feathers on a woman's hat

COQ-A-L'ANE an incoherent or ridiculous story; a satire

COQ AU VIN chicken stewed in a sauce of red wine (Random House)

FAQIH a Moslem theologian

FAQIR var. of *fakir,* a Moslem mendicant or ascetic

FIQH Moslem jurisprudence based on theology (Random House)

FUQAHA plural of *faqih*

MIQRA the Hebrew text of the Bible

NASTALIQ an Arabic script used in Persian poetical writings

PAQ var. of *paca,* a South American rodent (Funk & Wagnalls)

QABBALA(H) var. of *cabala,* a mystical interpretation of the Bible

QADI a Moslem judge dealing in religious law

QAF the twenty-first letter of the Arabic alphabet (Random House)

QAID var. of *caid,* a local official in Spain or North Africa

QAIM(M)AQAM var. of *kaimakam,* a minor Ottoman Empire official

QANEH an ancient Hebrew measure of length

QANTAR var. of *kantar,* a Mediterranean unit of weight

QASAB an ancient Near East unit of length

QASABA an ancient Arabian measure of area

QASIDA var. of *kasida,* a laudatory or satiric Arabian poem

QAT (Q'AT) var. of *kat,* an Arabian shrub used as a narcotic

QAZI var. of *qadi*

QERE var. of *kere,* a marginal reading in the Hebrew Bible

QERI var. of *qere*

QIBLA(H) var. of *kiblah*, the direction to the Kaaba, in Mecca
QINAH var. of *kinah*, a Hebrew elegy
QINDAR var. of *qintar* (Random House)
QINOT(H) plural of *qinah*
QINTAR an Albanian unit of money
QIVIUT the wool of the undercoat of the musk ox
QIYAS analogical interpretation of Moslem law
QOBAR a dry fog of the upper Nile (Funk & Wagnalls)
QOPH var. of *koph*, the nineteenth letter of the Hebrew alphabet
QRE var. of *qere*
QRI (Q'RI) var. of *qere*
QVINT(IN) var. of *quint(in)*, a Danish weight
SAMBUQ var. of *sambuk*, a small Arabian dhow
SHOQ var. of *chogak*, an East Indian tree
SHURQUEE a southeasterly wind of the Persian Gulf (Funk & Wagnalls)
SUQ a marketplace in the Moslem world
TALUQ var. of *taluk*, an Indian estate including subtenants
TALUQDAR var. of *talukdar*, a collector of the taluk's revenues
TALUQDARI var. of *talukdari*, a landholding tenure in India
TAQIYA(H) outward Moslem conformity in a hostile environment
TAQLID uncritical acceptance of a Moslem orthodoxy
TARIQA(H) mystical communion; the Sufi path of spirituality
TARIQAT var. of *tariqa*
TRINQ an oracular statement in Rabelais' *Pantagruel*
WAQF var. of *wakf*, a charitable trust in Moslem law
YAQONA var. of *yanggona*, an intoxicating beverage (kava)
ZAQQUM a tree with bitter fruit, mentioned in the Koran
ZINDIQ a heretic extremely unfaithful to Islam

All unlabeled entries can be found in the unabridged Merriam-Webster.

The list could be lengthened by adding more dictionaries. Some examples: *muqaddam*, a headman, and *qi*, a Chinese borrowing meaning "life force," are in *Chambers Twentieth Century*; *qanat*, an underground tunnel, is in the *Dictionary of New English*; and *qcepo*, a form of the parasitic disease leishmaniasis, is in *Dorland's Medical Dictionary*.

A much more exclusive class of words is the one in which Q is followed by U but U is not followed by a vowel. These are given in Figure 18b.

Figure 18b   Words with *QU* Followed by a Consonant (*WW*, May 1976)

ALQUHAIR obs. form of *everywhere*

LONQUHARD obs. word for a small lodge or cottage

PIQURE a puncture or wormhole

QUBBA var. of *kubba*, a small domed Moslem shrine

QUHAIR var. of *quair*, an obs. word for a book

QUHILK obs. word for *which*

QUR(U)SH a monetary unit of Saudi Arabia

SQUDGE to ooze, as soft mud

SQUDGY squat and pudgy

SQUG a symmetrical inkblot, as in a Rorschach test (Funk & Wagnalls)

UMQUHILE formerly, of late

ZAQQUM a tree with bitter fruit, mentioned in the Koran

Kucera and Francis's million-word corpus of English-language text lists only twenty-one words with *Q* not followed by *U*. Of these, thirteen are *Istiqlal* or *Istiqlal's*, a Moroccan political party.

TWO
LETTER PATTERNS
AND DISTRIBUTIONS

MAN HAS BEEN intrigued by patterns ever since he first inscribed graffiti on cave walls in Neolithic times. Linguistic patterns are probably nearly as old as written language itself; the *SATOR* square and the Greek baptismal font that palindromically exhorts the user to wash his sins as well as his hands both date back to the earliest Christian era. Although recognizing the important role palindromes have played in the history of recreational linguistics, the purpose of this chapter is to show that many other word patterns can be discovered and appreciated by the wordplay aficionado. This chapter is distinguished from the following one by its emphasis upon *all* the letters in a word and their relationship to each other, rather than letter groups or single letters distributed within an otherwise immaterial word. The concept of letter distribution is closely related to that of letter pattern; it focuses upon the number of letters of different kinds in a word without regard to their position in the word.

The study of word patterns was enormously aided by the

1971–73 publication by Jack Levine of his computer-generated three-volume *A List of Pattern Words* of lengths two through sixteen letters. In these books, all words from the second and third editions of the unabridged Merriam-Webster, plus derived forms such as plurals, participles, and past tenses, were grouped together if they had the same letter pattern, such as *excess* and *bamboo*. Unfortunately, they were published in a small edition and have been long out of print and virtually unobtainable in the secondhand book market.

21 PALINDROMES

A palindrome is a word that reads the same in the reverse direction as the forward one, as *level, redder,* or *deified*. In English, most palindromes are seven letters or fewer; the only two examples of eight or more in the unabridged Merriam-Webster are *Malayalam* and *kinnikinnik*. The longest palindromic placename in the United States is probably *Wassamassaw,* a swamp in South Carolina. Languages addicted to the stringing-together of words into long compounds, such as Dutch, German, or Finnish, are more likely to generate really long palindromes such as *parterretrap* (a first-floor stairway), *reliefpfeiler* (a relief-decorated architectural column or pillar), or *saippuakivikauppias* (a soap dealer). In an effort to rectify this, various authors have proposed plausible coinages such as *detartrated,* or extended the concept of a word to include a hyphenated word or dictionary phrase such as *race car* or *stent nets*. Perhaps the most famous palindromic phrase is *Yreka Bakery,* the name of a former commercial establishment in Yreka, California. This oddity was first mentioned in the 1866 volume of *Our Young Folks,* a magazine for children. Figure 21a gives a type-collection of palindromic two-word combinations with all possible splits represented.

Figure 21a A Type-Collection of Palindromic Word Pairs (*WW*, Aug. 1979)

o-go, as-a
l-eel, no-on, add-a
a-pupa, to-pot, not-on, agog-a
y-array, we-Llew, are-era, pull-up, belle-b
a-minima, so-memos, top-spot, daft-fad, noses-on, potato-p

g-nipping, an-Innina, Ona-llano, trap-part, tepee-pet, simoom-is, grammar-g

y-rotatory, no-stetson, eta-pupate, evil-olive, truck-curt, eroded-ore, forever-of, igniting-I

h-cailliach, li-keffekil, dey-allayed, lair-oorial, rebut-tuber, burgee-grub, burette-rub, rosettes-or, ?????????-?

?-?????????, ai-Rotatoria, nib-urorubin, live-nonevil, drawn-onward, regnal-anger, trapeze-part, sublevel-bus, underbred-nu, levitative-l

?-??????????, ??-?????????, eta-collocate, emit-noontime, retem-oometer, diaper-repaid, referee-refer, bardelle-drab, cordelled-roc, castallets-ac, ??????????-?

s-sensuousness, ??-?????????, set-apocopates, name-garageman, model-titledom, onager-oregano, reliant-nailer, relapses-paler, rosanilin-asor, hawsepipes-wah, ??????????-??, ???????????-?

... rete-millimeter, Setim-Assamites, ??????-????????, reified-deifier trigness-engirt, Saramacca-maras, remodelled-omer,...

... noit-apocopation, supra-Conocarpus, redart-nontrader, retinue-reuniter, dioramas-amaroid, enamorata-Romane, nigranilin-argin, analyticity-lana,...

... Etanim-effeminate, ???????-?????????, desserts-stressed,...

... Etanim-regerminate, ???????-?????????, laciness-Essenical, redrawers-rewarder,...

... rotatively-levitator,...

If any word or phrase from a printed source is allowed, including palindromes in other languages, thousands can be identified. Jeff Grant's *Palindromicon*, published in 1992 as part of the Word Ways Monograph Series, lists 2,332 with brief definitions; he includes a certain number of reasonable coinages as well, such as *derotored* or *reteeter*. Figure 21b hints at the richness of this corpus by exhibiting a complete set of three-letter palindromes from *AAA* to *AZA*.

Figure 21b Palindromes from *AAA* to *AZA* (WW, Nov. 1982)

AAA chief of the signet-bearers in the land of Kens (*Archaic Dict.*)
ABA an altazimuth for either astronomical or terrestrial use
ACA var. of *Aka,* an African Pygmy group (*New Cent. Cyclopedia*)
ADA a village in Hardin County, Ohio (*Webster's Geog. Dict.*)
AEA the chief town of ancient Colchis (*Webster's Geog. Dict.*)
AFA a river in Tahiti (*Times Index-Gazetteer*)
AGA a commander or chief officer in the Ottoman Empire (*OED*)
AHA expression of surprise, triumph, satisfaction, or irony (*OED*)
AIA var. of *ayah,* an Indian nurse or maid (*Chambers Twentieth*)
AJA a town in lower Egypt (*Columbia-Lippincott Gazetteer*)

AKA any of several species of a woody New Zealand vine
ALA a side apartment or recess in a Roman house (*OED*)
AMA the float of a Hawaiian outrigger canoe
ANA notes and scraps of information about a person or place (*OED*)
AOA a town and bay in American Samoa (*Times Index-Gazetteer*)
APA a valuable timber tree of the Guianas and northern Brazil
AQA in Aqa Hasan, a populated place in Iran (*Off. Standard Names Gaz.*)
ARA a genus of macaws
ASA a biblical king of Judah
ATA a predominantly pagan people of central Mindanao, Philippines
AUA an island in the Bismarck Archipelago (*Times Index-Gazetteer*)
AVA var. of *kava,* an intoxicating beverage of central Polynesia
AWA eighteenth- to nineteenth-century Scottish form of away (*OED*)
AXA a name appearing in the Douay Bible
AYA the consort of Shamash in Babylonian religion
AZA another name found in the Douay Bible

Unattributed definitions are found in the unabridged Merriam-Webster.

Palindromic phrases and sentences such as *A man, a plan, a canal—Panama!* and *Was it a bat I saw?* have been popular for a century or so; fine collections can be found in many sources, such as Dmitri Borgmann's *Language on Vacation* (Scribner's, 1965) and Howard Bergerson's *Palindromes and Anagrams* (Dover, 1973). No doubt the largest collection of palindromic phrases and sentences (more than seven thousand) has been compiled by Stephen Chism, whose *From A to Zotamorf: The Dictionary of Palindromes* was published in the Word Ways Monograph Series in 1991. Figure 21c presents one hundred palindromes by Leigh Mercer, perhaps the most noted palindromist of all time.

Figure 21c Leigh Mercer's 100 Palindromes in Notes & Queries
(*WW*, Aug. 1991)

Rise to vote, sir / Name now one man / Was it a rat I saw? / In a regal age ran I / "Rats gnash teeth," sang star / No slender evil was I ere I saw live red Nelson / Tense, I "snap" Sharon's roses, or Norah's pansies net /"Stop!" nine myriad murmur, "put up rum, rum, dairymen, in pots" / See, slave, I demonstrate yet arts no medieval sees / Desserts I'd reviled, drawn onward, deliver distressed

Live time, never even emit evil / "Now saw ye no mosses or foam, or a redder aroma of roses"—so money was won / Now Ned I am a maiden won / Here so long? No loser, eh? / Trade ye no mere moneyed art / Dora tones area; erase not a rod / Evil is the name of a foeman as I live / In airy Sahara's level, Sarah a Syrian I / Ban campus motto "Bottoms up, MacNab" / Bob, a Sugar Pool's foreman, madam, namer of sloop *Ragusa Bob*

No dot nor Ottawa "legal age" law at Toronto, Don / I made Border bards' drowsy swords: drab, red-robed am I / Now ere we nine were held idle here, we nine were won / "Deliver," demanded Nemesis, "emended, named, reviled" / Egad, a base life defiles a bad age / Name I, Major-General Clare, negro Jamie Man / No; relate, Mat, Aesop's Elba Fables—pose a tame tale, Ron / "Reviled did I live," said I, "as evil I did deliver" / I saw desserts, I'd no lemons, alas, no melon, distressed was I / Now debonair dahlias, poor, drop or droop—sail, Hadrian, Obed won

Live not on evil / Sue, dice, do, to decide us / Ah, Aristides opposed it, sir, aha! / Paget saw an inn in a waste gap / Diapered art as a trade repaid / Sir, I demand—I am a maid named Iris / No, set a maple here, help a mate, son / "Slang is not suet, is it?" Euston signals / Rise, morning is red, no wonder-sign in Rome, sir / Doom, royal panic, I mimic in a play or mood

Salisbury Moor, sir, is roomy; rub, Silas / Are we not drawn onward, we few, drawn onward to new era? / 'Tis Ivan, on a visit / See few owe fees / "Not New York," Roy went on / Poor Dan is in a droop / Harass sensuousness, Sarah / Yawn a more Roman way / Won't lovers revolt now? / No mists or frost, Simon

Never a foot too far, even / "Now dine," said I as Enid won / A man, a plan, a canal—Panama / I saw thee, madame, eh, 'twas I / Draw, O Caesar, erase a coward / Resume so pacific a pose, muser / "Pooh," smiles Eva, "have Selim's hoop" / Six at party, no pony-trap, taxis / "Not for Cecil?" asks Alice Crofton / No, I save on final plan if no evasion

Pull a bat, I hit a ball up / Red root put up to order / Selim's tired, no wonder, it's miles / Refasten gipsy's pig-net safer /

Tennis set won now Tess in net / Draw pupil's lip upward / Sums are not set as a test on Erasmus / Nurse's onset abates, noses run / Lapp, Mac? No sir, prison-camp pal / Egad, Loretta has Adams as mad as a hatter—old age?

Sue, Tom smote us / Too bad, I hid a boot / Anne, I stay a day at Sienna / Too far, Edna, we wander afoot / Nurse, I spy gypsies, run! / Drab as a fool, as aloof as a bard / Goddesses so pay a possessed dog / Reg, no lone car won, now race no longer / Mother Eve's noose we soon sever, eh, Tom? / Saladin enrobes a baroness, Senora—base-born Enid, alas

Niagara, O roar again / Deer frisk, sir, freed / Dora tendered net, a rod / No word, no bond—row on / Did Hannah say as Hannah did? / So remain a mere man—I am Eros / A gas, an age, bore Cicero, began a saga / Yes, Mark, cable to hotel "Back Ramsey" / Yale democrats edit "Noon-tide Star"— come, delay / Stephen, my lad—ah, what a hymn, eh, pets?

Ten dip a rapid net / Pull up if I pull up / Di, did I as I said I did? / So may Obadiah aid a boy, Amos / Remit Rome cargo to Grace Mortimer / Tide-net safe soon, Alin—a manila noose fastened it / Gate-man sees name, garage-man sees name-tag / Pusillanimity obsesses Boy Tim in "All Is Up" / Yes, Syd, Owen saved Eva's new Odyssey / Anne is not up-to-date, godmother, eh? Tom, do get a dot put on Sienna

References: 1–12 7 Sep. 1946, 13–30 2 Nov. 1946, 31–42 10 Jan. 1948, 43–51 16 Oct. 1948, 52–60 13 Nov. 1948, 61–70 8 Jul. 1950, 71–80 30 Aug. 1952, 81–100 Feb. 1953.

Palindromic phrases can be cleverly woven together to form a story, as illustrated by J. A. Lindon in Figure 21d.

Figure 21d In Eden, I (WW, Nov. 1970)

ADAM: Madam—
EVE: Oh, who—
ADAM: [No girl-rig on!]
EVE: Heh?
ADAM: Madam, I'm Adam.
EVE: Name of a foeman?
ADAM: O, stone me! Not so.
EVE: Mad! A maid I am, Adam.
ADAM: Pure, eh? Called Ella? Cheer up.
EVE: Eve, not Ella. Brat-star ballet on? Eve.
ADAM: Eve?

EVE: Eve maiden name. Both sad in Eden? I dash to be
    manned. I am Eve.
ADAM: Eve. Drowsy baby's word. Eve.
EVE: Mad! A gift. I fit fig, Adam—
ADAM: On, hostess? Ugh! Gussets? Oh, no!
EVE: ? ? ?
ADAM: Sleepy baby peels.
EVE: Wolf! Low!
ADAM: Wolf? Fun, so snuff "low."
EVE: Yes, low. Yes, nil on, no linsey-wolsey.
ADAM: Madam, I'm Adam.
        Named under a ban, a bared, nude man…
        Aha!
EVE: Mad Adam!
ADAM: Mmmmmmmm!
EVE: Mmmmmmmm!
ADAM: Even in Eden I win Eden in Eve.
EVE: Pure woman in Eden, I win Eden in—a mower-up!
ADAM: Mmmmmmmm!
EVE: Adam, I'm Ada.
ADAM: Miss, I'm Cain, a monomaniac. Miss, I'm—
EVE: No, son.
ADAM: Name's Abel, a male, base man.
EVE: Name not so, O stone man!
ADAM: Mad as it is, it is Adam.
EVE: I'm a Madam Adam, am I?
ADAM: Eve?
EVE: Eve mine. Denied, a jade in Eden, I'm Eve.
ADAM: No fig. [Nor wrong if on!]
EVE: ? ? ?
ADAM: A daffodil I doff, Ada.
EVE: 'Tis a—what—ah, was it—
ADAM: Sun ever. A bare Venus.
EVE: 'S pity! So red, ungirt, rig-nude, rosy tips—
ADAM: Eve is a sieve!
EVE: Tut-tut!
ADAM: Now a seesaw on—
EVE: On me? [O poem!] No!
ADAM: Aha!
EVE: I won't! O not now, I—
ADAM: Aha!
EVE: NO! O God, I—[Fit if I do?] Go on.
ADAM: Hrrrrrrh!
EVE: Wow! Ow!
ADAM: Sores? [Alas, Eros!]
EVE: No, none. My hero! More hymen, on, on—
ADAM: Hrrrrrrrrrh!

EVE: Revolting! Is error! Resign it, lover!
ADAM: No, not now I won't. On, on—
EVE: Rise, sir!
ADAM: Dewy dale, cinema-game—nice lady wed?
EVE: Marry an Ayr ram!
ADAM: Rail on, O liar!
EVE: Live devil!
ADAM: Diamond-eyed no-maid!
EVE: Mmmmmmmmmmmmmm!

However, it is only since 1970 that palindrome constructors realized that palindromic phrases and sentences could be made as long as one pleased, providing that not too much overall sense was required. Most read like the ravings of a maniac. They make local sense, albeit with strained syntax, but have the disconcerting habit of suddenly shifting the subject being discussed. The production of ever-longer palindromic stories was undoubtedly encouraged by the fact that, starting in 1971, the *Guinness Book of World Records* gave official recognition to the genre; from 1971 through 1980 the longest palindrome recognized by Guinness increased from 242 words to 11,125, a factor of 46.

At least two of these monster palindromes have been published in limited editions. David Stephens constructed a 58,795-letter palindrome, *Satire: Veritas*, "a gallimaufry of epistles, manuscripts, memoranda and critical notes found on the desk of Giles Selig Hales, editor of an avant-garde journal with literary pretensions but minuscule circulation," published in the Word Ways Monograph Series in 1980. In 1986 Lawrence Levine issued *Dr. Awkward & Olson in Oslo*, a "palindromic novel" of 31,954 words, in mimeograph form.

22 TAUTONYMS

A tautonym is a word of two identical parts, such as *beriberi* or *murmur*. Eight-letter tautonyms are not hard to find, but ten-letter or longer ones are unusual, particularly if written without hyphens; the only ones appearing in the unabridged Merriam-Webster are the ten-letter *Bellabella, chimachima, kerrikerri, quinaquina, strumstrum* and *Wallawalla,* and the twelve-letter *antinganting, chiquichiqui* (palm), *killeekillee,* and *tangantangan.* If hyphens are allowed, Merriam-Webster lists *bumpety-bumpety* (or *bumpity-bumpity*), and if spaces are allowed there is the eighteen-letter *per second per second.* The commonest sources of two-word tautonyms are found in the field of biology (*Buteo buteo*) and gazetteers, par-ticularly ones specializing in Philippine and Ma-laysian placenames.

The tautonymic concept can be extended to three or more repeti-tions. The only two unabridged Merriam-Webster examples, *tat-tat-tat* and *cha-cha-cha,* are hyphenated. There are many triple tau-tonyms in biology, as illustrated in Figure 22a.

Figure 22a   A Bestiary of Triple Tautonyms (*WW,* May 1983)

> *Bufo bufo bufo,* the European toad
> *Naja naja naja,* the black cobra
> *Alces alces alces,* the Scandinavian elk
> *Bison bison bison,* the Great Plains bison
> *Buteo buteo buteo,* the common buzzard
> *Gallus gallus gallus,* the Cochin-Chinese red junglefowl
> *Quelea quelea quelea,* the African weaverbird
> *Rattus rattus rattus,* the common rat
> *Caretta caretta caretta,* the Atlantic loggerhead turtle
> *Gorilla gorilla gorilla,* the coastal gorilla
> *Lagopus lagopus lagopus,* the willow ptarmigan
> *Redunca redunca redunca,* the Bohor reedbuck
> *Panthera panthera panthera,* the Barbary leopard
> *Capreolus capreolus capreolus,* the European roebuck
> *Francolinus francolinus francolinus,* the black francolin
> *Crossoptilon crossoptilon crossoptilon,* the Szechuan white-eared
> pheasant

Even higher tautonymic multiples exist. *Kukukuku* can be found in the unabridged Merriam-Webster, *Fofo Fofo* is a town in eastern Papua, and *angang-angang* is a Javanese gong described in Sibyl Marcuse's *Musical Instruments: A Comprehensive Dictionary* (1964). There is one seven-repeater: *bubububububububu,* a word suggestive of the sound of flight, appearing in F. G. Cassidy and R. B. LePage's *Dictionary of Jamaican English* (1967).

A literary version of the tautonym akin to the palindromic phrase or sentence is the charade sentence. This wordplay was introduced to American readers by Dmitri Borgmann in *Language on Vacation* (1965); typical examples are:

> Flamingo pale, scenting a latent shark
> Flaming opalescent in gala tents—hark!

> O, fly, rich Eros—dogtrot, ski, orbit eras put in swart
> of lyric heros. Dog Trotski or bite Rasputin's wart

Two more extended examples, constructed by James Rambo and Bonita C. Miller, are presented in Figure 22b.

Figure 22b   The Poet's Reply (*WW*, May 1977)

> Use fulsome howl or direst word in galling us; toil over a shoddy ode?
> Listen, dressed in gyves, tiger, allies fall, ensnared in timeless eras, mentally in agony, essays in gall.
> Outwit Hades, ignore verses, you real lover? Come!

> Useful somehow, Lord, I rest, wording all in gusto I love.
> Rash odd yodel is tendresse; dingy vestige rallies fallen snared.
> Intime, lesser as men tally, I nag on—yes, say, sing all out—with a design.
> O reverses, you're all overcome!

The Cynic's Soliloquy; Her Reply (*WW*, May 1974)

> Wit: howl on, gibe: rate the semen
> Of thy men "waste." Stedfast—be low!
> Be foul, men, ever. No moralist and
> Ho! nor able to go do good.

> With Ow! long I berate these men.
> Oft hymen was tested fast below.
> Befoul me never. No; moral I stand,
> Honorable to God. O, good.

23 SWITCH WORDS

Consider the four-armed box below, somewhat resembling a railway switch, containing twelve movable blocks. Select a word of twelve letters, and place one letter in each block. Then, in the fewest moves possible, slide the blocks one at a time into the vertical arms of the box, so that the word reads correctly from top to bottom. A move is defined as the sliding of one letter any distance within the box, including the turning of a corner if desired. However, the blocks may not be removed from the box, so that jumps of one letter over another are forbidden. The theoretical minimum number of moves is twelve; can one find a word transferrable from horizontal to vertical in exactly twelve moves?

This problem was originally proposed by Henry Ernest Dudeney, who discussed it in *The World's Best Puzzles* (London: The Daily News Publishing Department, 1925). He stated that this puzzle was sent him by Sam Loyd twenty-six years previously. Dudeney revealed that the word *interpreting* was a solution, and wondered whether or not others existed.

Dudeney's problem can be readily generalized to words of any length and switch points at any position within the word. If a word of *n* letters can be moved from horizontal to vertical in *n* moves for at least one switch point, it is termed a switch word.

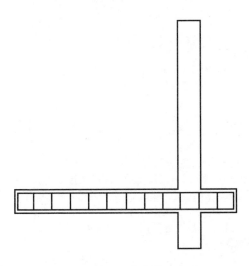

Switch words come in a number of different letter patterns, but the basic one is of the form *spsq* or *psqs,* where *p* and *q* are palindromic sequences and *s* an arbitrary sequence of letters. For example, *interpreting* is divided according to *in-terpret-in-g,* where the second palindrome is only one letter long. Switch words are, in effect, interleaved palindromes and tautonyms. Figure 23a is a type-collection of all possible switch-word patterns for words of five through eight letters.

Figure 23a   A Type-Collection of Switch Words (WW, Feb. 1969)

Five-letter words switching on letter
5 ROTOR
4 ONION, DEEDS, AMASS
3 AMASS, CEDED, LLAMA, CACAO
2 ONION, BELLE, LLAMA
1 ROTOR

Six-letter words switching on letter
6 REDDER
5 SHOOSH, TENETS, APPALL
4 MURMUR, TESTER, APPALL, aabcbc
3 MURMUR, PICNIC, aabccb, SUSURR
2 SHOOSH, PREFER, aabccb
1 REDDER

Seven-letter words switching on letter
7 REPAPER
6 EDIFIED, NIPPING, REFEREE
5 DERIDER, RATTRAP, REFEREE, UKULELE
4 CARCASS, OPPOSES, RINGING, aabcdcb, PIPETTE, MURMURS
3 DERIDER, PIERRIE, aabcdbc, TOTOABA
2 EDIFIED, GRAMMAR, aabcdbc
1 REPAPER

Eight-letter words switching on letter
8 abcddcba
7 TEAMMATE, SELFLESS, RAPPAREE
6 abcddabc, ANTITANK, RAPPAREE, abbacdcd
5 BERIBERI, LOGOLOGY, abccabdd, REVERSES, aabcdbcd
4 BERIBERI, SENTIENT, aabcddbc, NONLEVEL, PREPRESS
3 abcddabc, GESTATES, aabcddcb, ababcddc
2 TEAMMATE, DYSPEPSY
1 abcddcba

Armed with this understanding of switch-word formation, one can return to Dudeney's original query: Are there any other words that can be processed through the Dudeney switch in twelve moves?

There are four possible patterns: *abcdeffedabc, abcdefedcabg, abcdeedcbafg,* and *abcddcbaefef.* However, no other Merriam-Webster words satisfying these patterns exist. In fact, there are only four twelve-letter switch word patterns for which Merriam-Webster words can be found: the words are *antinganting* (1, 12), *rough-wrought* (7), *curliewurlie* (6), *huckermucker* (6), *huddermudder* (6), *huggermugger* (6), *cuggermugger* (6) and *sensuousness* (11). The number in parentheses indicates the location of the switch point (10, for *interpreting*).

24   WORD GRAPHS

Place the different letters of a word (for example, *I, N, O, T* in *notion*) on a sheet of paper and spell out the word by a connect-the-letters tour by pencil. The result is a word graph, a method for classifying words into groups. For example, all words having three different letters are represented either by three letters with two lines connecting them (*arm, here, banana*) or by letters at the vertices of a triangle (*area, tests*). By suitable placement of the letters, all graphs can be constructed with straight lines.

Each graph can be characterized by the number of connector lines emanating from each letter; for example, the graph of *arm* is (1,1,2) and the graph of *area* (2,2,2). These numbers enable one to determine whether or not each connector line can be traversed exactly once. This feat is possible only if there are at most two letters having an odd number of connectors; if there are three or more such letters, at least one connection line must be traversed twice. For instance, if one considers words with four different letters, the graph having all letters connected to each other, a triangle with three additional lines connected to a central letter (a flattened tetrahedron) is (3,3,3,3); one connector line must be traversed twice, and the shortest word having such a graph is eight letters in length (*unendued*).

Words having the same graph can be further categorized according to their letter pattern, as discussed at the beginning of this chapter. For example, there are three different letter patterns corresponding to a graph of four letters consisting of a square with a connecting diagonal: *people, extent, anyway.*

For each graph, one can define the minimum-length letter pattern needed to traverse it. For all graphs with four or fewer letters, words with minimum-length patterns can be found; however, for graphs of words with five or more different letters this is not always possible. For example, the (3,3,3,3,4) graph consisting of a square with all corners connected to a fifth letter in the center (a flattened pyramid) has no minimum-length ten-letter word; the shortest that can be found is the thirteen-letter *prepossessors*. Often, words with far more than the minimum number of letters can be found; *people* and *senselessnesses* share the same graph.

Figure 24a exhibits nineteen of the twenty-one different graphs of words with five different letters; for each of these, a minimum-length word can be found. The two for which this cannot be done are the pentagon with an inscribed star, discussed below, and the flattened pyramid described in the preceding paragraph.

Figure 24a   A Bestiary of Word Graphs With Five Different Letters
(*WW*, Feb. 1995)

Doubled lines are traversed twice in spelling out the word.

```
O—R            E        H  N       A—P              F
|   |          |        |＼|       |／|             |
F—E—B      S—T＝A    T—I—W     R＝E—D       T＝U—R—E
before       state     within    prepared       future


E—C            Y  N     R—A        P—S            A—P
|  |＼         |／|      |    ＼     |＼|＼         |／|
R—N—O      C＝E—D    E—H—T      E—R—O        R＝E—D
concern      decency   rather    prospers       prepared


        /I     A——R            /I     R ＝＝E       M
       /       |＼  |          /       |＼／|        |
C—S  /       |  V  |       T—N/       |／＼|     T＝I＝L
|＼ |/        |     ＼       |＼ |/      |    ＼       |
N—E           G——E        R—O        I ——— P     A
sciences     average     intortion  perspires   militia


W—O—U—L—D       S              I            G—O
would           |             /|＼          |   |
                U            / E ＼         N—I
               /|＼         / /|＼ ＼        going
              / T ＼       / /S＼ ＼
             //    ＼＼   N———C
            O ＝＝ R      insciences
            torturous
```

For some words, no matter how the corresponding graph is drawn, two connector lines must cross. A word with such a graph is called an *eodermdrome*. This word was coined by Gary Bloom, John Kennedy, and Peter Wexler when they were unable to find a minimum-length Merriam-Webster word with an obligatory connector line crossing.

Most words are not eodermdromes. If a word is an isogram (no repeated letters), a graph with no line crossings is trivial to construct. Experimentation with non-isograms soon convinces one that, in order to be an eodermdrome, a word must contain a considerable number of repeated letters. It is not easy to identify eodermdromes by trial and error; an inept positioning of letters may lead to an unnecessary line crossing. What is needed is a set of rules that identifies word patterns that lead to eodermdromes.

The necessary rules are drawn from a branch of mathematics known as graph theory. A famous theorem proven by Kuratowski in 1930 characterizes graphs with essential line crossings (called nonplanar graphs by graph theorists). To understand Kuratowski's Theorem, a bit of preliminary definition is needed. Illustrated below are two relatively simple nonplanar graphs, K(5), the complete graph on five points, and K(3,3), the bipartite graph on six points.

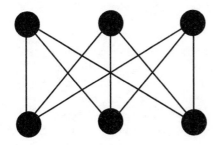
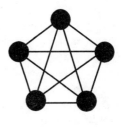

Kuratowski's Theorem states that a graph is nonplanar if and only if it can be reduced to either K(5) or K(3,3) by eliminating superfluous connector lines and by eliminating all points that have only two connector lines emanating from them (note that all points in K(5) and K(3,3) have three or more connector lines emanating from them).

Kuratowski's Theorem enables one to eliminate a large number of words from consideration without even drawing their word graphs. To contain K(5), a word must have at least four different letters each repeated at least twice, and at least one letter repeated at least three times. To contain K(3,3), a word must have at least six different letters repeated at least twice. If a word passes either of these preliminary tests, then it is necessary to draw its word graph. Figure 24b lists all known unabridged Merriam-Webster words whose word graphs contain K(3,3); it also contains the shorter list of all Merriam-Webster words whose word graphs contain K(5) alone. The shortest known K(3,3) word is *metasomatoses;* the shortest K(5) word, *saponaceousness.* The word graph of the former is drawn by connecting *M, T,* and *S* to *E, A,* and *O* in every possible way; the word graph of the latter is drawn by forming a pentagon with vertices *S, A, O, N* and *E* and joining all letters to each other (*C* interrupts the *EA* line, *U* the *SO* line, and *P* the *AO* line).

Figure 24b   Eodermdromes That Reduce to K(3,3) (*WW,* Aug. 1980)

metasomatoses	orthopsychiatrist	electrohorticulture
orchioscirrhus	colicystopyelitis	unconscientiousness
supersaturates	proletarianization	pectinatodenticulate
satellitesimal	hyperbrachycephaly	electrometallurgical
electroculture	transrectification	ophthalmodiastimeter
duodenojejunal	orthopsychiatrical	hydroxyanthraquinone
hyperpharyngeal	tetrachloromethane	thoracogastroschisis
preconspiracies	tuberculosectorial	spinulosodenticulate
enterogastrones	intercontradictory	disproportionateness
ethnohistorians	microrefractometer	protransubstantiation
intranscalencies	ultraconscientious	mandibulosuspensorial
magnetogenerator	pharyngorhinoscopy	duodenopancreatectomy
postconvalescent	Heautontimorumenos	aminoacetophenetidene
unprosperousness	superconsciousness	microseismometrograph
Sericostomatidae	erythrocytoschisis	pseudohermaphroditism
transformationist	duodenojejunostomy	lymphangioendothelioma
unadulteratedness	forethoughtfulness	pancreaticoduodenostomy
tetrachloroethane	Helminthocladiaceae	blepharosphincterectomy
intraorganization	ultradolichocranial	formaldehydesulphoxylate
transexperiential	hyperarchaeological	tetraiodophenolphthalein
transportationist	monochloranthracene	tetrabromophenolphthalein
antispectroscopic	encephalomyelopathy	hydroxydeoxycorticosterone
historicocultural	counterorganization	cystoureteropyelonephritis
overconcentration	hyperdolichocephaly	hydroxydesoxycorticosterone
contradictoriness	cholecystolithiasis	trinitrophenylmethylnitramine

Eodermdromes That Reduce to K(5) (WW, Aug. 1980)

saponaceousness   craniorhachischisis   hypsibrachycephaly
sphincteroscopes

The shortest possible eodermdrome is formed from the word
graph K(5) that has no connector lines that need to be traversed
twice. There are twenty-two different patterns of eleven letters that
can traverse K(5), but none of them form Merriam-Webster words;
they are listed in Figure 24c.

Figure 24c   Minimal Eodermdrome Patterns, and a Poem (WW, Aug.
1980)

12314253451	12314254351	Tears at Rest
12314352451	12314354251	
12314524351	12314534251	Stray satyrs,
12341352451	12341354251	Dense and sad,
12341524531	12341542531	Tip tan paint.
12342513541	12342514531	Teaser's tart
12342531451	12342531541	Pursues prep ...
12342541351	12342541531	Yearly relay.
12345135241	12345142531	Sweat wastes.
12345241351	12345241531	Science sins ...
12345324251	12345315241	Ah ... rather tea.

Two Merriam-Webster words reduce to both K(3,3) and K(5):
overconscientious and *phenoltetrachlorophthalein*.

Philip Cohen proved that the Merriam-Webster *pneumonoultramicroscopicsilicovolcanoconiosis* word graph requires two connector
line crossings. To see this, construct a graph with *A, I,* and *O* in a vertical line, each connected to *C* on the left and *M* on the right. If the
OULTRA sequence is to avoid a crossing, it must lie outside this
graph; but then *LI* demands a line crossing. A second crossing is
induced by the fact that *N* must join *O, I,* and *A*.

There are two thirty-four-letter words in the unabridged
Random House that are not eodermdromes: *diaminopropyltetramethylenediamine* and *supercalifragilisticexpialidocious*.

Word graphs are closely related to word molecules, a concept
introduced by David Morice. In a word molecule, one places each
different letter of a word at the center of a circle (each circle can have

a different radius, if necessary), and then arranges these circles on a sheet of paper so that two circles touch if and only if the two letters these circles represent are adjacent in the word. If a letter is doubled, as *o* in *bamboo*, two circles are used to represent that letter. To construct the word molecule for a long word, it is usually necessary to employ circles of vastly different sizes.

Word molecules and eodermdromes are mutually exclusive concepts; if a word is not an eodermdrome, it can be depicted as a word molecule, and vice versa. Of course, it is necessary to modify a word molecule before constructing the corresponding word graph; one must cancel doubled letters before replacing circles with connector lines.

25   WORD TILES

Word tiles are a restricted form of word graphs in which the positions of the different letters are restricted to a regular geometric array, such as a pavement tiling. Usually, it is assumed that two tiles are adjacent if they have a common line boundary, but adjacency can also be assumed if the two tiles touch only at a corner of each (a single point). This difference is illustrated by a checkerboard tiling in which only rectilinear one-step moves are allowed, versus a checkerboard tiling that allows diagonal one-step moves as well (king's move in chess). Note that the former tiling does not allow connector line crossings, whereas the latter does.

In unpublished research, Lee Sallows and Stan Wagon have been able to prove that word graphs based on king's move, christened *K-graphs* by Leonard Gordon, are closely related to eodermdromes. In particular, they have shown that neither the K(3,3) nor the K(5-) graph can be traced out by king's moves (the K(5-) graph is the K(5) graph with one connector line left out). Intuitively, this result is quite reasonable. Four letters can mutually touch each other if arranged in a square, but a fifth letter can touch only two of these. Similarly, if each of the letters *ABC* must touch each of the letters *DE*, it is not hard to do this with an array consisting of *ABC* in a horizontal line, *D* above *B*, and *E* below *B*, but there is no place left to put *F* so that it touches *ABC*. There exist twenty-two ten-letter patterns that can trace out K(5-) but only one, *insciences*, is a Merriam-Webster word. This is the shortest known word that is not K-graphable. The twenty-two patterns are deducible from the ones listed in Figure 24c by omitting the final letters.

In general, neither word graphs nor K-graphs dominate the other. There are words such as *inscience* that are word graphs but not K-graphs; conversely, there are at least nine Merriam-Webster words that can be K-graphed but are eodermdromes: *arterioplasties, enterogastrones, sphincteroscopes, hypsibrachycephaly, proletarianization, intracontradictory, hyperarchaeological, cholecystolithiasis, pectinatodenticulate,* and *electrometallurgical.*

The longest known K-graphable words are *ethylenediaminetetraacetate, octamethylpyrophosphoramide,* and *diaminopropyltetramethylenediamine,* the latter thirty-four letters long.

```
       L            L P S              L H
   D E N Y        Y H O C            E T Y
   C I T H        R T E D          D M N R P
   M A R            A M I            I A O
```

Supercalifragilisticexpialidocious cannot be K-graphed because there are ten letters adjacent to *I: ACDFGLOPST.*

The K-graph dominates a hierarchy of pavements in which only edge crossings (not corner ones) are allowed. The first of these are the hexagonal pavement and the alternating octahedron-square pavement. Neither of these dominates the other, but both dominate the square pavement, and this in turn dominates the least usable pavement, the triangular one. All have been studied by Leonard Gordon, who has identified both the longest graphable and the shortest nongraphable words for each pavement. Words traced out on these pavements are, respectively, called H-graphs, OS-graphs, Q-graphs (for quadrature), and T-graphs. The shortest and longest words are:

K-graph	insciences	diaminopropyltetramethylenediamine
H-graph	unendued	magnetohydrodynamically
OS-graph	unendued	dioxydiamidoarsenobenzol
Q-graph	area	hyperthyroidization
T-graph	area	dicyclopentadiene

Although neither hexagonal nor octahedron-square pavements dominate each other in word graphability, the latter is clearly the more potent array. There are quite a number of words that can be OS-graphed but not H-graphed, including *horseshoers, constrictions, corticotropic,* and *osteosteatoma* (what is the shortest such word?). Contrariwise, there is no known word that can be H-graphed but not OS-graphed; it would be interesting to construct the shortest letter string that fulfills this requirement.

Leonard Gordon also identified a hybrid form of word graph that relies on a pavement but does not insist on side-adjacency: rook's move in chess. Words that are traced out by rook's move (up and down, right and left, but not diagonal) on a chessboard are said to be R-graphed. The shortest word that cannot be R-graphed is *area,* and the longest ones that can be R-graphed are *laryngopharyngectomies* and *sulfamethoxypyridazine.*

```
    L       S       ULM   ETH
  ARYNGEC       SFAD    O
  H   P   O   T       ZIN   X
      MI              R   YP
```

R-graphable and Q-graphable words have the interesting property that repeated letters must always be an even number of spaces apart.

There is no reason why word graphs cannot be extended to three dimensions. Of course, an unrestricted word graph in three dimenions is trivial, but those based on three-dimensional lattices have some interest. Leonard Gordon has examined the cubic lattice and the stacked hexagonal lattice; the former can accommodate the twenty-letter *dimethyltubocurarine* and the latter, the twenty-five-letter *occipitoroscipitoscapular.* The more versatile tetrahedral (cannonball) lattice, with offset hexagonal arrays on adjacent levels, enables each letter to contact twelve others; *supercalifragilisticexpialidocious* can be graphed in this lattice. A C-graph (a graph based on a cannonball lattice) neither dominates nor is dominated by a word graph or a K-graph. *Spectroheliokinematographs* can be diagrammed as a word graph but not a C-graph or a K-graph; *diaminopropyltetramethylenediamine* can be diagrammed as a K-graph but not a word graph or C-graph; *hepatocholangioenterostomy* can be diagrammed as a C-graph but not a word graph or K-graph.

Finally, one can construct word graphs, either unrestricted planar ones or ones on pavements, to accommodate groups of words. The most natural exercise is to see how many of the cardinal numbers *one, two, three, four*... can be so diagrammed on a single template. For planar graphs or K-graphs, the answer appears to be nine.

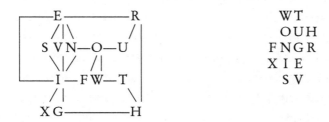

If any cardinals can be used, Leonard Gordon has packed sixty-four into a planar graph, and thirty-seven into a K-graph. What planar graph or K-graph template can incorporate the largest number of words from a specified dictionary? Even for the Pocket Merriam-Webster, one hundred or more should be possible.

A related challenge consists of packing twenty-five different letters of the alphabet in a 5-by-5 array to maximize (or to minimize) the number of words traceable by king's move, again with respect to a specified dictionary.

Lee Sallows has proved that there are certain pairs of six-letter words that are incompatible—that is, cannot be traced out as a K-graph on a single template. Some common examples: *pearly-player, unable-nebula, aspire-praise, listen-tinsel.*

26 ISOGRAMS

A word is an isogram if it contains no more than one of any letter. The longest Pocket Merriam-Webster isogram is *ambidextrously*, and the longest unabridged Merriam-Webster word, *dermatoglyphics. Uncopyrightable*, also fifteen letters in length, is found as an adjective in the Tenth Collegiate Merriam-Webster. If this can be used as a noun to describe uncopyrightable material, it could be pluralized to yield a sixteen-letter isogram. At Edward Wolpow's suggestion, dermatologist Lowell Goldsmith used the seventeen-letter isogram *subdermatoglyphic* in his article "Chaos: To See a World in a Grain of Sand and a Heaven in a Wild Flower" in the September 1990 issue of the *Archives of Dermatology*. This coinage describes the skin directly below the well-known fingerprint ridges. If place-names are allowed, *South Cambridge, NY* contains sixteen different letters.

The word *isogram* was apparently coined by Dmitri Borgmann; it appears in *Language on Vacation*. Unfortunately, the word has another meaning, being used by cartographers and the like to denote a line connecting a set of points having the same numerical value on a map (such as elevation above sea level, or barometric pressure). Ted Clarke has proposed that it be changed to *disogram* or *heterogram*, the latter coined by Susan Thorpe. Dr. J. H. Marshall, Senior *OED* editor, has proposed *haplogram*. However, *isogram* is so well established a usage that any replacement would have to be accompanied by a reference to the original terminology.

The advent of national telephone directories on CD-ROMs has made it an easy task to discover persons whose full names are isograms; the problem is to identify relatively long surnames that are isograms. The longest isogrammatic name belonging to a person is *Melvin Schwarzkopf* of Alton, Ill. If his surname were spelled *Schwartzkopf*, then this name would be eighteen letters long. Other plausible seventeen-letter names include *Floyd Braunschweig, Floyd Kirschenbaum*, and *Barney Wolfschmidt*, but none of these appear to exist. Three-part names as long as twenty-one letters are theoretically possible: *Emily Jung Schwartzkopf.*

Literary isograms can, of course, be no longer than twenty-six letters (see the following section, on Pangrams, for examples). However, one can write much longer texts in which each word, rather than each letter, is unique; Figure 26a gives an example of this genre.

Figure 26a   Metalingustic Thoughts Set Down **at** Random (WW, Feb. 1995)

Below, dear reader, **you** will encounter perhaps **the** longest English-language literary isogram ever constructed: every word therein **is** unique. While reading, please watch carefully

for inadvertent duplications (hopefully, **they** appear impossible **to** find). Professor H. J. Verschuyl has written **a** Dutch example three times longer (see Battus's *Opperlandse taal- & letterkunde,* page 62); however, **this** work does **not** translate very felicitously. **Had he,** perchance, too many foreign idioms **in his** account?

Formerly, some writers piled **one** adjective **on** another ad nauseum, **but** such concatenation **was** often criticized **as** making humdrum narrative. My essay employs those 33 words (emphasized **with** boldface type) rated most common **by** Kucera **and** Francis.

Note **that I have** <u>used</u> an article here—profligate wastefulness, because **it** may never **be** <u>reused</u>. Why underline these? Similarities among letter sequences raise perplexing questions; can prefixing legitimatize root <u>reuse</u>? What about changes **of** tense, shown above? **Or** plurals? Hyphenated terms cause additional problems; **are** their component parts disallowed? Clearly, different spellings must always generate admissible lexical forms.

Who shall write more extensive prose passages **which,** free **from** any repetition whatever, sound natural throughout?

27 PANGRAMS

A pangram can be defined as a group of words using the twenty-six letters of the alphabet exactly once. Historically, the additional restraint has been imposed that these words be assembled into a sentence making some degree of sense. If abbreviations are not allowed, most pangram sentences use outré words and tortured syntax, requiring lengthy explanations of their meaning. The following two examples by Dmitri Borgmann are taken from Martin Gardner's *Notes* in C. C. Bombaugh's *Oddities and Curiosities of Words and Literature* (Dover, 1961): *Cwm, fjord-bank glyphs vext quiz,* and *Zing! Vext cwm fly jabs Kurd qoph.* These mean, respectively, "Carved figures on the bank of a fjord and in a circular blind valley irritated an eccentric person," and "Zing! An irritated valley fly jabs at the Hebrew letter qoph, as written by a Turkish tribesman."

According to David Kahn in a letter to *The New York Times* on 16 August 1972, Claude Shannon, the founder of information theory, was responsible for the pangram *Squdgy fez, blank jimp crwth vox,* which says that a man orders his squashed-down hat to mute the skimpy voice of a Welsh violin.

A very sensible sentence can be constructed by allowing just one extra letter, as demonstrated by Sir Jeremy Morse: *Bawds jog, flick quartz, vex nymph.*

If abbreviations are allowed, sentences can be written using common words and more reasonable syntax. A classic example is *D. V. Pike flung J. Q. Schwartz my box.* Clement Wood's *Mr. Jock, TV quiz Ph.D., bags few lynx* is very good, as is one from the August 1986 issue of *Games* magazine: *New job: fix Mr. Gluck's hazy TV, PDQ.* Ted Clarke proposed *Meg Schwarzkopf quit Jynx Blvd.* This, describing a lady's move away from Wryneck Street, works better in Great Britain than the United States; the jynx is a British bird listed in desktop dictionaries there but only in unabridged ones in the United States.

If one regards a pangram as only a word list, many can be constructed. Dennis Ritchie programmed a computer in the late 1970s to search the second edition of the unabridged Merriam-Webster for (1) twenty-six-letter pangrams consisting of words of two or more letters, and (2) twenty-five-letter pangrams leaving out the letter *S* (appending the *S* to a suitable word in the list to complete the pangram). He found 3,330 pangram lists, 2,005 of the first type and 1,325 of the second. The number of pangrams based on the second edition is undoubtedly far larger, for a number of words from the dictionary were not included on the tape, including such prime pangrammatic possibilities as *wuz* (dialect variant of was), *qvint* (variant of *kwint*), *suq* (variant of *sooq*), and *waqf* (variant of *wakf*).

What is the commonest pangram? The word list *fjord quiz vex balks nth gyp cwm* is in the Pocket Merriam-Webster except for the last word, found in the Collegiate. Other pangrams located entirely in the Collegiate are given in Figure 27a.

Figure 27a Webster's Collegiate Pangrams (WW, Nov. 1983)

jab qoph vug Fritz lynx desk cwm	jug qoph vex blitz fry dank cwms
jug qoph vex blintz fard sky cwm	jug qoph vex Fritz bland sky cwm
fjord quiz vex balk gyp nth cwms	fjeld qursh vat zig pyx knob cwm
junk qoph vex Fritz by glad cwms	junk qoph vex blitz dry fag cwms

junk qoph vex blitz fry gad cwms   jag qoph vex blitz fry dunk cwms
jag qoph vex blitz dry funk cwms   jag qoph vex blintz fry dusk cwm
jib qoph vug zed kraft lynx cwms   jud qoph vex blintz fry skag cwm

Cwm is by far the most prevalent word in the 3,300 pangrams, appearing in 92 percent of them; other common words are *qoph* (65 percent) and *jynx* (52 percent). In fact, 44 percent of the pangrams contain all three of these words. There are 104 pangrams of six words and 3,226 of seven. Unless the pangram has six words, including a Q-word with only one vowel, it is clear that one or more words of the pangram must be vowelless (no *AEIOUY*). This, of course, accounts for the great popularity of *cwm;* other words not using *AEIOUY* include *crwth* (in 166 pangrams) and *nth* (in 11, always in conjunction with *cwm*).

Because Q ordinarily requires two vowels to follow it (see Section 18), very few Q-words are suitable for pangrams; 3,307 of the pangrams use *qoph, shoq, qung,* or *qursh*, while the remaining twenty-three are scattered among *squdgy* (12 examples), *quiz* (4 examples), *squdge, squab, quab, quak, quark, squawk*, and *quick.*

Is a five-word pangram possible? Dmitri Borgmann used two previously mentioned unabridged Merriam-Webster words to construct *Qvint jackbox wuz phlegm fyrds.* This pangram can be combined with five Ritchie ones to form six pangrams with no words in common, depicted in Figure 27b.

Figure 27b   Six Pangrams with No Words in Common (*WW*, Nov. 1983)

shoq fjeld vug zink pyx brat cwm   Qung fjord vext biz swack lymph
qursh jynx veldt zimb gowf pack   qoph jambs vex Fritz wynd gluck
squdgy job vamp knex flix crwth   qvint wuz jackbox phlegm fyrds

A one-word pangram is, of course, impossible to find. The only way it might arise is as a law, vaccine, syndrome, or medical procedure named after its joint discoverers. Figure 27c gives a fictional account of this possibility.

Figure 27c　The Syndrome (WW, May 1987)

Dr. Edward Wax carefully inserted the cassette in the player as he glanced at the other four sitting around the conference table. "I'm glad you could find the time to listen to my problem," he began. "I realize that the Psychiatric Institute is ordinarily concerned with research into phobias or psychological aberrations that have resisted treatment by the foremost psychiatrists, not the routine neuroses encountered by a GP like myself. Were it not for my neighbor, Mr. Pfund of your Institute, I suppose I should never have been given this hearing." He nodded toward the short cherubic man sitting across from him.

"You make too much of my influence here," protested the latter. "I'm an administrator, not a doctor, and my word counts for nothing in determining which patients are examined or research undertaken. It was the bizarre nature of your patient's symptoms that I related to Professor Hjelmqvist that convinced him to listen to your tape."

"Yah," said the Professor in an accent hinting of his Scandinavian origin. "Mr. Pfund tells me that your patient speaks in an oddly stilted manner. I am very curious to see just what you mean by this, and to aid in diagnosis I haf called in two colleagues, Dr. Alexander Gryb, a speech therapist, and Dr. Friedrich Zock, a psycholinguist. I expect," he complacently added, "we should have no trouble pinpointing the exact nature of your patient's syndrome."

Dr. Wax pressed the play button. The recorder began to whirr, and the voices of doctor and patient filled the room.

> What advice do you give new employees at the post office, Harry?
> *Just be very quick when fixing zip code mail*
> But isn't that hard to do?
> *Such a job requires extra pluck and zeal from every wage-earner*
> No staring out the window, eh?
> *No—all you can see is five thickets of quaking aspen, box elder and juneberry lining a frozen swamp...*

Dr. Wax hit the stop button. The Institute members looked at each other blankly. The Professor nervously tapped his pencil on the table. "Very curious—very curious indeed. Vot do you make of it, Dr. Zock?"

"I don't know," the latter replied thoughtfully. "He certainly seems to be a keen observer of nature. Let's hear another part of the tape."

Dr. Wax hit the fast forward, then the play button.

So she's been very busy lately?
My girl wove six dozen plaid jackets before she quit
What did her friend Zelda do when she heard about this?
Zelda quickly wove eight nubby flax jumpers
What did she give you for Christmas?
Her gift box of jigsaw puzzles quickly drove me nuts

Dr. Gryb shook his head in perplexity. "Do you think there's any significance in the fact that he always works the letter X into his answer—six, box, flax?"

Dr. Zock's eyes widened. "Yes, that's a strange compulsion, and not the only one he shows. He always uses the letter Q, and Z, and J, and..."

Professor Hjelmqvist clapped his hand to his head. "Uff course! I should haf seen it at vunce! The patient is suffering from the necessity to use efery letter of the alphabet in each sentence he utters—a pangram, I think you call it?" Dr. Zock nodded assent. "All my life, I have dreamed of being the discoverer of a syndrome new to the medical world, and I may haf found it! Who knows what this may lead to?" he mused, more to himself than the others at the table. "The Freud Medal, the Nobel Prize for the Hjelmqvist syndrome..."

He stopped, aware that the others were frowning at him. "The Hjelmqvist syndrome?" cried Dr. Gryb. "I was the one who first called your attention to the repetition of a letter..."

"And I," put in Dr. Zock, "built on Gryb's idea, giving you the flash of insight. What about credit for us?"

"Vell," said the professor grudgingly, "I guess we might call it the Hjelmqvist-Gryb-Zock syndrome, yah?"

"Wait a minute," cried Pfund. "Aren't you forgetting that I was the one who brought this patient to your attention? And what about Dr. Wax, who told me about it? If credit is to be given for this discovery, let it be meted out equally: I propose that it be christened the Hjelmqvist-Gryb-Zock-Pfund-Wax syndrome..."

The concepts of pangram and isogram can be combined in the following way: How much of the alphabet can be exhausted by a set of *n* isograms? For the Pocket Merriam-Webster, the answer appears to be

ambidextrously (14)
blacksmith, gunpowder (19)
humpbacks, frowzy, tingled (22)
humpbacks, frowzy, veldt, jinx (24)
chintz, plumbs, fjord, gawky, vex (25)

Since there is no Pocket Merriam-Webster pangram, this is as far as one can go. For the unabridged Merriam-Webster, the analogous lists are

dermatoglyphics (15)
blacksmith, gunpowdery (20)

The maximum-letter three-word and four-word lists are not known; they probably use twenty-three and twenty-five letters, respectively.

If the isogram requirement is waived, one can squeeze more different letters into n words. Once the entire alphabet has been included, the objective changes; one then tries to use as few total letters as possible in n words. For the Pocket Merriam-Webster:

ambidextrously (14)
ambidextrously, watchmaking (20)
ambidextrously, foreknowledge, receivership (23)
zipping, foxhound, jabberwocky, ventriloquism (39 letters)
plumbing, chintzy, squawk, fjord, vex (29 letters)
lamb, squawk, fjord, chintz, vex, gyp (27 letters)

Since there is no Pocket Merriam-Webster pangram, this is the end of the line. It seems likely that the thirty-nine-letter set can be improved. If *bezique* were in the Pocket dictionary, it could be combined with *fixedly*, *jackpots* and *overwhelming* for a total of thirty-four letters. For the unabridged Merriam-Webster, the corresponding lists are

superacknowledgement (16)
formaldehydesulphoxylates, backjawing (23)
benzoxycamphors, quick-flowing, juventude (36 letters)
jukebox, viewfinders, phlegmy, quartz (31 letters)

The latter can almost certainly be improved, since it is possible to construct a pangram with five words.

If all words must be of the same length, one can form various near-pangrams. For words of three, four, five, six, and seven letters the best examples are:

> nth vex jug rip adz sky fob cwm
> cyst flex whiz jump knob drag
> dzong crwth jumps flaky vibex
> blowzy frumps jading kvetch
> jackbox freshly dumping

The five-letter set has been proposed as a strategy in the game of Jotto. The five-letter set is due to Robert Levinson, and the six-letter set to Leonard Gordon.

Pangrams can be embedded in crosswords. Figure 27d shows a minimum-area one using Pocket Merriam-Webster words, as well as one using just five words, due to Leslie Card. A four-word crossword appears impossible.

Figure 27d   Pangrammatic Crosswords (*WW*, Feb. 1970, Feb. 1977)

```
    Q    V                 S
  J UG  WAX                J
    I   B  S              WAQF
    CRYPT                  M
    K    L          L    B      V
  F EZ  OHM          UNCOPYRIGHTED
    N    D           X    K      Z
```

28   THE PANGRAMMATIC WINDOW

The pangrammatic window is closely related to the pangram. In English-language text, what is the fewest number of consecutive letters that include all the letters of the alphabet? Excluding deliberate efforts to shorten it (such as a discussion of pangrams), the current record-holder contains only sixty-seven letters, reported in A. Cyril Pearson's *Pictured Puzzles and Word Play* (George Routledge & Son, London, 1910?). The passage in question is found on page 217 of Sarah Grand's novel *The Beth Book* (1897):

Then Ruth sat with her work on her lap for a little, looking up at the summer sky. It was an e[xquisitely deep blue just then, with filmy white clouds drawn up over it like gauz]e to veil its brightness.

Kyle Corbin found a seventy-four-letter window in the 2 August 1987 issue of *Parade Magazine:*

How do people in show business regard Vanna White, the young lady who turns the letters on the "Wheel of [Fortune" TV quiz show? What is her great talent, or is she considered a joke? —Kimberly Poindex]ter, Birmingham, Ala.

The next-shortest pangrammatic window, of seventy-five letters, was reported by Tom Pulliam, who found it in an article called "Constructing Good Questionnaires" in the June 1983 *Training and Development Journal:*

The advantages of questionnaires over interviews is that many more people can complete a questionnaire than can be inter[viewed. The major drawback to open-ended questions is the complexity of scoring and analyz]ing the responses.

Had the *V* only occurred beyond the word *major,* this would have been a sixy-four-letter window! There is a seventy-six-letter window in Book I of Milton's *Paradise Lost:*

Likening his Maker to the gra[zed ox,
Jehovah, who, in one night, when he passed
From Egypt marching, equalled with one stroke
B]oth her first-born and all her bleating gods.

The probability that a set of *n* consecutive letters of text will contain all the letters of the alphabet can be approximated by a simple mathematical model. Assume that English-language text is mimicked by a random process that selects letters according to their text frequencies, independently of the letters that have been chosen previously. (The assumption embodied in the last sentence is not true in reality, but rare letters such as *J, Q, X,* and *Z* nearly always appear at widely scattered points in text, and their behavior is not likely to be much affected by this simplification.) Let $p(n)$ be the probability that the *n*th letter of the alphabet appears in text; reasonable values are

$p(z)$ = .00084 (counting doubled letters as one appearance), $p(q)$ = .0010, $p(j)$ = .00161, and $p(x)$ = .00657. (These have been taken from the million-word corpus of English-language prose by Kucera and Francis.) The probability that a pangrammatic window of length m will contain one or more of the nth letter is

$$P(n) = 1 - (1 - p(n))^m$$

where the asterisk directs one to raise $1 - p(n)$ to the mth power. The probability that the window will contain all 26 letters is

$$P = P(a)P(b)...P(z)$$

To have a fifty-fifty chance of including all letters, the window must be about 2,000 letters in length. For shorter lengths, the probabilities rapidly decrease to .26 for 1,000 letters, .060 for 500 letters, .0018 for 200 letters, and .000049 for 100 letters. Computers could be programmed to validate this approximate formula against actual texts.

29 LETTER DISTRIBUTIONS

Words can be classified not only according to their letter patterns, but also by their letter distributions: the number of letters of each kind in a word, without regard to location. A pair isogram is a word in which each letter appears exactly twice. J. H. Marshall, senior editor of the *OED,* proposes the term diplogram. The longest unabridged Merriam-Webster pair isograms are *Taeniodontidae, scintillescent,* and *unsufficiences;* the word *inaccidentated* appears in a 1579 citation in the *Oxford English Dictionary. Unprosperousness,* a sixteen-letter pair isogram, is marred by the appearance of four Ss. In the May 1995 issue of *Wordsworth* (a privately published magazine), Ted Clarke notes the sixteen-letter pair isogram *esophagographers.* Although this appears in no dictionary, *esophagography* (roentgenography of the esophagus) is in the twenty-fourth edition of *Dorland's Illustrated Medical Dictionary.* The inferred Merriam-Webster plural *antianthropomorphisms* would be a pair isogram except for the extra O. *Taeniodontidae* is a special case of a pair isogram: the second half of the word rearranges to letters of the first half. Tautonyms (Section 22) are a further specialization.

A trio isogram is a word in which each letter appears exactly three times. Six-letter examples are *deeded, essees, seeses,* and *geggee;* a nine-letter example is *sestettes. Feffee* is in the *Oxford English Dictionary* and *sheeshehs* in the unabridged Funk & Wagnalls. The *Oxford English Dictionary* word *monimolimnion* would be a trio isogram were it not for the *L.*

Pyramid words contain one of one letter, two of a second letter, three of a third letter, and so on. Ten-letter pyramid words are not too difficult to find. The only Pocket Merriam-Webster example is *sleeveless;* Figure 29a lists unabridged Merriam-Webster examples.

Figure 29a   Ten-Letter Pyramid Words (*WW,* May 1982)

ACTAEACEAE a group of plant genera typified by the baneberry
BEERBIBBER one who drinks beer, especially to excess
CHACHALACA the Texan guan, a bird of the order Gallinae
DEADHEADED   treated as one who isn't required to pay for a ticket
DISSEISSEE a person ousted from tenancy or possession of land
ENTETEMENT state or quality of being opinionated
ISOOSMOSIS equality of diffusion through a semipermeable membrane
KEENNESSES states of sharpness
KINNIKINIC a mixture of dried leaves and bark smoked by Ohio Indians
KOTUKUTUKU the New Zealand native fuchsia
NAGNAGGING   nagging
NESHNESSES states of softness, weakness, or fastidiousness
REDEFERRED deferred again
REMEMBERER one who remembers
REREMEMBER remember again
RERENDERED rendered again
RERESERVES reserves again
REREVERSES reverses again
RESTRESSES converts an unstressed monosyllable to a stressed form
SANENESSES states of being mentally sound or rational
SASSANIANS members of a dynasty of Persian kings, A.D. 226–641
SERENENESS quality or state of being calm, quiet, or composed
SLEEVELESS lacking sleeves
SUSURRUSES whispering or rustling sounds

These can be augmented by *shahanshah,* the Persian word for king of kings, and *pepperette,* a word in the 1969 *Britannica Yearbook* denoting a girl who does a dance routine during an intermission at an athletic event. No dictionary fifteen-letter pyramid words are known to exist, although Dmitri Borgmann has proposed *knell-lessnesses,* the respective conditions of church bells that have ceased to sound because of mechanical or other defects; Sir Jeremy Morse has suggested *linenlessnesses,* states of being without linen; and Ralph Beaman has coined *resuppresseress,* a woman who suppresses once more, and *teletattletales,* persons or their statements revealing by telephone, telegraph, or television gossip about others. In Figure 29b Howard Bergerson introduces the concept of pyramidal sentences.

Figure 29b   Addleheaded Lads Scale the Pyramid (*WW,* Aug. 1980)

Addleheaded Dale
Dale, the addleheaded lad
Let Dale, the addleheaded lad, melt
Lead, mild addleheaded lad; let the hate melt
Lead, Dale, mild addleheaded lad; let mirth melt the hate
Lead them, Dale, mild addleheaded lad; let glad mirth melt their hate
Lead them all, Dale, mild addleheaded teen lad; glad mirth might melt their hatred
Dale, a mild addleheaded teen lad, led them—old men all—a-right; glad mirth might melt their hatred
Ted Alden, a mild addleheaded lad, led them—grim old men all—to land: rare mirth's glad height might melt their hate
Dell, dim addleheaded giant liar, led them—grim old men all—home to land; rare mirth's glad height might melt, then, a dread death lust
Alec, dim addleheaded giant liar, led them—grim old men all—to their homeland; rare mirth's glad height might melt, then, glum Donald's dread death lust

To give an idea of the variety of letter distributions, a type-collection of unabridged Merriam-Webster words of three through twelve letters is presented in Figure 29c. In each case, the commonest known word is given, and the word is starred if it is not in the Pocket Merriam-Webster.

Figure 29c   A Type-Collection of Letter Distributions (WW, Nov. 1974)

the, 2 all

with, 2 that, 3 lull, 22 mama

would, 2 which, 3 added, 22 sense, 23 mamma

should, 2 before, 3 seemed, 4 assess, 22 people, 23 needed, 24 muumuu, 33 deeded, 222 murmur

another, 2 through, 3 between, 4 Alabama*, 22 thought, 23 minimum, 24 referee, 33 seeress*, 34 seesees*, 222 opinion, 223 alfalfa

children, 2 American, 3 business, 4 sessions, 5 Swissess*, 22 national, 23 tomorrow, 24 stresses, 25 assesses, 33 refereed, 34 redeeded*, 44 kukukuku*, 222 pressure, 223 remember, 224 teeterer*, 233 susurrus*, 2222 teammate

something, 2 president, 3 determine, 4 elsewhere, 5 assessors, 22 different, 23 available, 24 possessed, 25 possesses, 33 preferred, 24 senseless, 44 seeresses*, 222 sometimes, 223 beginning, 224 teeterers*, 225 anapanapa*, 233 sleepless, 234 sassarara*, 2222 classical, 2223 recherche

importance, 2 university, 3 facilities, 4 experience, 5 dispossess, 6 beeveedees*, 22 government, 23 themselves, 24 everywhere, 25 possessors, 26 Swissesses*, 33 settlement, 34 reassessed, 35 reassesses, 44 Sassabasar*, 222 conditions, 223 conference, 224 remembered, 225 recercelee*, 233 nineteenth, 234 sleeveless, 244 Wallawalla*, 333 repressers, 2222 throughout, 2223 intonation, 2233 couscousou*, 22222 intestines

personality, 2 responsible, 3 development, 4 experiences, 5 acataphasia*, 22 performance, 23 corporation, 24 represented, 25 possessions, 26 sissynesses*, 33 refrigerate, 34 assassinate, 35 uselessness, 44 sweetnesses, 222 information, 223 temperature, 224 tresspassers, 225 abracadabra, 233 independent, 234 senselessly, 235 taratantara*, 244 kinnikinnic*, 333 intenseness*, 334 kinnikinick*, 344 kinnikinnik*, 2222 association, 2223 thermometer, 2224 tattletales, 2233 engineering, 2234 senescences, 2333 couscousous*, 22222 unconscious, 22223 intensities

considerably, 2 considerable, 3 developments, 4 civilization, 5 invisibility, 22 professional, 23 distribution, 24 nevertheless, 25 greenskeeper*, 26 dispossesses, 33 missionaries, 34 hopelessness, 35 assassinates, 44 corroborator*, 45 fiddledeedee*, 222 particularly, 223 significance, 224 interference, 225 dispossessed, 226 assassinists*, 233 availability, 234 independence, 235 selflessness, 244 Mississippi*, 245 serenenesses*, 333 highlighting, 344 kinnikinnick*, 2222 organization, 2223 constitution, 2224 intermittent, 2225 sensuousness, 2233 efficiencies, 2234 resuppresses*, 2235 lenslessness, 2244 killeekillee*, 2333 inconcoction*, 22222

Philadelphia*, 22223 ingratiating, 22224 antinganting*, 22333 inefficience*, 222222 happenchance

The longest unabridged Merriam-Webster words containing two, three, and four different letters are, respectively, *kukukuku, kinnikinnik,* and *senselessnesses;* all have been previously encountered in this chapter. Dmitri Borgmann proposed the nondictionary phrase *Miss Mississippis,* denoting the winners of the Miss America pageant in 1959, 1960, and 1980.

In his unpublished book *Our Fabulous Language: The Alphabet Dictionary,* Murray Geller notes that there are four unabridged Merriam-Webster words having sixteen different letters: *blepharoconjunctivitis, pseudolamellibranchiata, pseudolamellibranchiate,* and *psychogalvanometric.* All can be found in the third edition; *superacknowledgement* can be added from the second. *Sulfamethoxypyridazine,* in the twenty-fourth edition of *Dorland's Illustrated Medical Dictionary,* has eighteen different letters; this is matched by three chemical compounds in the 1976 *Merck Index: monohydroxymercuridiiodoresorcinsulfonphthalein, chlorsulfonamidodihydrobenzothiadiazine,* and *dihydroxydiphenylethanedisulfonic.*

THREE
WORD FRAGMENTS

IN THE PRECEDING chapter, each letter in a word played an important role in the patterns or distributions displayed. In contrast, this chapter looks at word fragments having various characteristics—internal palindromes, consecutive identical letters, regularly spaced identical letters, anchored letters, and the like. In examining word fragments, three cases can be distinguished: words containing specified letters in order and adjacent, words containing specified letters in order but not necessarily adjacent, and words containing specified letters with no further restriction.

31 BIGRAMS, TRIGRAMS, TETRAGRAMS

A logologist, like a collector of stamps, coins, or baseball cards, always strives for a complete collection of linguistic types. The trick is to define a collection that is neither too easy nor too hard to assemble. Finding words containing each of the 676 possible bigrams from *bazAAr* to *puZZle* has been an alluring goal for the logologist for at least three decades. A complete collection is exhibited in Figure 31a.

Figure 31a A Type-Collection of Bigrams (WW, Nov, 1982)

bazAAr, ABout, bACk, hAD, AEsthetic, AFter, AGainst, AHead, sAId, mAJor, mAKe, ALl, sAMe, ANd, extrAOrdinary, perhAPs, AQueous, ARe, AS, AT, becAUse, hAVe, AWay, tAX, mAY, magAZine

BAck, loBBy, suBCommittee, suBDivision, BE, cluBFoot, suBGroup, cluBHouse, BIg, suBJect, suBKingdom, puBLic, suBMarine, oBNoxious, aBOut, bomBProof, suBQuality, BRought, oBServed, oBTained, BUt, oBViously, suBWay, suBXerophilous, BY, suBZone

CAn, eCBolic, aCCording, aneCDote, sinCE, fliCFlac, eCGonine, whiCH, CIty, arCJet, baCK, CLose, aCMe, piCNic, COuld, eCPhonesis, aCQuire, aCRoss, politiCS, faCT, CUt, MechaniCVille [Rand McNally, N.Y.], CWm, aCXoyatl, poliCY, CZar

DAy, gooDBye, broaDCast, aDDed, maDE, granDFather, knowleDGe, chilDHood, DId, aDJustment, hanDKerchief, harDLy, aDMinistration, diDN't, DO, stanDPoint, heaDQuarters, chilDRen, hanDS, wiDTh, DUring, aDVantage, DWelling, ToloDXi [Phonedisc, Rockford, Ill. and Tampa, Fl.], boDY, aDZ

yEAr, basEBall, bECause, usED, bEEn, bEFore, bEGan, bEHind, thEIr, rEJected, weEK, wELl, thEM, beEN, pEOple, keEP, rEQuired, wERe, thESe, gET, nEUtral, EVen, nEW, nEXt, thEY, squeEZe

FAct, halFBack, brieFCase, serFDom, liFE, oFF, aFGhan, ofFHand, FIrst, FJord, calFKill, FLoor, feofFMent, alooFNess, FOr, ofFPrint, FutalauFQuen [Times Index-Gaz.], FRom, belieFS, aFTer, FUll, arFVedsonite, halFWay, aFXentiou [Phonedisc; West Orange, N.J.], identiFY, styFZiekte

aGAinst, peGBoard, doGCart, kinGDom, GEt, meaninGFul, suGGested, throuGH, GIve, loGJam, ginGKo, EnGLish, judGMent, foreiGN, GOod, baGPipe, nGQika [Cent. Cyc. Names 1954], GReat, thinGS, WashinGTon, fiGUre, doGVane, doGWood, LonGXuyen, enerGY, ziGZag

tHAt, neigHBorhood, fortHComing, birtHDay, tHE, youtHFul, churcHGoing, witHHeld, HIs, higHJacker, latcHKey, higHLy, establisHMent, tecHNical, wHO, birtHPlace, eartHQuake,

tHRough, montHS, migHT, cHUrch, boscHVark, higHWay,
meoHX [*OED*, under *mix*], wHY, maHZor

socIAl, possIBle, whICh, saID, experIEnce, IF, mIGht,
likelIHood, skIIng, marIJuana, lIKe, wILl, hIM, IN, natIOnal,
equIPment, technIQue, theIR, IS, IT, medIUm, gIVe,
handIWork, sIX, bIYearly, sIZe

JAzz, raJBansi, WoJCik [1429 in Phonedisc], sloJD, subJEct,
FaJFer [5 in Phonedisc], BaJGier [12 in Phonedisc], JHeel, JIg,
haJJi, riJKsdaalder, maJLis, jaJMan, JNana, maJOr, raJPramukh,
feJQien [Maltese for 'cure'], baJRa, WiJS method, muJTahid,
JUst, bliJVer, biJWoner, DiJXhoorn [*Web. Bio. Dic. 1966*],
JYngine, GiJZegem [*Times Index-Gaz.*]

remarKAble, worKBench, booKCase, breaKDown, liKE,
breaKFast, bacKGround, stocKHolder, KInd, blacKJack,
booKKeeping, quicKLy, worKMen, KNow, recKOn, cocKPit,
cucKQuean, banKRuptcy, weeKS, cocKTail, picKUp, KVass,
bacKWard, kicKXia, sKY, AchaKZai

LAst, eLBow, weLCome, wouLD, peopLE, himseLF, piLGrim,
schooLHouse, LIke, kilLJoy, waLKed, aLL, aLMost, ilLNess,
LOng, heLP, catafaLQue, aLReady, aLSo, feLT, vaLUe,
themseLVes, aLWays, caLX, onLY, coLZa

MAy, nuMBer, arMChair, filMDom, soME, coMFort,
sluMGullion, farMHouse, MIght, gyMKhana, firMLy,
coMMunity, coluMN, MOre, iMPortant, kuMQuat, coMRade,
hiMSelf, warMTh, MUst, circuMVent, teaMWork, XeMXija
[*Off. Stand. Names Gaz.*, Malta], MY, haMZa

NAtional, uNBroken, siNCe, aND, oNE, iNFormation, loNG,
iNHerit, uNIted, eNJoyed, thiNK, oNLy, goverNMent,
caNNot, NOt, iNPut, iNQuiry, suNRise, agaiNSt, iNTo,
NUmber, iNVolved, meaNWhile, aNXiety, aNY, broNZe

bOArd, prOBlem, sOCial, goOD, dOEs, OF, prOGram,
cOHerent, gOIng, prOJect, toOK, OLd, frOM, ON, tOO,
peOPle, elOQuent, fOR, mOSt, nOT, yOU, OVer, nOW,
bOX, bOY, dOZen

PArt, shiPBuilding, toPCoat, uPDated, PEople, helPFul,
camPGround, PHysical, sPIrit, skiPJack, uPKeep, peoPLe,
develoPMent, PNeumonia, uPOn, suPPort, poPQuiz,
PRogram, perhaPS, kePT, PUblic, hoPVine, uPWard, Q'oa'PX
[Hodge, *Handbook of Amer. Indians*], happY, LeiPZig

tariQA, ShuQBa [*Times Index-Gaz.*], QCepo [*Dorland's Med. Dict.*], taluQDar, QEre, cinQFoil, IraQGate [*neologism*], fiQH [*Random House*], QIviut, FeQJakuqe [*Off. Stand. Names, Albania*], aQKiyenik [Hodge, *Handbook of Amer. Indians*], taQLid, LuQMan, QNaitra [*Times Index-Gaz.*], QOph, MaQPiato [*14th Report Bur. Amer. Ethology,* 1896], zaQQum, miQRa, buQSha, QTrah [*Times Index-Gaz.*], QUite, QVint, acQWyte, ClerQX [*De Nederlandse Geslachtsnamen* 1971], QYrghyz, AhmaQZai [*Times Index-Gaz.*]

geneRAl, uRBan, chuRCh, towaRD, aRE, suRFace, laRGe, peRHaps, RIght, peRJury, woRK, woRLd, foRM, goveRNment, fROm, puRPose, toRQue, caRRied, fiRSt, paRT, tRUe, seRVice, foRWard, MaRXist, veRY, scheRZo

SAid, huSBand, SChool, TueSDay, theSE, succesSFul, diSGuised, SHe, SInce, miSJudged, aSKed, iSLand, SMall, waSN't, SO, SPecial, SQuare, clasSRoom, leSS, firST, SUch, tranSVerse, anSWer, MeSX [*Current Trends in Linguistics,* Vol. 1, Soviet & East European, 1963], SYstem, groSZ

sTAte, fooTBall, kiTChen, ouTDoor, afTEr, plaTForm, ouTGoing, THe, TIme, booTJack, caTKin, litTLe, deparTMent, wiTNess, TO, ouTPut, coTQuean, counTRy, iTS, beTTer, TUrn, posTVocalic, TWo, posTXyphoid, ciTY, bliTZ

individUAl, pUBlic, sUCh, stUDy, qUEstion, sUFficient, throUGh, broUHaha, qUIte, hallelUJah, dUKe, woULd, nUMber, UNder, continUOus, UP, boUQuet, oUR, mUSt, bUT, vacUUm, jUVenile, raUWolfia, flUX, bUY, pUZzle

aVAilable, VBerte [*OED* under *ubeity*], noVCic, heaVD, haVE, thraVFfe [*OED* under *thrave*], aVGas, GiVHans [*Rand McNally,* S.C.], serVIce, eVJe [*Times Index-Gaz.*], soVKhoz, VLei, tradeVMan, czareVNa, VOice, soVPrene, SoVQuinet [*Dorland's Med. Dict.*], cheVRon, reVS, PoloVTsian, VUlnerable, fliVVer, VWang [*Times Index-Gaz.*], MolyneVX [Phonedisc; Williamstown, Mass.], heaVY, eVZone

WAs, coWBoy, neWComer, croWD, WEre, aWFul, bloWGun, WHich, WIth, ploWJogger, haWK, knoWLedge, shoWManship, doWN, WOuld, vieWPoint, caWQuaw, WRote, neWS, groWTh, sWUng, loWVeld, gloWWorm, HaWXhurst [44 in Phonedisc], laWYer, froWZy

eXAmple, oXBow, eXCept, seXDecillion, fiXEd, oXFord, foX-
Glove, eXHibit, eXIstence, VaXJo [*Times Index-Gaz.*],
boXKeeper, aXLe, aXMinster, laXNess, eXOtic, eXPerience,
eXQuisite, banXRing, coXSwain, neXT, seXUal, poXVirus,
boXWood, waXXenn [*OED* under *wax*], oXYgen, eXZodiacal

YArd, maYBe, cYCle, hYDrogen, YEar, plaYFul, oxYGen,
anYHow, trYIng, pYJamas, tYKe, stYLe, sYMbol,
polYNomial, YOu, tYPe, triptYQue, thYRoid, alwaYS,
anYThing, picaYUne, polYVinyl, anYWay, asphYXiate,
gaYYou, analYZed

organiZAtion, whiZBang, meZCal, MaZDaism, siZE, topaZFels,
whiZGig, muZHik, amaZIng, muZJik, blitZKrieg, puzZLe,
miZMaze, GhaZNevid, horiZOn, miZPah, meZQuit,
arZRunite, vammaZSa, aZTec, seiZUre, rendeZVous,
ZWieback, ZzyZX [*Rand McNally;* Calif.], craZY, puZZle

Well over 90 percent of the bigrams can be found in unabridged
Merriam-Webster words, but a handful have proven remarkably
recalcitrant: *FX* requires an unusual Greek surname, and *QJ, MX,*
QP, and *QK* are found only in transliterations of obscure
Amerindian placenames.

For trigrams or tetragrams, a complete collection is impossible to
assemble, and it is necessary to define more specialized type collections. For example, there are six different ways in which three different letters can be arranged to form a trigram; can one discover a single unabridged Merriam-Webster word containing all six? The
answer appears to be no, although it is possible to specify a nine-
letter letter pattern that would accomplish it: abcabacba. A more
fruitful quest consists of identifying twenty-four unabridged
Merriam-Webster words that exhibit all possible permutations of
four different letters; groups based on *AIRT, AGIN, AIST, AGIR,*
ADIR, and *AGIL* have been found. The first two sets are given in
Figure 31b.

Figure 31b All Tetragram Permutations in Twenty-four Words (*WW,*
May 1984, Aug. 1984)

paRTIAl	TRIAl	TIARa	mARITal
cuRTAIn	TRAIl	sTAIR	veRITAble

pARTIcle	mATRIx	milITARy	RATIng
flIRTAtion	nITRAte	sATIRe	laRIAT
AIRTight	dIATRibe	TIRAde	tRAIT
semIARTiculate	wAITRess	sTARIng	admIRATion

imAGINe	aGAIN	dIAGNose	maNAGIng
mAGNIfy	orGANIc	trIANGle	NAIGie
campAIGN	GIANt	shenanIGAN	uNGAInly
visAING	vaGINA	sIGNAl	sporaNGIA
ANGIna	hanGNAIl	coINAGe	NIAGara
shenANIGan	laGNIAppe	martINGAle	shenaNIGAn

Perhaps the best-known logological question involving a trigram is the following one:

> There are only three words in the English language, all adjectives, which end in -gry. Two are angry and hungry; the third word describes the state of the world today. What is it?

The question first came to broad public consciousness on the Bob Grant radio talk show on WMCA in New York City in the spring of 1975; soon it was widely cited in the media. Ignoring the adjectival restriction, it is possible to identify nearly one hundred -gry words, including gry itself, but none of these are common, other than the two cited above. In fact, there is only one other adjective, meagry, meaning "meager"; it is listed in the Oxford English Dictionary. Figure 31c exhibits a considerable number of -gry words, ignoring a host of compound words like fire-angry or dog-hungry found in various dictionaries. Also omitted is the plausible nondictionary word ulgry, an unattested modification of ulgrie, an unidentified animal mentioned five times in John Smith's The True Travels, Adventures and Observations (London, 1630).

Figure 31c Dictionary Words Ending in -gry (WW, Nov. 1989, Feb. 1990, Nov. 1992)

AGGRY BEAD an African glass bead
ANGRY, HANGRY (OED), NANGRY (OED), UNANGRY angry
BEGRY (OED under beggary)
BEGGRY (Eng. Dial. Dict. under peel)
BRAGGRY (OED under braggery)
CONYNGRY, CONY-GRY (OED under conyger) a rabbit warren

GRY horse, in Gypsy dialect
HAEGRY (*Eng. Dial. Dict.* under *hagery*)
HIGRY PIGRY (*OED*) a purgative drug
HOGRY, HOGRYMOGRY, HUGGRYMUGGRY (*Eng. Dial. Dict.* under *huggerie*)
HUNGRY, AHUNGRY, ANHUNGRY, HONGRY (*OED*) hungry
IGGRY (*OED*) to hurry up, in Arabic
KAINGRY (*Eng. Dial. Dict.* under *caingry*)
MAGRY, MAUGRY, MAWGRY (*OED* under *maugre*) ill will; in spite of
MEAGRY (*OED*) meager
MENAGRY, MANAGRY (*OED*) domestic economy
MESSAGRY (*OED* under *messagery*) office of a messenger
PODAGRY the plant disease dodder
POTTINGRY (*OED* under *pottingary*) an apothecary
PUGRY (*OED*), PUGGRY a scarf on a sun-helmet
RUNGRY (*Eng. Dial. Dict.*)
SCAVENGRY (*OED* under *scavengery*)
SHIGGRY (*Eng. Dial. Dict.*)
SKUGRY (*OED* under *scuggery*) secrecy
YMAGRY (OED under *imagery*)

Placenames ending in -*gry* (*WW*, Nov. 1989, Feb. 1990)

AGRY DAGH (11th *Britannica*) Mount Ararat
BADAGRY (11th *Britannica*) Nigerian placename
BALLINGRY (*Bartholomew Gaz. of British Isles,* 1887) British placename
BUGRY (*Times Index-Gaz.*)
CHOCKPUGRY (*Worcester's Universal Gaz.*)
COGRY (*BBC Pronouncing Dict.*) British placename
DSHAGRY, DZAGRY, JAGRY (11th *Britannica*) Russian placename
ECHANUGGRY (*Century Atlas of World,* 1898) Indian placename
EGRY (*Times Index-Gaz.*) French placename
GAGRY (11th *Britannica*) Caucasus placename
LANGRY (*Times Atlas*) Siberian placename
LISNAGRY (*Bartholomew Gaz. of British Isles,* 1887) British placename
PINGRY (*Handbook of Private Schools,* 1985) New Jersey private school
SEAGRY, SEGRY (11th *Britannica*) British placename
SHCHIGRY, SCHTSCHIGRY, SHTCHIGRY, SHTSHIGRY, TCHIGRY (*Times Index-Gaz.*) Russian town
TANGRY, TINGRY (11th *Britannica*) French placename
TCHANGRY (*Index Geographicus,* 1864)
VIGRY, WIGRY (*Times Atlas*) Polish placename

Surnames in U.S. Telephone Directories (*WW*, May 1995)

KINGRY (94 in Phonedisc)   ANGRY (11 in Phonedisc)
PINGRY (47 in Phonedisc)   SHOGRY (11 in Phonedisc)
BENGRY (36 in Phonedisc)   BARAGRY (9 in Phonedisc)
EGRY (26 in Phonedisc)   STANGRY (4 in Phonedisc)
LANGRY (Austin, Tex.; Walnut Creek, Calif.; Cupertino, Calif.)
GINGRY (Indianapolis, Ind.; Greens Fork, Ind.; Silvis, Ill.)
TANGRY (Thomas of Sodus, N.Y.; Thomas J. of Rochester, N.Y.)
UNGRY (Brad of Lincoln, Neb.; Evelyn of Aurora, Col.)
GRIGRY (Beulah of Wharton, Tex.; Stephen W. of Monahans, Tex.)
BARRAGRY (Mary A. of Thiersville, Wis.; John J. of Appleton,
    Wis.)
LEGRY (John P. of Vancouver, Wash.)
MAGRY (T. H. of Beaumont, Tex.)
MCGRIGRY (Donna of Lewisville, Tex.)
MARGRY (Jean of New Castle, N.H.)
GRIGGRY (Houston of Flint, Mich.)
AGRY (B. W. of New York, N.Y.)

32 CONSECUTIVE IDENTICAL LETTERS

There are only a handful of words in the unabridged Merriam-Webster that exhibit three identical letters in a row without hyphens, apostrophes, or other punctuation: *headmistressship, goddessship, patronessship* and *wallless*. The latter word illustrates the inconsistencies that plague dictionary-makers; *gall-less* and *wall-like* are both hyphenated, as is *demigoddess-ship*. The unabridged Random House dictionary also admits *goddessship*, and the *Oxford English Dictionary* adds *countessship, frillless,* and *duchessship. Hostessship* appears in Shakespeare's *The Winter's Tale*, in Act IV, scene iv.

What about letters other than *S* or *L*? One can find many non-dictionary examples in abbreviations, ejaculations, comic books, nonce-words, trademarks, surnames, and the like. The nonvowel *brrr* appears in the *Oxford English Dictionary Supplement,* and *zzz* is in the unabridged Random House. The words *bzzzbzzz,* to gossip, and *pffft,* to go to ruin, are in Berrey and van den Bark's *American Thesaurus of Slang.* The word *weeest* is found in an 1878 citation in the Oxford, and *vertuuus* and *uuula* are early spellings of *virtuous* and *uvula* in the same source. The medical jawbreaker *laparohys-*

terosalpingoooophorectomy is usually hyphenated, but it appears solidly in William J. Robinson's *Medical and Sex Dictionary* (1933).

The *Oxford English Dictionary* is the source of three dictionary-sanctioned four-consecutive-identical-letter words: *eeeeve*, a variant of *iiwi* in a 1779 citation; *esssse*, an old spelling of *ashes;* and *brrrr*, a variant of *brrr*. The *American Thesaurus of Slang* adds *zzzz* and *hmmmm*.

Gazetteers contain *Kaaawa*, a town in Hawaii (*Times Atlas of the World*) and *Yyyezu* (*Official Standard Names Gazetteer,* USSR). Four-letter geographical names also exist: *Kyyyy*, a variant of *Kyyy* (*Official Standard Names Gazetteer,* USSR) and the Welsh town *Llanfairpwllgwyngyllgogerychwyrndrobwllllantysiliogogogoch*, cited in the *Guinness Book of World Records*. (This name appears in full on the railway station sign, but is usually abbreviated to Llanfairpwll on maps and highway signs.)

Figure 32a presents a collection of sentences that string together identical letters separated by punctuation marks (as in *Ross's seal* or *Ross's snow goose*, entries in the unabridged Merriam-Webster).

Figure 32a   Sentences with Consecutive Identical Letters

Nausicaa's typing was erratic, and she kept doubling words. When Aaron asked for "aa," he got from Nausicaa "aa aa." "Aa aa," Aaron said, "is redundant." (12 A)

The farmer's wife shouted at her son, "Stop shooting, Robb; BB bullets can injure the chickens!" (5 B)

With unemployment rising, the USA needs a program of public service jobs such as those the energetic CCC completed in the 1930s. (5 C)

I know a chap called Davy Judd who really loved his beer; he'd sup his Double Diamond till it made him feel quite queer. And when you think he'd had enough and couldn't take no more, then Davy Judd'd, D.D.'d, drink till he slumped to the floor. (7 D)

Lucinda was struggling to remember how many *Es* there were in the first syllable of *tepee;* "E?...EE?...eeney-meeney-miney-mo," she muttered to herself. (7 E)

Wagner's music is full of loud stuff; FFF figures prominently in many of his compositions. (6 F)

The Roman vase was priced XV denarii, IIII librae. (6 I)

Although on his sixth hajj, J. J. Jinnah was as excited as the first time. (5 J)

The black leader referred to the "sick KKK kids." (5 K)

"If the LL in the word MALL in the marquee won't turn on
automatically," said the supervisor, "then maybe Lavill,
L.L.'ll l—"; "L.L.L.'ll? LL'll!" L. L. Lloyd interrupted.
(20 L)

The chess player made a booboo (O-O-O); O-O obviously
was better. (8 O)

I used to enjoy concerts by the family von Trapp; PPP passages as well as FFF ones were both possible for this tal-
ented ensemble. (6 P)

The children's answers were incorrect except for Bess's "SS's
S's stand for Schutzstaffel." (9 S)

There is one unabridged Merriam-Webster word with four consecutive pairs of doubled letters: *subbookkeeper.*

33   CADENCES

It is difficult to find unabridged Merriam-Webster words having
more than two consecutive identical letters. To overcome this defi-
ciency, consider the idea of a cadence in a word: a set of identical letters spaced at equal intervals. The special case in which the cadence
spacing is two was long ago dubbed an alternating monotony.

Long words are more likely to contain cadences than short ones.
Not surprisingly, the longest word in the unabridged Merriam-
Webster contains one cadence of length four and five of length three:

pneumOnoultramicrOscopicsilicOvolcanoconiOsis
pneumonoultramicroscOpicsilicOvolcanocOniosis
pneumonoultramIcroscopicsillIcovolcanoconIosis
pneumonoultramicroscopiCsiliCovolCanoconiosis
pneumonoultramiCrosCopiCsilicovolcanoconiosis
pneumonoultramicrosCopicsiliCovolcanoConiosis

In order that a word contain no cadences of length two or more, it
must contain no repeated letters—that is, it must be an isogram, as
discussed in Section 26. The longest unabridged Merriam-Webster
word containing no cadences of length three or more is the twenty-
nine-letter *trinitrophenylmethylnitramine.* For various spacings, the
longest unabridged Merriam-Webster cadences are:

spacing 2: hUmUhUmUnUkUnUkUapuaa (8),
   mOnOgOpOrOus (6)
spacing 3: noNcoNdeNsiNg eNgiNe (6), EffErvEscEncE,
   sigmOidOprOctOstOmy, unExpEriEncEdnEss (5)
spacing 4: StreSsleSnesS, dAcryAdenAlgiA (4)
spacing 5: NoncoNtamiNatioN (4)

Cadences of length three can be found with all spacings from six through eleven; the latter is illustrated by *TransubstanTiationalisT* and *syNgenesiotraNsplantatioN*.

There are no unabridged Merriam-Webster words other than the forty-five-letter lung disease that have more than three cadences of length at least three. Three triple-three examples are given by *coNsubsTaNTIaTIoNIst* (spacings 7,3,3), *NoNINsTITuTIon* (spacings 2,4,2), and *succESSlESSnESS* (spacings 4,4,4).

The book *Combinatorics on Words* (Addison-Wesley, 1983) considers cadences in alphabets having fewer than twenty-six letters, in which any sequence of letters is counted as a "word." Depending on alphabet size and cadence length, there exists a letter-sequence length such that all letter sequences at least that long must contain a cadence. For an alphabet size of two (sequences consisting only of *A*s or *B*s), a cadence length of three must appear with a sequence length of 9, a cadence length of four must appear with a sequence length of 35, and a cadence length of five must appear with a sequence length of 178. For an alphabet size of three, a cadence length of three must appear with a sequence length of 27. For example, no cadences of length three appear in the sequences *aabbaabb, abbaabba,* or *ababbaba.*

In a pair isogram, discussed in Section 29, every letter participates in a cadence of length two. There exist eight-letter pair isograms in which cadence spacings of one, two, three, and four are all represented: *appeases* and *appearer.* However, no unabridged Merriam-Webster pair isograms of length ten exist for which the cadence spacings are one, two, three, four, and five.

34   LETTERS ANYWHERE IN THE WORD

There are 3,276 ways that three letters can be chosen from the alphabet with repetition allowed. It is possible to assemble a type-collection of these almost entirely from the unabridged Merriam-Webster dictionary; the seventeen that do not fall into this category are enumerated in Figure 34a.

Figure 34a Three-Letter Combinations not in Merriam-Webster (WW, May 1982)

FJQ jiffy-quick (*Oxford English Dictionary*)
FXZ Xhafzotaj (*Off. Stand. Names Gaz., Albania*)
JJQ Qingjujie (*Rand McNally New International Atlas*)
JJX jejunohepatopexy (*Index Medicus*)
JQV quasi-objective (*Random House*)
JQX Quxingji (*Rand McNally New International Atlas*)
JQZ jazzotheque (*Barnhart Dictionary of New English*)
JXX Xixiaojie (*Rand McNally New International Atlas*)
JXZ Xudzej (*Modern Language Assoc. International Bibliography,* 1974)
KQX squawkbox (Mary Peiter, *Dictionary of New Words,* 1955)
KXX jukebox-axiom (Hofstadter, *Gödel, Escher, Bach,* 1979, p. 155)
QQW Quweiq river (*Times Index-Gaz.*)
QQX Qixingqiao (*Rand McNally New International Atlas*)
KQX squaw-axe (*Oxford English Dictionary*)
QXX xaxaquine (H. Bennett, *Chemical & Technical Dict.,* 1974)
XXX hexahydroxycyclohexane (*Random House*)
XXZ oxybenzoxazole (*Hackh's Chemical Dict.,* 1969)

If one is restricted to the Pocket Merriam-Webster, it is possible to find all of the 351 two-letter combinations but *QQ*. A few are found in only two or three words: *JJ* jejune, jujitsu, jujube; *JQ* jonquil, jacquard; *JX* juxtapose, jinx; *QW* squaw, squawk; *QX* exquisite, quixotic, exchequer; *XX* executrix.

Logologists have also collected unabridged Merriam-Webster words containing as many as possible of each letter. A type-collection of these is given in Figure 34b.

Figure 34b Most Repeated Letters in Merriam-Webster Words (WW, Feb. 1969, Nov. 1970, Feb. 1995)

[*pneumonoultramicroscopicsilicovolcanoconiosis* omitted]

6A tAthAgAtAgArbhA
5B huBBle-BuBBle (BuBByBush)
5C CirCumCresCenCe

6D DiDDle-DaDDle (DisDoDecaheDroiD)
7E EthylEnEdiaminEtEtraacEtatE
4F riFFraFF
5G hiGGlehaGGlinG
4H tHymolsulpHonepHtHalein
7I IndIvIsIbIllItIes
4J JeJuno-JeJunostomy (JeJune)
4K KnicKKnacK
5L aLLopLasticaLLy
4M MuMMydoM
6N NoNaNNouNcemeNt
6O mOnOgOnOpOrOus
4P whiPPersnaPPer
3Q QaraQalpaQ
5R feRRipRotopoRphyRin
9S poSSeSSionleSSneSSeS
6T TaT-TaT-TaT (ToTipoTenTialiTy)
9U hUmUhUmUnUkUnUkUapUaa
3V oVoViViparous
4W WoW-WoW (WilliWaW)
2X eXecutriX
4Y dacrYocYstosYringotomY
4Z raZZmataZZ

It is possible to find seven-letter words in which all six possible arrangements of three different letters appear. The possible letter patterns consist of *ABCABCA* alfalfa, entente, Samsams, Sarsars, Semsems (Simsims); *ABACABA; ABACBAB* cachaca, tathata; *ABCBACB* Barabra; *ABCBABC* patapat, Sarasar (Sereser); *ABCABAC; ABCACBA.* Many longer words possess the same property.

There are a handful of unabridged Merriam-Webster words that contain all twenty-four possible arrangements of four different letters: *eint* in *intestinointestinal, cilo* in *pneumonoultramicroscopicsilicovolcanoconiosis,* and *inrt* in *trinitrophenylmethylnitramine;* these are exhibited for the latter word in Figure 34c.

Figure 34c All Twenty-four Possible Orders of Four Different Letters

INRT	trINitRophenylmeThylnitramine	EGOR	gEorGe O. gRegory
INTR	trINiTRophenylmethylnitramine	EGRO	gEorGe o. gRegOry
IRNT	trInitRopheNylmeThylnitramine	EOGR	gEOrGe o. gRegory
IRTN	trInitRophenylmeThylNitramine	EORG	gEORGe o. gregory

ITNR	trIniTropheNylmethylnitRamine	ERGO	gEoRGe O. gregory
ITRN	trIniTRopheNylmethylnitramine	EROG	gEoRge O. Gregory
NIRT	triNItRophenylmeThylnitramine	GEOR	GEORge o. gregory
NITR	triNITRophenylmethylnitramine	GERO	GEoRge O. gregory
NRIT	triNitRophenylmethylnITramine	GOER	GeOrgE o. gRegory
NRTI	triNitRophenylmeThylnItramine	GORE	GeORgE o. gregory
NTIR	triNiTrophenylmethylnItRamine	GREO	GeoRgE O. gregory
NTRI	triNiTRophenylmethylnItramine	GROE	GeoRge O. grEgory
RINT	tRINiTrophenylmethylnitramine	OEGR	geOrgE o. GRegory
RITN	tRIniTropheNylmethylnitramine	OERG	geOrgE o. gReGory
RNIT	tRiNITrophenylmethylnitramine	OGER	geOrGE o. gRegory
RNTI	tRiNiTrophenylmethylnItramine	OGRE	geOrGe o. gREgory
RTIN	tRiniTrophenylmethylnItramiNe	OREG	geORgE o. Gregory
RTNI	tRiniTropheNylmethylnItramine	ORGE	geORGE o. gregory
TINR	TrINitRophenylmethylnitramine	REGO	geoRgE o. GregOry
TIRN	TrInitRopheNylmethylnitramine	REOG	geoRgE O. Gregory
TNIR	TriNItRophenylmethylnitramine	RGEO	geoRGE O. gregory
TNRI	TriNitRophenylmethylnItramine	RGOE	geoRGe O. grEgory
TRIN	TRINitrophenylmethylnitramine	ROGE	geoRge O. GrEgory
TRNI	TRiNItrophenylmethylnitramine	ROEG	geoRge O. grEGory

The unabridged Funk & Wagnalls permutes *eort* in *electrotelether-mometer,* and the *Oxford English Dictionary* exhibits *einv* in *nievie-nievie-nick-nack* and *einz* in *zenzizenzizenzic.* Dmitri Borgmann noted that the plausible name *George O. Gregory* contains all arrangements of *eogr.* A man with this name was listed in the 1981 Richmond, Va., telephone directory; his permutations are shown in Figure 34c.

In order for all twenty-four permutations of four different letters to occur, the word containing them must have at least twelve letters. No such words of only twelve letters are known, but the following letter patterns (and their reversals) satisfy the requirements: *ABCDACBADCBA, ABCDACBADBCA, ABCDACBADCAB, ABCDABCADBAC.* These letter patterns all have a 4,3,3,2 distribution with the twice-appearing letter located in the fourth and ninth positions; it is conjectured that all qualifying letter patterns exhibit these properties. Some plausible twelve-letter names include *Roger O. Gregor, Ernie N. Reiner,* and *George O. Grego;* however, no individuals bearing these names have been discovered.

35 ANCHORED LETTERS

In the preceding sections, letters or letter groups were allowed to appear anywhere within a word. It is well known that *X* is by far the rarest letter occurring at the beginning of a word. More generally, what letters of the alphabet are most likely to shun certain positions in words? The leading candidates appear to be *Q* in the next-to-last position and *Q* and *J* in the last position. Unabridged Merriam-Webster dictionary uncapitalized words of four letters or more are quite scarce: for next-to-last *Q*, *waQf*, *burQa*, and *tariQa* (plus plurals of words ending in Q); for final *Q*, *shoQ*, *cinQ*, *taluQ*, *trinQ*, *sambuQ*, *zindiQ*, and *nastaliQ*; for final *J*, *benJ*, *gunJ*, *hadJ*, *hajJ*, *munJ*, *kaliJ*, *samaJ*, *somaJ*, *kaleeJ*, *kharaJ*, *khiraJ*, *kurunJ*, *sohmaJ*, *swaraJ*, *kankreJ*, and *hajiliJ*. If capitalization is permitted, *IraQi* is a common name that can be added to the list. The word *fiQh* is found in the unabridged Random House.

There is no complete set of Pocket Merriam-Webster words of a given length exhibiting all letters in all positions; the closest one can come to this ideal is with four-letter words, lacking only ---Q, --Q-, and ---J. Five-letter and six-letter words lack these patterns, plus words ending in *V*. Seven-letter words also lack examples having *J* in the next-to-last position.

Acrostic dictionaries were compiled in the last century arranging words by first and last letter, from *A--A*, *A--B*, through to *Z--Z*. All but 39 of the 676 possible categories can be filled with unabridged Merriam-Webster words, as Figure 35a illustrates (in a few cases, common proper names have been substituted for less-common Websterian examples). The longest and shortest Merriam-Webster words have also been compiled.

Figure 35a   A Type-Collection of Anchored Merriam-Webster Words

AreA, AraB, AcademiC, AnD, ArE, AlooF, AmonG, AlthougH, AlkalI, A--J, AsK, AlL, AM, AN, AlsO, AsleeP, A--Q, AfteR, AS, AT, AdieU, AnalaV, AlloW, AX, AnY, AdZ

BacteriA, BomB, BasiC, BehinD, BE, BrieF, BeinG, BotH, BroccolI, BenJ, BacK, BeautifuL, BedrooM, BeeN, BuffalO,

BishoP, B--Q, BetteR, BusinesS, But, BureaU, BonaV, BeloW, BoX, BY, BuzZ

ChinA, CluB, CatholiC, CoulD, ComE, ChieF, CominG, ChurcH, ConfettI, ChuJ, ChecK, CalL, ClaiM, CaN, ChicagO, CamP, CoQ, CaR, CarS, CannoT, ChateaU, ChiV, CoW, CompleX, CitY, ChintZ

DatA, DumB, DemocratiC, DiD, DonE, DeaF, DurinG, DeatH, DzigettaI, D--J, DarK, DeaL, DreaM, DowN, DO, DeveloP, D--Q, DooR, DoeS, Don'T, DamoiseaU, DeV, DreW, DupleX, DaY, DaeZ

ExtrA, EbB, EconomiC, EnD, ExamplE, ElF, EveninG, EacH, EnnuI, E--J, EmbarK, EquaL, ElM, EveN, EgO, EquiP, E--Q, EveR, EyeS, EighT, EmU, EmanatiV, ElboW, EquinoX, EverY, ErsatZ

FormulA, FiB, FantastiC, FounD, FacE, FlufF, FiG, FrencH, FungI, FunJ, FranK, FederaL, FroM, ForeigN, FrescO, FriendshiP, F--Q, FoR, FriendS, FirsT, FlU, FestiVe, FeW, FoX, FamilY, FuzZ

GrandmA, GraB, GeographiC, GooD, GivE, GolF, GoinG, GrowtH, GraffitI, GunJ, GreeK, GeneraL, GriM, GiveN, GO, GrouP, G--Q, GovernoR, GirlS, GeT, GurU, GaV, GreW, GreX, GraY, GrosZ

HysteriA, HuB, HistoriC, HaD, HE, HimselF, HavinG, HigH, HindI, HadJ, HooK, HoteL, HiM, HumaN, HerO, HelP, H--Q, HeR, HiS, HoT, HindU, HeaV, HoW, HoaX, HistorY, HumbuzZ

IdeA, IamB, InorganiC, InsteaD, IssuE, IF, IncludinG, IncH, IsraelI, I--J, InK, InternationaL, IteM, IN, IntO, ImP, IraQ, InterioR, IS, IT, ImpromptU, InvolV, IntervieW, IndeX, IndustrY, IneZ

JuliA, JoB, JudaiC, JoineD, JusticE, JefF, JoininG, JewisH, JacamI, J--J, JacK, JournaL, JiM, JohN, JumbO, JumP, J--Q, JunioR, JameS, JusT, JujitsU, JugoslaV, JeW, JasponyX, JurY, JazZ

KoreA, KnoB, KoraniC, KinD, KnifE, KerchieF, KinG, KetcH, KhakI, KhawariJ, KicK, KilL, KingdoM, KnowN, KangaroO, KeeP, K--Q, KilleR, KnowS, KnighT, KudzU, KisleV, KnoW, KyliX, KeY, KibitZ

LindA, LamB, LogiC, LookeD, LikE, LeaF, LonG, LengtH, LocI, L--J, LooK, LocaL, LooM, LearN, LeO, LeadershiP, L--Q, LateR, LesS, LasT, LieU, LeitmotiV, LaW, LateX, LikelY, LiederkranZ

MA, MoB, MusiC, MinD, MorE, MyselF, MakinG, MucH, MacaronI, MunJ, MarK, MateriaL, MaximuM, MaN, MoroccO, MembershiP, M--Q, MatteR, MemberS, MosT, MenU, MordV, MeadoW, MiX, MaY, MuzZ

NauseA, NumB, NeurotiC, NeeD, NamE, NeckerchieF, NothinG, NortH, NucleI, N--J, NecK, NationaL, NationalisM, NatioN, NO, NaP, NastaliQ, NeveR, NumberS, NoT, NoyaU, NerV, NeW, NartheX, NobodY, NatcheZ

OrchestrA, OrB, OrganiC, OlD, OnE, OF, OperatinG, OH, OkapI, O--J, OaK, OiL, OptimuM, ON, OntO, OverlaP, O--Q, OR, OtherS, OuT, OrmulU, OllaV, OverthroW, OX, OnlY, OyeZ

PA, ProverB, PubliC, PerioD, PeoplE, ProoF, PlayinG, PatH, PI, P--J, ParK, PoliticaL, PrograM, PositioN, PianO, PartnershiP, PontacQ, PoweR, PerhapS, ParT, PlateaU, PshaV, PilloW, ParadoX, ProbablY, PhiZ

QuA, QuaB, QuadratiC, QuestioneD, QuitE, QuafF, QuestioninG, QuasH, QuasI, Q--J, QuicK, QuilL, QualM, QuestioN, QuO, QuiP, QaraqalpaQ, QuarteR, QuestionS, QuieT, QuipU, QualitatiVe, QuartersaW, QuadrupleX, QualitY, QuiZ

ReplicA, RoB, RepubliC, ReD, RangE, RelieF, RinG, ResearcH, RabbI, RaJ, RocK, RolL, RooM, ReasoN, RadiO, RelationshiP, R--Q, RatheR, ReligiouS, RighT, RondeaU, ReV, RevieW, RelaX, ReallY, RazZ

SeA, SuperB, SpecifiC, SaiD, ShE, SelF, SomethinG, SucH, SkI, SaJ, StocK, StilL, SysteM, SeeN, SO, SteP, SuQ, SimilaR, StateS, SeT, SoU, SlaV, SaW, SiX, SaY, SpitZ

TeA, TuB, TraffiC, TolD, ThE, TurF, ThinG, ThroughH, TaxI, TaJ, ThinK, TelL, TheM, ThaN, TO, ToP, TaluQ, TheiR, ThiS, ThaT, ThoU, TaV, TomorroW, TaX, TheY, TopaZ

UtopiA, UnsiB, UnscientifiC, UseD, UsE, UnbelieF, UsinG, UnderneatH, UterI, U--J, UnlocK, UntiL, UniforM, UpoN,

UndO, UP, U--Q, UndeR, US, UniT, UrdU, U--V, UndertoW, UnorthodoX, UnitY, UnfrizZ

VirginiA, VerB, VolcaniC, VieweD, VoicE, VeinstufF, VotinG, VanisH, VermicellI, V--J, VolK, VitaL, VictiM, VisioN, VetO, VamP, V--Q, VinegaR, VariouS, VisiT, VirtU, VaV, VieW, VerteX, VerY, ViZ

WisteriA, WeB, WhimsiC, WoulD, WerE, WolF, WorkinG, WitH, WadI, W--J, WorK, WilL, WilliaM, WheN, WhO, WorshiP, W--Q, WaR, WaS, WhaT, WamefoU, WeaV, WindoW, WaX, WaY, WaltZ

XanthomA, X--B, XanthiC, XiphoiD, XylophonE, XerifF, XeroprintinG, XenolitH, XenomI, X--J, XicaK, XanthophylL, XanthiuM, XenoN, XibarO, XylocarP, X--Q, XysteR, XanthouS, XysT, XanadU, X--V, X--W, XylanthraX, XenogamY, X--Z

YeA, YoB, YttriC, YielD, YokE, YourselF, YounG, YoutH, YogI, Y--J, YorK, YelL, YaM, YarN, YahoO, YelP, Y--Q, YouR, YearS, YeT, YoU, YugoslaV, YelloW, YeX, YesterdaY, YeZ

ZebrA, ZimB, ZinC, ZoneD, ZonE, ZarF, ZigzaG, ZenitH, ZucchinI, Z--J, ZwiebacK, ZeaL, ZooM, ZeN, ZerO, ZiP, ZindiQ, ZippeR, ZeroS, ZesT, ZulU, ZhadnoV, ZiW, ZaX, ZoologY, ZizZ

The acrostic type-collection can be used to answer a question posed by Henry Dudeney in *The World's Best Word Puzzles* (London: The Daily News Publication Department, 1925): Can one embed the alphabet in words joined at their ends, as in *AraBloColDirgE...*? The answer is no for the unabridged Merriam-Webster, for there is no *I--J* or *U--V* word in Figure 35a. Darryl Francis suggested completing the word chain with two placenames from the *Times Index-Gazetteer, Inathganj* (in Pakistan) and *Ulanov* (in the former USSR). For other types of *A*-to-*Z* word lists, see Section 53.

36 INTERNAL PALINDROMES AND TAUTONYMS

Palindromes and tautonyms, the two most readily perceived word patterns, were discussed in Sections 21 and 22. These patterns can often be detected within words as well. Type-collections of internal palindromes and internal tautonyms of six or more letters are presented in Figures 36a and 36b. The latter list separately identifies tautonyms that are more than double but less than triple, such as *ALFALFA* or *ParINTINTIN*. Special attention should be paid to triple internal tautonyms, the only Websterian examples known being *AIAIAI*, *sHEHEHEyanu*, and *lOGOGOGue*.

Figure 36a A Type-Collection of Internal Palindromes of Six or More Letters in Merriam-Webster (*WW*, Feb. 1974, Nov. 1986)

gAILLIArde, AKAAKAi, cANAANAean, LecANIINAe,
tambAROORA, BARRABle, BATTABle, aBITTIBi,
CANNACeae, CARRACk, baCILLICide,
COCCOChromatic, COLLOCate, CONNOChaetes,
DAFFADowndilly, moDELLED, DIFFIDent,
ArmaDILLIDium, CyDIPPIDa, DISSIDent, fiddlEDEEDEe,
GALLAGe, GAMMAGraphic, cHALLAH,
cHATTAHoochee formation, occipITOOTIc, KEFFEKil,
KILLIKinick, KINNIKinick, thaLASSAL, swelLDOODLe,
gLISSILe, gLOSSOLogy, gLOTTOLogist, MATTAMore,
MILLIMeter, MITTIMus, MURRUMbidgee pine,
meNACCANite, aNALLANtoic, NANNANder,
kNAPPAN, uNARRANged, uNECCENtric,
syNEMMENon, uNESSENtial, bruNETTENess, sNIBBINg,
sNIFFINg, sNIGGINg, vaNILLIN, NIMMINg, NIPPINg,
kNITTINg, PINNIPed, bRAGGARt, gRAMMAR,
RAPPARee, bRASSARd, RATTARee, shREDDER,
gREGGER, tREKKER, quaRELLER, pRESSER, fRETTER,
corROBBORee, arROWWORm, hoSANNAS, miSDEEDS,
mademoiSELLES, SENNESer, asSESSES, roSETTES,
riSOTTOS, STAATSraad, SUCCUSation, SUFFUSe,
suSURRUS, sTACCATo, TAFFATa, sTANNATe,
TARRATine, casTELLET, inTERRETicular, TILLITe,
TINNITus, gUARRAU, WALLAWalla, WILLIWaw

opACIFICAtion, extrACIVICAlly, ADINIDAn, tAKAMAKA,
opAKAPAKA, mAKARAKA, gALAGALA, pALAPALAi,
cALCICLAse, guANABANA, ANAPANApa, rAMARAMA,
squAMOSOMAxillary, upANAYANA, anAPANAPa,
APOCOPAte, bARABARA, cARACARA, cARAJARA,
ASSESSAble, mATAMATA, lATINITAster, AVADAVAt,
kAVAKAVA, lAVALAVA, kAWAKAWA, BIAJAIBa,
CALCLACite, riCININIC acid, unDERBRED, prECIPICE,

weEDICIDE, rEDIVIDE, stEERTREE, ThymELAEALEs,
rELEVELEd, sEMITIME, distENDEDNEss,
splENDIDNEss, ethylENIMINE, TaENIOINEi,
pregnENOLONE, rEREFEREnce, ThEROMOREs,
rETINITE, prEVISIVE, iGNITING, recoGNIZING,
lIBIDIBI, ethICOSOCIal, coccIDIOIDIan, tIKITIKI,
awIKIWIKI, antILEVELIng, wILIWILI,
anchIMONOMIneral, chINAMANIac, hINAYANIst,
PhthIRACARIdae, bIRIBIRI, pIRIJIRI, pIRIPIRI,
eISEGESIs, ISOROSIndone, mISSISSIppi, nITIDITIes,
vITILITIgate, sensITIVITIes, excITOMOTIon, kIVIKIVI,
kIWIKIWI, phlorhIZINIZIng, bewiLDEREDLy,
huLLABALLoo, LLEWELLyn, skiLLIGILLee, MESOSEMe,
MONONOMial, gyNECOCENtric, saNITATINg,
uNLEVELNess, NONANONymity, lOCOFOCO,
mOCOMOCO, explOITATIOn, cOLOCOLO,
kOLOKOLO, hOMOEOMOrph, hOMONOMOus,
chrOMOSOMOlogy, tOMTITMOuse, bONAMANO,
mONOGONOporic, mONOTONOus, fOOTSTOOl,
cOROCORO, pOROPORO, tOROTORO, pOSSESSOr,
pOTAWATOmi, mOTTETTO, suPERPREParation,
PROCORPoration, PROMORPhology, coPROPORPhyrin,
PSOROSPerm, pROMEMORial, pROTUTOR,
cROWNWORt, counteRREFERRing, ipSEITIES, SELFLESs,
SEMIMESsianic, abSENTNESs, hawSEPIPES, miSERERES,
SERORESistance, deSERTRESs, SINONISm, miSREFERS,
TARTRATe, inTERFRET, inTERPRET, inTERURETeric,
inTRACARTilaginous, inTRAPARTy, elecTROCORTin,
elecTROHORTiculture, hUMUHUMUnUKUNUKUapuaa,
kUKURUKU, tUKUTUKU, okUPUKUPU fern,
kURUKURU, mURUMURU oil, pURUPURU,
graVITATIVe, dYSPEPSY, analYTICITY

CAILLIACh, ovERAPPAREled, caSTELLETS

wALLAWALLA, countERREFERREd, lEVITATIVE,
kINNIKINNIck, pREDIVIDER, aSSERTRESS

SENSUOUSNESs

Figure 36b A Type-Collection of Internal Tautonyms of Six or More
Letters in Merriam-Webster (WW, Feb. 1980)

ACEACEnaphthene, stomACHACHe, AKAAKAi, pALLALL,
crAMBAMBuli, slAMPAMP, cANAANAean,
OvANGANGela, TurANIANIsm, kANSANS, chANTANT,

nARSARSukite, cASEASE, ASSASSin, rATCATCher,
sATIATIon, nAYSAYS, BARBARic, BOOBOOk,
BORBORygmus, fiBROBROnchitis, BULBULe,
muCHACHA, CHECHEn, CHICHIbe, isoCHOCHOlia,
paCHYCHYmia, CINCINnati, COCCOChromatic,
CONCONscious, COXCOXtli, arCTICTIs, CUSCUSu,
hyDRODROme, antECAECAl, rECTECTomy, rEDEEDEd,
dENSENS, sENTENTial, palEOGEOGraphy, gERAERA,
camERIERI, hetEROEROtism, vERSERS, FARFARa,
FOOFOOrah, FULFULde, FURFURaceous, GARGARize,
GUAGUAnche, wretcHEDHED, dagHESHES,
paHOEHOE, chiHUAHUA, aHUEHUEte, LouisIANIAN,
fIERIER, pimperlIMPIMP, tINEINE, rINGING, seISMISM,
dISTISTyle, JOOJOOb, KANKANai, KHAKHAm,
KINKINess, SinupalLIALIA, alLIKLIK, veLLALLA,
paraLLELLEss, MARMARize, MIAMIAn, MORMORando,
cheMOSMOSis, NANNANder, uNCONCOrdat,
maNIENIE grass, uNINNINg, aNOUNOU, noNSENSE,
uNTANTAlized, coNTENTEd, dOLIOLIdae,
hOMEOMErous, nONCONCern, lONDONDerry,
nONIONIzed, spONSONS, bOOHOOHing, cOOLOOLy,
lOPHOPHytosis, cOPIOPIa, cOPROPRietor, mORIORI,
cOSTOSTernal, pediPALPAL, suPERPERfect,
scyPHOPHOre, paPIOPIO, PORPORate, PROPROvost,
PURPUReal, QUAQUAversal, sesQUIQUIntal,
veRATRATe, REDREDge, REPREPare, tRIARIAn,
farRIERIEs, nitROPROPane, fuSCESCEnt, eSCHSCHoltzia,
SCISCItation, viSCOSCOpe, obSESSES, SHASHAi,
SHISHIng, SHOSHOne, SIKSIKa, aSSESSEd,
insTANTANeous, TARTARic, meTASTASis, TAUTAUg,
counTERTERm, THATHAnai, THETHEr,
gnaTHOTHOrax, insaTIETIEs, TINTINnabulation,
TOKTOKje, ecTOSTOSis, inTRATRAcheal,
TRITRIacontane, elecTROTROpism, TSITSIhar,
TSUTSUgamushi, gUANUANche, UNIUNIvalent,
UNNUNNed, caUSEUSE, WARWARds

sACHACHA, piCROCROCin, fiddlEDEEDEE, mISSISSIppi,
KASKASKia, uNKINKINg, clOGDOGDO,
trOPHOPHOre, PREPREParation, aSSESSES, TSITSITh,
gERAERAE

prelINPINPIN, ParINTINTIN, TSUTSUTSi

ACETACETic, pACKSACKS, ANTIANTIbody,
ARCHARCHitect, grATINATINg, aliBANGBANG,
CHINCHINg, raCHISCHISis, CLEMCLEMalats,

CORACORAdiales, aHOLEHOLE, notIDANIDAN,
jINGLINGLy, quINOLINOL, homoIOUSIOUS,
hooMALIMALI, aNCIENCIEs, paNGUINGUI,
OPHIOPHIlism, OSTEOSTEatoma, pOSTROSTRal,
oPAKAPAKA, PALAPALAi, PERIPERIcarditis,
camPHORPHORone, PHOSPHOSilicate, PICOPICOgram,
POOHPOOHist, supRACORACOideus,
sTOMATOMAlacia, koTUKUTUKU, aWIKIWIKI

kAMEHAMEHA, dENIZENIZE, CarPHIOPHIOPs

mETHYLETHYLacetic, KINNIKINNIck, MICROMICROn,
    PHILOPHILOsophy, SUPERSUPERb

NEURONEURONal

GASTROGASTROtomy, QUADRIQUADRIc

Does *mANANAN* mean "pertaining to the Isle of Man"? This word
appeared on a postal cancelation advertising a music and arts festival
there. The *Oxford English Dictionary* contains the remarkable triple
internal tautonym *ZENZIZENZIZENZIc,* a word that also has six
Zs (see Section 34).

One can extend the idea of internal tautonyms to encompass sen-
tences such as the following: John and Mary are brINGING IN
GINGer snaps to eat; The Irish republican having his emblem, and
the English monarcHIST HIS, THIS THISTle must belong to the
Scottish nationalist. The latter sentence was constructed by Sir
Jeremy Morse. Figure 36c gives an example by Edward Wolpow.

Figure 36c   Falalalala-lala-la-la (*WW,* Feb. 1982)

Honolulu Lulu lullabied her baby and greeted the elderly
lady from Nassau, "Whom may you be?"

"I'm Bahama Mama, Ma'am—am amazed at how lovely it
is in Hawaii. What a joy to hear arara (rara avis) and see one
nene nesting."

"I can show you kukukuku, kusain and all the Pacific
islanders and their crafts. The Filipino's shop is down the
street and the Chinese's, ESE, seseli herbs planted nearby.
Tell me about yourself."

"I've had adventures all my life," sighed Mama. "I
encountered a bear in Argentina, on a safari joined for so

many pesos. Oso! S.O.S. O! So-so solution was to climb a tree. We met a French Guyana shepherd and with our new ewe we were stranded in the rain in Inini, nine miles from camp. I, out hunting nilgai, aiaiai, aimed my gun, but missed each time."

"Couldn't you see well?"

"I'm 83 now. When I was one and twenty ('20): 20/20. Twenty ('t went, yes) years later, I needed glasses. I used to live on First St., St. Stephen, SC, but then I went to the University of Maine, but in Orono, no nononerous work was to be had. The same was true in Albany, NY, Nyack and Troy. I've just opened a store in Meeker, Colorado, to sell South Seas produce. It's called the Rio Blanco Co. CO Coco Co. Cocozelles are also sold, in season."

"I'd love to chat some more," said Lulu, "but I'm going to a performance of my favorite Bach cantata. Ta-ta!"

"Ta-ta, take care!"

The book *Combinatorics on Words* (Addison-Wesley, 1983) considers internal tautonyms in alphabets having fewer than twenty-six letters, in which any sequence of letters is counted as a word. For an alphabet containing only *A* and *B*, all letter sequences of four or more must contain an internal tautonym; the three-letter exceptions are *ABA* and *BAB*. However, if the alphabet has three letters, then it is possible to construct arbitrarily long sequences of letters that have no internal tautonyms. To make a mathematically interesting problem, one must impose an added condition: What is the longest letter sequence using a three-letter alphabet that contains no internal tautonyms or permuted internal tautonyms (sequences such as *ABC-CAB* or *ABCCBCAC*)? The answer is seven, and the corresponding patterns of letters are *ABCBABC, ABACABA,* and *ABACBAB.* It is possible to find unabridged Merriam-Webster words matching two of these patterns: *sereser* (or *sarasar*), *patapat, cachaca,* and *tathata.*

For alphabets with four or more letters, it is conjectured that arbitrarily long letter sequences can be formed that do not have either internal tautonyms or permuted internal tautonyms. The longest Websterian words using four, five, or six different letters satisfying these requirements appear to be *taratantara, nonintention,* and *intertrinitarian.*

FOUR
TRANSFORMING ONE WORD INTO ANOTHER

THIS CHAPTER FORMS the core of letterplay. Words may be transformed into other words by inserting or omitting letters (*at* to *art, sand* to *sad*), or by rearranging them (*ocean* to *canoe*). In recent years, such changes have been viewed as transformations linking words in elaborate networks, the characteristics of which can be studied in their own right. It is through concepts such as these that logology has begun to transcend its reputation as a mere collection of curiosa, or a taxonomy of word types. By drawing on ideas from mathematics—in this case, graph theory—logology gains additional respectability and legitimacy.

41 INSERTIONS AND DELETIONS

The simplest operation that can be performed on a word is the deletion of a letter from it. In the inverse operation, a letter is inserted to make the word one letter longer, while preserving the letter order. If the deletion occurs at the beginning or the end of a word, it is known as a *beheadment* or a *curtailment*. The terms *hydration* and *caudation* have been suggested as names for insertions at the beginning or end of a word.

The longest chain of successive deletions using unabridged Merriam-Webster words is *strangelings-strangeling-strangling-stranging-stanging-staging-saging-aging-ging-gin-in-i*. For the Pocket Merriam-Webster, the corresponding chain is *sheathed-sheathe-sheath-heath-heat-eat-at-a* (achieved exclusively by beheadments or curtailments). On the other hand, Jeff Grant discovered that *Oxford English Dictionary* words allow a fourteen-step chain: *strengthenings-strengthening-strengthning-strengthing-strenghing-strenging-strening-streing-string-sting-sing-sin-in-I*. Figure 41a lists the longest beheadable words for each letter of the alphabet found in two Merriam-Webster dictionaries. These words were the subject of a *Games* magazine contest in January/February 1979.

Figure 41a   Longest Beheadable Words in the Pocket Merriam-Webster (*WW*, Aug. 1980, Nov. 1983) and the Third Edition of the Unabridged Merriam-Webster (May 1990)

a-pathetically, b-rightness, c-hastening, d-enunciation, e-numerating, f-rightfulness, g-astronomical, h-airbrush, i-slander, j-unction, k-nightly, l-ionization, m-eagerness, n-evermore, o-esophagus, p-rearrangement, q-s, r-evolutionary, s-peculation, t-reasonable, u-praise, v-indication, w-hereabouts, x-s, y-ourselves, z-one

a-pathetically, b-rightness, c-hastening, d-emulsification, e-motionlessness, f-utilitarianism, g-astronomically, h-edriophthalma, i-dentification, j-unctional, k-inaesthetic, l-imitableness, m-ethylacetylene, n-eopaleozoic, o-enanthaldehyde, p-redetermination, q-uinta, r-evolutionary, s-electiveness, t-reasonableness, u-praiser, v-indication, w-henceforward, x-anthophyllite, y-ourselves, z-oosporiferous

David Silverman introduced the concept of a charitable word, which remains a word no matter what letter is deleted, and a hospitable word, which can be transformed to another word by adding a letter in any position. To avoid uninteresting examples, consider only words having no doubled letters. The longest charitable word from the unabridged Merriam-Webster is *pleats: pleat, pleas, plets, plats, peats, leats;* the word *chains* offers a second example. The longest hospitable word from the unabridged Merriam-Webster is *cares: scares, cadres, caries, carets, caress.*

It is possible to find four-letter words in the unabridged Merriam-Webster that are both charitable and hospitable. *Anis*, a Scottish word meaning "once," deletes to *ani, ans, ais,* and *nis,* and inserts to *manis, arnis, antis, anils,* and *anise.*

Successive deletions and insertions can be used to transform one word into another quite different, as *stop-top-to-tot-tout-out-gout-got-go.* Two words joined by such a chain are said to be in the same insertion-deletion network. The majority of short words belong to a main network, with a number of much smaller ones not connected with it. The main network for Pocket Merriam-Webster words in boldface type (disallowing most plurals and past tenses) consists of approximately 2,800 words of one to eight letters in length. Much of the network is a hard-to-diagram thicket of interlocking cycles such as *-to-ton-on-one-tone-toe-* or *-planet-plane-plan-plant-.* All cycles are of even length, with the minimum being four. In addition, there are many peripheral branches that have a more treelike appearance, and even some long single strands. Most chains leading to eight-letter words are of this nature:

```
                   chatter
                     |
         shatter—hatter    theater
                  |           |
         HATE—hater——heater——heather——heathery


                            mutter
                              |
         BUT--butt--butte--butter--utter--putter--sputter--splutter
                              |
                       cutter--clutter
```

Other eight-letter words in the main network include *wrangler, masteryly, leathern,* and *leathery.*

Let the distance between two words in the main network be

defined as the minimum number of steps needed to transform one into the other (eight, for example, for *stop* to *go*). The span of a network is then defined as the maximum possible distance between two words in the network. For the main network of the Pocket Merriam-Webster, the span is not known for sure, but the distance between *dud* and *miserly* has not been reduced to fewer than thirty-four steps:

> DUD-dude-due-dune-dun-dung-dug-drug-rug-rung-RUN-runt-rut-rout-out-pout-pot-poet-pet-pert-per-pier-pie-pice-ICE-mice-mince-mine-miner-minter-miter-mister-miser-misery-MISERLY

All known paths from *dud* to *miserly* go through *run* and *ice;* the only likely place to reduce the steps is between these words.

The calculation of the span is a very difficult computer problem for networks of any size. Leonard Gordon calculated the span between end-words of equal length for various limited networks in which the maximum word allowed was three, four, or five letters in length. The span varied from eight (between two-letter end-words in a network allowing words at most three letters long) to twenty-six (between four-letter end-words in a network allowing words at most five letters long). Since the span increases with both the length of the end-words and the maximum word allowed, one can conjecture that the span for the Pocket Merriam-Webster network is forty.

One can define an idealized distance between words that consists of the number of steps necesssary if any letter-combination forms a "word." To calculate the idealized distance, cancel the maximum subsequence of letters common to both words, as, for example, *MTL* in *MasTerLy* and *MenTaL,* and count the remaining letters in the two words. If two words have no common letters, such as *dud* and *miserly,* the idealized distance is the total number of letters they contain. Using this concept, one knows that it is impossible to reduce the distance between *run* and *ice* to less than six no matter what dictionary is used.

There exist word-pairs with distance and idealized distance both equal to fourteen: *LEATHERY-leather-lather-lathe-late-ate-at-a-an-wan-wain-win-wing-swing-SOWING.* No doubt longer such chains can be found; the one above can be extended to fifteen with *snowing*, not a Pocket Merriam-Webster word in boldface type. If the difference between the distance and the idealized distance is not zero, it must be an even number.

Figure 41b diagrams the two largest known insertion-deletion networks outside the main network for the Pocket Merriam-Webster.

Figure 41b The Two Largest Insertion-Deletion Networks Outside the Main Network in the Pocket Merriam-Webster (*WW*, Aug. 1987)

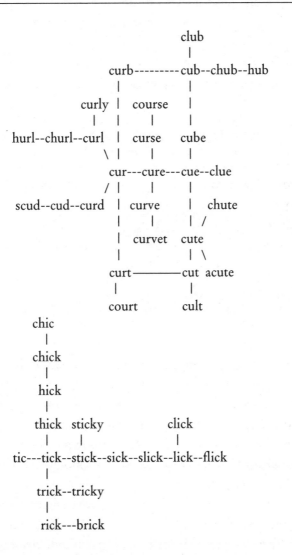

42 FROM LADDERS TO WORD NETWORKS

If a letter is deleted from a word and another letter inserted at the same place, the operation is known as a letter-change. A sequence of words, each one a letter-change of its predecessor, is known as a *word ladder*. Lewis Carroll christened word ladders *doublets,* and challenged readers to connect antonymic words of the same length by means of a word ladder, such as *LESS-loss-lose-love-move-MORE.*

If one considers words in boldface in the Pocket Merriam-Webster (barring most inferred forms such as plurals or past tenses), the words most susceptible to letter-changes are presented in Figure 42a.

Figure 42a Pocket Merriam-Webster Words with the Most Changes

> AN: ad am as at ax ay in on (8)
> SAY: sac sad sag sap sat saw shy sky sly soy spy sty bay cay day fay gay hay jay lay may nay pay ray way (25)
> WARE: ward warm warn warp wart wary wade wage wake wale wane wave were wire wore bare care dare fare hare mare pare rare tare (24)
> SHARE: shard shark sharp shade shake shale shame shape shave shire shore spare scare snare stare (15)
> BATTER: batted batten bather banter barter better bitter butter hatter latter matter patter tatter (13)
> PETTING: patting pitting potting putting betting getting jetting letting netting setting wetting (11)
> SLIPPING: slapping slopping shipping skipping snipping clipping flipping (7)

If inferred forms are allowed, these records are easily broken; there are nineteen letter-changes on *mates.* Corresponding studies of unabridged Merriam-Webster words have not been made. However, Jeff Grant has discovered in the *Oxford English Dictionary* forty-two letter-changes on *ea,* fifty on *say,* fifty-three on *were,* thirty-six on *share,* thirty-four on *better,* twenty-eight on *betters,* twenty on *slatters,* fourteen on *slattered* and fourteen on *slattering.*

Many words, of course, do not admit even a single letter-change; David Silverman christened these *isolanos.* In the Pocket Merriam-Webster, there are no isolanos of length two, but twelve of length three: *ebb, emu, gnu, imp, ism, its, nth, obi, ohm, ova, urn,* and *use.* In the unabridged Merriam-Webster, three-letter isolanos are impossible to find, and even four-letter ones are unusual: *ecru, ziim, ukaz.* In the *Oxford English Dictionary, tprw* and *umff* qualify.

David Silverman called a word an *onalosi* if any of its letters can be replaced with other letters to form other words. The longest onalosi formed from boldface words in the Pocket Merriam-Webster is *shore: chore, store, share, shone, short;* if one allows inferred forms, *canter: banter, center, caster, canker, cantor, canted* qualifies. In the unabridged Merriam-Webster the longest onalosi known is *pasters: tasters, posters, patters, passers, pastors, pastels,* and *pastern,* found by Mary J. Hazard.

David Morice rechristened onalosis *friendly words,* and added some new wrinkles to the concept. A friendlier word is one in which the replaced letters also spell out a word, as in CANTER: pANTER, CeNTER, CArTER, CANnER, CANToR, CANTEd, yielding *Pernod.* Other six-letter examples include *bracks* (to *clinty*) and *paster* (to *consol*). A friendliest word is a friendlier word that, in a second substitution, can return to itself, such as CAT: hAT, CoT, CAd to HOD and HOD: cOD, HaD, HOt back to CAT.

By successively changing each of the letters in a word, one can convert a word to one with different letters in all positions. In the Pocket Merriam-Webster, *settle* can be converted to *banner, filler, banker,* or *barter* in six moves, the minimum possible.

SETTLE, settee, setter, better, batter, banter, BANNER
SETTLE, settee, setter, fetter, fitter, filter, FILLER
SETTLE, settee, setter, better, batter, banter, BANKER
SETTLE, settee, setter, better, batter, barter, BARKER

For the third edition of the unabridged Merriam-Webster, the record is eight, demonstrated by Kyle Corbin: THUMBING-*thumping-trumping-tramping-trapping-crapping-crappins-crappies*-CRAP-POES. If the first, second, and third editions of the unabridged Merriam-Webster are allowed, a nine-letter solution is possible: CANCERATE, *cancerite, cancerine, cancering, cantering, bantering, battering, battening, battoning,* BUTTONING.

Two words that can be joined by a word ladder are said to be in the same word network. Unlike insertion-deletion networks discussed in Section 41, word networks consist entirely of words of the same length. Figure 42b depicts the main network for seven-letter words in the Pocket Merriam-Webster; since all the words end with -*ing*, this has been omitted.

As the word length increases, the networks become smaller and more fragmented, and the number of isolanos (words belonging to networks of size one) increases. In the *Official Scrabble Players Dictionary*, 901 of the 907 three-letter words (99 percent) are in a single main network. For four-letter words, the numbers are 3,550 and 3,670 (97 percent); for five-letter words, 6,950 and 8,200 (85 percent); for six-letter words, 7,750 and 14,300 (40 percent).

For any pair of words in a network, there is a minimum-step ladder joining them. The span of a network is defined as the length of the longest of these minimum ladders; the corresponding pair of words are the farthest apart of any word-pair in the network. In Figure 42b, it is not difficult to determine that the span is seventeen (from *parting* to *longing*).

The spans of the four *Official Scrabble Players Dictionary* networks are, respectively, ten, fourteen, twenty-nine, and forty:

> IVY-icy-ice-ace-aye-tye-the-thy-try-fry-FRO
> INCH-itch-etch-each-eath-eats-pats-pals-aals-alls-ills-illy-idly-idle-ISLE
> GENRO-genre-genie-genic-xenic-xeric-ceric-ceria-curia-curie-curse-purse-purge-surge-sarge-saree-spree-sprue-sprug-sprig-sprit-split-uplit-unlit-unlet-inlet-islet-isles-idles-IDLER
> PAINCH-paunch-launch-launce-jaunce-jounce-bounce-bouncy-bounty-county-counts-mounts-mounds-pounds-poinds-points-joints-joists-jousts-rousts-roasts-coasts-coapts-compts-comets-comers-corers-carers-carets-carats-carate-cerate-derate-delate-relate-relace-reface-deface-defame-degame-DEGAGE

Other pairs of words achieve the span; for example, -*pry*-PRO can be substituted for -*fry*-FRO.

It is likely that the unabridged Merriam-Webster main networks consist of larger fractions of the total wordstock than do the *Official Scrabble Players Dictionary* networks; however, the spans may not change much. Details on the evolution of a network are given in Section 43.

Dmitri Borgmann once asserted that substituting *V* for *U* in a word is "one of the most difficult feats in English verbal acrostics,"

Figure 42b Seven-Letter Main Network of Pocket Merriam-Webster Words (WW, Aug. 1973)

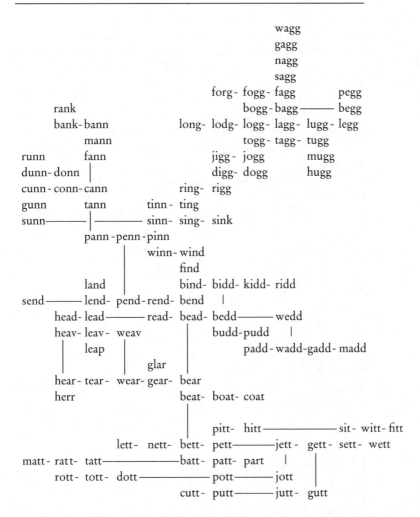

citing only *valUe-valVe, leU-leV, moUe-moVe, roUe-roVe* and *taU-taV*. Figure 42c examines this problem in depth, suggesting words for each of the 325 possible letter-pairs. In general, substitutes involving Q are more difficult; the word *coq* is extremely valuable to have.

Figure 42c All Possible Letter-Substitutions in Word Ladders (WW, May 1969)

Aid-Bid, peAk-peCk, Aim-Dim, sAt-sEt, Air-Fir, Around-Ground, Aide-Hide, An-In, Aurist-Jurist, Aid-Kid, coAt-coLt, alAs-alMs, beAt-beNt, An-On, sAy-sPy, Aue-Que, heAd-heRd, peAt-peSt, peA-peT, fAn-fUn, Aim-Vim, peA-peW, seA-seX, boA-boY, Aero-Zero

Ball-Call, Bark-Dark, Bat-Eat, Bill-Fill, Bin-Gin, Book-Hook, faBled-faIled, Bump-Jump, Bite-Kite, Bit-Lit, Be-Me, Bun-Nun, But-Out, Big-Pig, Built-Quilt, Bug-Rug, Been-Seen, Bee-Tee, Brine-Urine, Beer-Veer, Be-We, taB-taX, Bank-Yank, Best-Zest

Cog-Dog, peCk-peEk, Cat-Fat, Cap-Gap, Cot-Hot, Crony-Irony, Cam-Jam, sCull-sKull, Cow-Low, Can-Man, diCe-diNe, Cut-Out, Cast-Past, Cuit-Quit, Care-Rare, Came-Same, Cart-Tart, taCt-taUt, liCe-liVe, Can-Wan, aCe-aXe, Cam-Yam, maCe-maZe

corD-corE, golD-golF, hanD-hanG, Dog-Hog, aDd-aId, Dot-Jot, maDe-maKe, reeD-reeL, Dust-Must, Deed-Need, Dust-Oust, Dear-Pear, Duality-Quality, Dead-Read, Do-So, minD-minT, beaD-beaU, Dine-Vine, Din-Win, waD-waX, honeD-honeY, Done-Zone

Ear-Far, Eel-Gel, latE-latH, bEd-bId, Ear-Jar, worE-worK, talE-talL, East-Mast, beEt-beNt, nEw-nOw, carE-carP, coE-coQ, fuEl-fuRl, Eat-Sat, seE-seT, bEt-bUt, Ease-Vase, Earn-Warn, seE-seX, feE-feY, fuzE-fuzZ

Fun-Gun, Fat-Hat, waFt-waIt, Fog-Jog, Fill-Kill, Fast-Last, Fan-Man, oF-oN, Far-Oar, Fair-Pair, Fuelled-Quelled, oF-oR, iF-iS, iF-iT, loFt-loUt, File-Vile, Food-Wood, waFer-waXer, Four-Your, Foster-Zoster

Gate-Hate, Grate-Irate, Gay-Jay, thinG-thinK, Get-Let, Gate-Mate, Go-No, Gut-Out, Gale-Pale, Guest-Quest, Gum-Rum, Gin-Sin, panG-panT, revenGe-revenUe, Gain-Vain, Good-Wood, boG-boX, baG-baY, raGe-raZe

tHe-tIe, Hug-Jug, Hiss-Kiss, Hate-Late, Heat-Meat, Hear-Near, tHe-tOe, Hat-Pat, Hua-Qua, Ham-Ram, Have-Save, Hail-Tail, sHe-sUe, Heal-Veal, Here-Were, aH-aX, Hour-Your, Heal-Zeal

Iamb-Jamb, locI-locK, faIl-faLl, claImed-claMmed, saId-saNd, In-On, Irate-Prate, waIf-waQf, laId-laRd, waIted-waSted, baIted-baTted, bId-bUd, serIes-serVes, aIl-aWl, poI-poX, dIe-dYe, tIar-tZar

Jilt-Kilt, Jog-Log, Jar-Mar, Jot-Not, Jar-Oar, Joke-Poke, Juey-Quey, Jam-Ram, Jay-Say, Joy-Toy, taJ-taU, Jest-Vest, Jar-War, raJ-raX, maJor-maYor, Jest-Zest

taKe-taLe, saKe-saMe, liKe-liNe, silK-silO, looK-looP, trinK-trinQ, peeK-peeR, Kale-Sale, booK-booT, Knit-Unit, caKe-caVe, Kill-Will, taKes-taXes, treK-treY, maKe-maZe

Let-Met, taLk-taNk, silL-silO, Lost-Post, coL-coQ, baLk-baRk, Laid-Said, maLe-maTe, sLit-sUit, stoLe-stoVe, Line-Wine, coaL-coaX, paL-paY, Lone-Zone

Mine-Nine, Mat-Oat, Man-Pan, Muid-Quid, Main-Rain, Met-Set,

Men-Ten, beaM-beaU, saMe-saVe, Mind-Wind, heM-heX, theM-theY, priMe-priZe

Nut-Out, Nine-Pine, coN-coQ, eveN-eveR, iN-iS, iN-iT, laNd-laUd, saNe-saVe, Near-Wear, fiN-fiX, baN-baY, None-Zone

sOar-sPar, coO-coQ, foOt-foRt, loOt-loSt, sOar-sTar, shOt-shUt, Oat-Vat, tOo-tWo, coO-coX, whO-whY, quartO-quartZ

coP-coQ, Pan-Ran, Pit-Sit, Pore-Tore, sPite-sUite, Pine-Vine, Paste-Waste, siP-siX, raP-raY, doPe-doZe

Quinate-Ruinate, Quit-Suit, Quart-Tuart, coQ-coU, Qat-Vat, coQ-coW, coQ-coX, coQ-coY, coQ-coZ

theRe-theSe, ouR-ouT, taRt-taUt, caRe-caVe, Ripe-Wipe, taR-taX, baR-baY, Real-Zeal

iS-iT, poSt-poUt, Seal-Veal, Say-Way, miSer-miXer, Sear-Year, Seal-Zeal

beaT-beaU, haTe-haVe, That-What, siT-siX, haT-haY, maTe-maZe

valUe-valVe, sUing-sWing, taU-taX, dUe-dYe, feU-feZ

Vest-West, waVy-waXy, braVed-braYed, haVe-haZe

boW-boX, saW-saY, West-Zest

boX-boY, siXes-siZes

braYing-braZing

A minimum-length pangrammatic word ladder is one that uses all the letters of the alphabet in as few steps as possible. They come in two varieties: the twenty-six-step ladder in which the last word circles back to rejoin the first one, and the less elegant (but slightly shorter) ladder which can begin and end anywhere. The former is possible for four-letter *Official Scrabble Players Dictionary* words. In the closed ladder below, capital letters are the ones that change as one reads from left to right; a different arrangement of the alphabet ensues if one reads the ladder from right to left.

-maZe-Faze-Gaze-gaVe-Wave-wavY-waXy-waRy-warN-waIn-wHin-Shin-shiT-sUit-Quit-Duit-duCt-ducE-duPe-Jupe-juKe-jOke-jAke-Bake-baLe-Male-

Leonard Gordon discovered a pangrammatic ladder of the second variety using words from the unabridged Merriam-Webster.

FAQIRS-faKirs-fakErs-Nakers-Bakers-Takers-taVers-taWers-taXers-taLers-Halers-haYers-haZers-Gazers-gaPers-Japers-Capers-cOpers-Mopers-Dopers-dUpers

If letters can also be rearranged from one step to the next, see Section 49 for a closely related study of substitute-letter transpositions.

43   A MATHEMATICAL DIGRESSION: THE STRUCTURE OF WORD NETWORKS

This section is more technical in character than others in this book, and may be omitted by the casual reader. However, it does offer further insight into the character of word networks.

How does a network of words form as words are added one at a time to a collection? Figure 43a shows what happens if one adds three-letter words in decreasing order of frequency in English-language text as tabulated by Kucera and Francis in *Computational Analysis of Present-Day American English* (Brown University Press, 1967). Each word is followed by its Kucera and Francis rank (*the 1, and 2, was 3, for 4*, etc.)

The initial linkage of words into a network occurs when *him 15* joins *his 5;* the next word selected, *has 16*, joins these two with *was 3* and *had 6* in the mini-network

HAD
|
HIM--HIS--HAS--WAS

No further accretions occur to this until *way 29* creates a nine-word network that also captures the previously formed fragment of *can 20, may 23* and *man 27*.

HAD WAY--MAY--MAN--CAN
  | |
HIM--HIS--HAS--WAS

Little more happens for awhile except for the addition of *men 34, day 36, say 41, war 43, far 45* (which adds *for 4* as well), *saw 53, law 55* and *car 57. Nor 69* unites this eighteen-word network with a fourteen-word one that started with *not 7, new 21* and *now 25*, to make a network of thirty-three words, 48 percent of all the three-letter words thus far encountered in Kucera and Francis. For

Figure 43a   The Evolution of a Three-Letter Word Network (*WW*, May
1989)

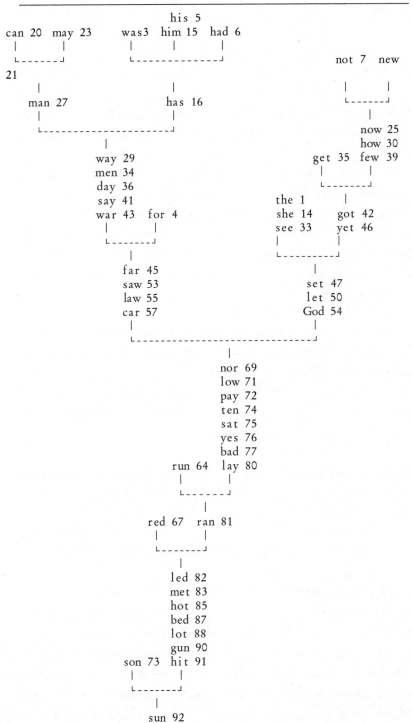

the first time this can be fairly regarded as the main network. (The only competitors are *put-but-out-our, any-and-end,* and *act-art-are-age-ago.*)

The main network continues to grow slowly, increasing its fraction of all the three-letter words sampled. By the time 169 words have been included, the main network contains 85 percent of the three-letter words. Occasional groups of two or more words are brought in (*who-why, her-per, all-ill,* and *two-too-top-ton* are waiting in the wings), but most additions are one word at a time.

It is even more interesting to study the fluctuations in the span as the network grows. Intuitively, one would expect the span to increase with network size, especially when large subnetworks coalesce as they did with *nor.* On the other hand, as isolated networks become ever more rare and most words are added singly, the increasing interconnectedness of the network should halt, or even reverse, the span growth.

Let us see what happens in the present case. Before *nor* is added, the two networks have spans of seven (*can* to *him*) and five (*the* to *few*); the new network has a span of fourteen: *THE-she-see-set-get-got-not-nor-for-far-war-was-has-his-HIM.* This is unusually large for a thirty-three-word network, reflecting the fact that it is very loosely connected. By contrast, the span of the 539 three-letter words in the Pocket Merriam-Webster is eleven, and the span of the 907 words in the *Official Scrabble Players Dictionary* is ten (see Section 42). By this time the main network has captured all but six words: *gnu, qua, ebb, ism, ugh, oxy.* The center of the network has become a luxuriant tangle of alternate routes. There are 33 words one step away from *pal,* and 244 more (over one-quarter of the whole) two steps away. Probably one-third of the words lie one or two steps away from *pat-pay-sat-say.*

Networks built from longer words behave in the same way, but because of their decreased density in word-space the effects take longer to show up. As a rule of thumb, it takes about five times as many words of length $n+1$ as words of length n to produce the same effect. Figure 43b omits much of the detail of Figure 43a, citing only those words such as *nor* that join various already-formed networks.

Figure 43b   Summary of the Evolution of a Three-Letter Word
Network

5 has (his 2, was 1, had 1)
9 way (was 5, may 3)
15 far (war 13, for 1)
33 nor (for 18, not 14)
42 ran (man 40, run 1)
44 led (let 42, red 1)
52 sun (run 50, son 1)
59 bit (hit 52, big 1, but 5)
71 sex (see 61, six 9)

76 die (did 74, due 1)
80 buy (but 77, boy 2)
83 dry (day 81, try 1)
103 odd (add 101, old 1)
109 Bob (boy 106, job 2)
119 aim (aid 111, arm 7)
143 fog (fig 141, dog 1)
148 Tim (aim 143, Tom 4)

The corresponding picture for four-letter Kucera and Francis words
is given in Figure 43c.

Figure 43c   Summary of the Evolution of a Four-Letter Word Network
(WW, May 1989)

Main Network
4 gave (give 2, have 1)
11 live (five 5, love 1, like 4)
13 move (love 11, more 1)
17 fine (five 13, find 3)
27 game (gave 17, same 9)
31 firm (fire 28, form 2)
37 Mike (like 33, make 3)
44 nine (line 39, none 4)
52 wine (line 48, wide 3)
57 Rome (come 52, role 4)
65 wore (more 58, were 2, work 4)
128 hole (home 71, hold 56)
156 lose (nose 128, lost 27)
165 fort (form 159, sort 2, foot 3)
176 lake (like 168, late 7)
188 mile (mine 186, milk 1)

196 wave (have 192, wage 3)
199 load (road 197, loan 1)
201 meat (meet 199, mean 1)
204 sale (same 202, salt 1)
222 seed (need 216, seen 5)
257 fail (fall 233, mail 23)
268 fool (foot 258, pool 9)
273 mood (food 270, moon 2)
277 cash (case 273, wash 3)
293 vary (Mary 291, very 1)
298 Jess (less 295, Jews 2)
309 lane (land 306, Jane 2)
320 cure (care 317, curt 2)
341 flew (fled 324, flow 16)
344 Fred (feed 341, free 2)

Network Leading to HOLE
3 held (head 1, help 1)
7 hold (held 4, told 2)
10 read (head 7, real 1, road 1)
13 hear (head 10, year 2)
31 hell (held 17, hall 13)
38 fell (hell 31, feel 6)
51 beat (heat 39, boat 1, best 10)
56 text (test 54, next 1)

Network Leading to LOSE
3 past (part 1, last 1)
9 lost (last 4, cost 4)
13 park (part 11, dark 1)
16 pass (past 13, mass 2)
18 loss (lost 16, less 1)
21 mark (park 18, Mary 2)
23 post (past 21, poet 1)

For four-letter words, the important accretions that first form what can be called the main network occur with the addition of *hole 330*, uniting a 71-word network with a 56-word one, followed immediately by *lose*, which joins the resultant 128-word network with a 27-word one. The resultant network contains 47 percent of the 331-word sample up to that point. By the time 513 words have been sampled, the main network contains 344 words, or 67 percent of the total. Surprisingly, eight of the twenty commonest four-letter words in Kucera and Francis (*that, this, they, when, what, than, them, then*) form a ten-word island with *thin* and *chin*, which does not join the main network until the 636th word is sampled. Another island of thirteen words, based on *does* and *goes*, does not join until the 784th word.

The span of the four-letter network is 23 just after *hold* and *lose* join it: *WAIT-want-went-west-best-beat-heat-head-held-hold-hole-role-rose-lose-lost-last-fast-fact-pact-part-park-mark-Mary-MANY*. The largest known span, 25, occurs when *very* is added to the network and it attains a size of 213: *VERY-vary-Mary-mark-park-part-pact-pace-pale-male-mile-file-fill-fall-fail-fair-pair-paid-laid-land-band-bank-back-lack-luck-LUCY*. For the 3,670 words in the *Official Scrabble Players Dictionary*, the span is only 14 (see Section 42). By this time the main network contains nearly 97 percent of the four-letter words.

For five-letter words, the grand coalition into a main network occurs when *beats* unites a 383-word network with a 233-word one, *blink* unites this 617-word network with a 69-word one, and *blots* unites this 687-word network with a 27-word one, to form a main network of 715 words, 43 percent of the 1,664 words sampled to that point. By the time *Beame* (the name of a New York City mayor of the 1970s) is reached, the main network, then 860 words in size, still contains only 46 percent of the words sampled; the growth of this network is agonizingly slow. However, if the entire *OSPD* network of 8,200 five-letter words is taken, then the main network contains 85 percent of them.

The span of the five-letter network is 52 when *beats, blink,* and *blots* have been added; by the time the full *OSPD* is included, however, it has reduced to 29. In general, the ratio of the maximum span achieved to the *OSPD* span is about 1.75. It is likely that these statistical characteristics—the maximum span associated with various word-lengths, as well as the proportional reduction in span size that later occurs—will remain much the same no matter how words are added to the sample.

In constructing word ladders, it is often easier to discover a link having the same vowel-consonant pattern than one with a different pattern. One can, in fact, visualize a network of three-letter words as a collection of eight subnetworks, of four-letter words as a collection of sixteen subnetworks, etc. Each subnetwork consists of a linked group of words having the same vowel-consonant pattern (call these internal links), and there are links joining different subnetworks to each other (call these external links).

Visually, it is difficult to see the subnetworks; the typical network does not divide into islands of densely connected words connected by isthmuses. Nevertheless, it can be quantified. To fix ideas, let Y be a consonant if it occurs at the start of a word, and a vowel otherwise. One can tabulate the average number of internal and external links emanating from a random word in each subnet

Average Number of Links to a Word in a Specified Subnetwork

From: | To:	CCVC	CCVV	CVCC	CVCV	CVVC	CVVV	VCCC	VCCV	VCVC	VCVV	VVCC	VVCV
CCVC|	_6.53_	.58			.42				.13			
CCVV|	2.17	_3.37_				.03				.16		
CVCC|			_11.72_	.78	.74						.19	
CVCV			1.27	_9.25_		.05						.09
CVVC|	.29		1.71		_8.88_	.05						
CVVV|		.10		1.86	1.33	_0.57_						
VCCC|							_2.62_	.36	.93		.50	
VCCV							.20	_1.53_		.17		.07
VCVC|	.37						.28		_4.00_	.19		
VCVV		.29						.43	.88	_1.62_		
VVCC			6.12				.74				_2.49_	.22
VVCV				3.26				.30			.39	_1.22_
Density	.008	.005	.026	.053	.038	.005	.015	.009	.016	.012	.003	.006

work. This is shown in the table above for *Official Scrabble Players Dictionary* four-letter words. To keep the statistics less volatile, only cases containing twenty or more internal links in a subnetwork have been included. The row of numbers at the bottom gives the word-density in each subnetwork: the ratio of the words to the theoretical maximum of all possible letter-patterns of that subnetwork.

The external-link averages are less than the internal-link averages (underlined) in thirty-two out of thirty-six cases—a fairly strong indication of the greater difficulty encountered in moving between subnetworks.

One can adduce a theoretical explanation of this increased difficulty, based on the idealized but unrealistic assumption that "words" are formed by random choices of letters with equal probabilities. To move from a word of, say, vowel-consonant pattern CVCV to another word with the same pattern, there are four possibilities: change the first consonant to another consonant (twenty cases, remembering Y is a consonant in the first position), change the second vowel to another vowel (five cases, counting Y now as a vowel), change the third consonant to another consonant (nineteen cases), or change the fourth vowel to another vowel (five cases). This sums to forty-nine possibilities, a far greater number than that allowed when moving from one subnetwork to another. For example, if CVCV is altered to CVCC, there are twenty possibilities, or if CVCV is to be altered to CVVV, only six. Analogous calculations could be made allowing letter-frequencies to mimic English text.

Why would any external links exceed internal ones in average value? This is explainable by the fact that the external link joins a less-dense subnetwork to a more-dense one; there are simply more opportunities for external links than internal ones. In the table above, all of the anomalous statistics (large external-link averages) correspond to such a situation.

An extreme illustration of this phenomenon is provided by the VVCCC subnetwork. Of the 19 such OSPD words, 10 are joined by a total of only 6 links (*airns-airts-airth, ought-aught, earls-earns, easts-oasts-ousts*), for an average of $6 \times \frac{2}{19} = 0.63$ links emanating from a random word; however, 14 of the words are united in 90 links with the CVCCC subnetwork, for an average of $\frac{90}{19} = 4.74$ links emanating from a random word. The CVCCC subnetwork is ten times denser (a fraction .00086 of all possible word positions occupied) than the VVCCC one (a fraction of .00008).

Having established the reality of subnetworks more loosely joined with external links to other subnetworks, what can be done with this structure? One can look for special types of word ladders that tour as many of the subnetworks as possible, lingering as little as possible in each subnetwork in turn. The ideal is a closed ladder (a cycle) of eight three-letter words, sixteen four-letter words, etc., which visits each subnetwork in turn and stays there for only one word. This is difficult to achieve because certain networks (notably the vowel-only or consonant-only ones) are very sparsely populated. Instead, one must allow various imperfections:

- ladders that visit all subnetworks but are not closed
- ladders that dwell in a given subnetwork for more than one word
- ladders that are closed but do not enounter all subnetworks
- ladders that visit as many subnetworks as possible without dwelling in any one
- trees that visit as many subnetworks as possible (if all are visited, this is a maximal spanning tree)

The network for the 907 three-letter *Official Scrabble Players Dictionary* words is presented below. The subnetwork size is given for each pattern, and the lines joining subnetworks are labeled with the number of links between them.

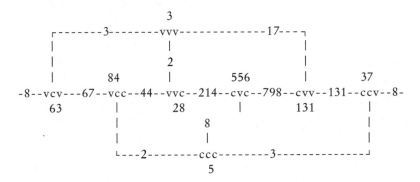

All subnetworks are represented (*cwm, nth, pht, shh,* and *tsk* in the *ccc* one, and *aye, eye,* and *eau* in the *vvv* one), and all connecting links exist. A closed completed no-dwell tour is impossible because the only ladder fragment through *vvv, tau-eau-ear* (or *-eat*), cannot be joined at both ends by the only ladder fragment through *ccc, phi-pht-pat* (or *-pet, -pit, -pot, -put*). A closed no-dwell tour of the six other subnetworks is achievable with the ladder *-bra-baa-bar-ear-err-era-*, as well as an open no-dwell tour of all eight, *poi-phi-pht-pit-ait-alt-ale-aye*, or a closed dwell tour of all eight, *-nth-[noh-nos-bos-bys]-ays-aye-tye-[the-tho-two-twa]-[awa-ewe-ere-era-eta]-eth-*. Finally, there exists a no-dwell spanning tree with a high degree of symmetry.

```
emu---eau
 |
eft---eat---pat---pay
           |
          pht---phi
```

If one uses words from the second edition of the unabridged Merriam-Webster, a closed complete no-dwell tour is at last possible: *-eau-pau-phu-ahu-aht-pht-pat-eat-*.

The study of four-letter word networks is more interesting. Of the sixteen subnetworks, fifteen contain words from the *Official Scrabble Players Dictionary* (no all-vowel words). The only three all-consonant words are *cwms, psst,* and *tsks.* There exists a closed no-dwell tour that visits eight subnetworks: *-eyes-eres-erns-erne-eyne-tyne-tyee-tyes-*. If the tour is open, it can be expanded to thirteen subnetworks: *flex-flea-olea-oles-eyes-tyes-tyee-tyne-eyne-erne-erns-eons-tons.* If one relaxes the no-dwell restriction, can an open tour visiting all fifteen subnetworks occupied by words be constructed? Trial and error suggests it is impossible, but the following open tour on fourteen exists: *cwms-[cams-cans-cons]-eons-erns-erne-eyne-tyne-tyee-tyes-oyes-oles-olea-flea-flex.* It is possible to connect all fifteen subnetworks with only nineteen words in a tree structure by appending the branch *thro-[tyro-tyre-* to *tyne* above.

The study of subnetworks of five-letter words is less complete. Figure 43d depicts a maximal spanning tree based on words in the *Official Scrabble Players Dictionary;* twenty-seven of the theoretically possible subnetworks are represented. The *OSPD* does not contain words for subnetworks *vvvvv, vvvcv,* and *vvvvc* (although the second edition has *aioli*), and there are no outside connections to *crwth* and *phhht,* or *schmo* and *schwa.*

Figure 43d A Maximal Spanning Tree for the Five-Letter Word Network (*WW*, Aug. 1994)

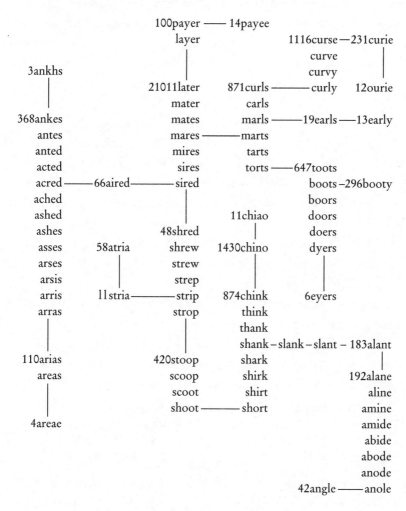

FROM STRINGS AND RINGS TO DIRECTED NETWORKS

Deletions and insertions can be combined in various ways to make words change into other words. Suppose that a word is changed into another by beheading it and inserting a new letter at the end. If this operation is continued on each new word thus formed, and the words are listed in an offset column so that each column consists of repetitions of the same letter, a *word stair* is formed. However, it is more compact to list the successive letters in a string: *spa-pal-ale-lea-*

eat-ate-tea compresses to *spaleatea.* In his 1925 book, *The World's Best Word Puzzles* (London: The Daily News Publications Department), Henry E. Dudeney presented several word-stair problems (also called word chains), claiming "this is an original form of Word Puzzle which was first introduced by the compiler of this volume a few years ago." Dudeney generalized the idea to include multiple beheadments and additions, as in *shrimp-impair-airway-waylay-layman.*

The longest word strings that can be constructed with no words repeated depend strongly on the word-length and dictionary size. For three-letter words using the Pocket Merriam-Webster the longest string is *waspantherayeatearevex.* Using the unabridged Merriam-Webster, Tom Pulliam constructed a string of three-letter words 437 letters long; no doubt this could be extended by computer. For four-letter words the Pocket Merriam-Webster record is *tsaridesk,* but again using the unabridged Merriam-Webster a far longer string, 296, is possible. Strings of five-letter words have also been investigated; the best unabridged Merriam-Webster example known is *sacaracharamanasalemaneth.*

The easiest way to shrink these string lengths to manageable size is to impose the added restriction that no letter in the string appears more than once. The longest strings then become:

	Pocket Merriam-Webster	Unabridged Merriam-Webster
3 letters	SPALEGOBINK	GJAWLOPSTYREDHUBINK
4 letters	ATOMENDS	KVASTONERICHUMP
5 letters	ALINERT	STOMANICER

By using a variety of dictionaries, Jeff Grant found a string of twenty three-letter words, only four short of the theoretical maximum: *gjudzostwnevrymphilack. Gju* is in the *Chambers Twentieth Century Dictionary,* and *udz, evr, ymp,* and *mph* are in the *Oxford English Dictionary.*

Word rings are word strings joined at the ends. These were first explored by Dudeney sometime before 1925, but the only examples he gave consisted of double beheadments, as in *-mean-anna-name-.* Word rings are difficult to form from Pocket Merriam-Webster words. There are only four rings of three-letter words known: *asp, are, aper,* and *anther.* Using the unabridged Merriam-Webster, the longest-known rings of three-letter and four-letter words are *anthye-*

dopsimul and *haloweris,* respectively. No doubt a computer could improve on these.

When the length of the word ring is the same as the length of the words comprising it, one is dealing with a cyclic transposition, discussed in Section 47. Alternatively, this is viewed in Section 62 as a cyclic word square.

Word strings can be generalized to word chains, in which more than one letter is replaced, as in *cone-near-arid-idea-each.* More generally yet, neither the word lengths nor the degree of overlap need remain constant. These have been called *ana-gram-mar* chains by Christopher McManus. There are so many ana-gram-mar chains possible that one must impose further restrictions, such as chains in which the compound words do not etymologically resemble their components, as in *cad-avers-ion* or *epic-enter-tain,* or chains in which each compound word must be one letter longer (or shorter) than its predecessor: *a-a-do-es-car-pal-mist-each-where-after-market-places.*

Word strings and word rings can be looked at in the more general framework of word networks, just as word ladders were in Section 42. However, these networks have a feature that the earlier ones did not: one can move in only one direction, from *ear* to *are* but not back from *are* to *ear.* In particular, there are some words that start networks, such as *die* or *gnu,* and others that end networks, such as *adz* or *end.* (Some words, such as *cwm* and *gyp,* have both characteristics; they are isolanos, unconnected with any other words.) We call these *directed networks* to distinguish them from the earlier ones.

In addition to isolanos, starters, and enders, directed networks contain many words that have neighbors preceding and following, such as *tan* (*eta-tan-and*) or *pya* (*spy-pya-yaw*). These words are called *intermediates.*

As more words are added to a directed network, new features appear. Certain sets of intermediates form word rings, enabling one to reach any word from any other: *-ant-nth-the-her-era-ran-, -era-rap-ape-per-.* These rings can be of any length (even two, as in *-aga-gag-*), and can intersect each other (as do the first two above, on *era*). As words continue to accrete, one witnesses a situation analogous to the coalition of various isolated small networks into a main network (Section 43). Isolated rings combine into a tangle of inter-

Figure 44a A Schematic Directed Network for Three-Letter Words in the Pocket Merriam-Webster

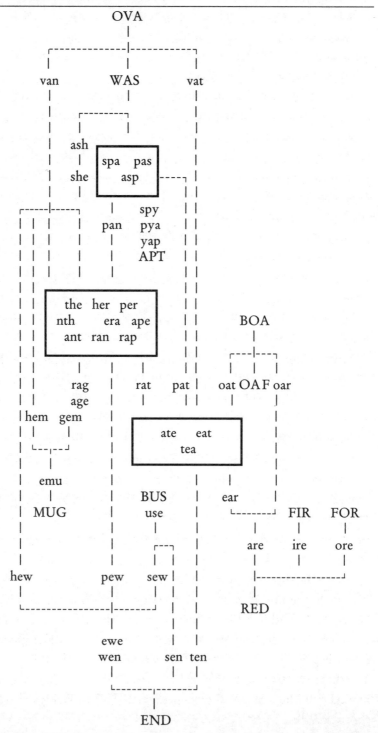

locking rings that is called a *core*. Eventually, one ends up with a main core, in which any word can be reached, albeit indirectly, from any other, and possibly one or more cores unconnected with the main one except via one or more word strings all running in the same direction.

The existence of cores calls for a refinement of nomenclature. The words in a core are called *insiders*. In turn, all words in any string connecting a starter with an insider are called *preceders*, and all words in any string connecting an insider with an ender are called *followers*. Words in strings that connect two cores are called *connectors*, and otherwise-unlabeled words in strings that bypass cores are called *bypassers*.

This terminology can be confusing, and is best seen by the examination of a relatively simple directed network. In this network, three-words overlap each other on two letters, a pattern which Leonard Gordon calls a (3,2) directed network. This network has been diagrammed in some detail, but in Figure 44a it is shown schematically. It is based on the set of 539 Pocket Merriam-Webster words, excluding initialisms such as *DDT* and *TNT*.

In this network, cores have just begun to form; two are three-word rings and the third is a six-word ring linked to one three-word ring by the word *era*. In addition to these 15 insiders (bounded on all sides by bold lines), the network contains 154 starters, 77 enders, 15 bypassers, 2 connectors, 4 preceders, and 81 followers, a selection of which is shown in Figure 44a. The capitalized words *OVA, WAS, BOA, FOR, FIR,* and *BUS* are starters, and the capitalized words *OAF, APT, MUG, RED,* and *END* are enders. All strings are read from top to bottom, following the connecting lines, except for the insiders, which are read in (sometimes intersecting) cycles. The four preceders (*ash, she, van, vat*) are all depicted, as are the three connectors (*pan, rat, pat*). Strings such as *spy-pya-yap* are not connectors but followers because *yap* directly joins the ender APT. Eight of the 15 bypassers are shown: *hew* joining the preceder *she* to the follower *wen*, *hem* joining the preceder *she* to the follower *emu*, and *oar* joining the starter *BOA* to the follower *are*. The other five bypassers (*ire, ore, use, sew, sen*) are perhaps less aptly named, for the starters they represent begin no strings that pass through a core.

As Figure 44a illustrates, starters and enders do not necessarily join each other. The starter *WAS* (along with *has* and *gas*, and the insider *pas*) joins 63 of the 77 enders; visualize it as a tree with 77 branches using a total of 154 words. The one-way span of the word *WAS* is defined as the minimum possible distance to its most distant ender—in this case, 9: *WAS-asp-spa-pal-ale-leg-ego-gob-obi-BID* (or *BIG*, or *BIB*). It is not possible to extend this string by adding *-bit-ITS* or *-bit-INK*, because other strings to *its* or *ink* are shorter: *WAS-ask-ski-kin-INK*, *WAS-ask-ski-kit-ITS*. The one-way span of the directed network is the maximum value of the one-way spans of the 154 possible starters. In this network the one-way span is 12: *OVA-van-ant-nth-the-her-era-rag-ago-gob-obi-bin-INK*. There is no way the string from *OVA* to *INK* can be reduced below 12, and there are no other starter-ender pairs that have a span exceeding 12.

Similarly, enders have reverse trees of starters which lead to them. In the Figure 44a network, the reverse tree ending at *END* has the largest number of words, 202, in it; 118 of the 154 starters join *END* using a total of 202 words.

Some trees or reverse trees are tiny. The starter *AVE*, for example, has a tree consisting only of the two enders *VET* and *VEX;* the ender *SKY* has a reverse tree containing only *ask, asp, spa, pas,* and the starters *GAS, WAS,* and *HAS.* The smallest reverse tree consists of *BOA* and *OAF,* matched by *BOA* and *OAK.*

In addition to the main network outlined in Figure 44a, there are several smaller networks that can be easily reconstructed by the reader from the following word lists:

> bur, cur, fur, our, out, urn, you
> aim, dim, him, imp, rim, vim
> ail, ill, ilk, mil, nil, oil
> axe, lax, tax, wax
> gnu, nub, nun, nut
> ace, act, lac, sac
> ice, icy, tic

The largest string constructible in the main network with no words repeated appears to be twenty words in length: *WAS-asp-spa-pan-ant-nth-the-her-era-ray-aye-yea-eat-ate-tea-ear-are-rev-eve-VEX.*

A final concept, the two-way span, is of little interest in the directed network of Figure 44a, but assumes greater importance in others. Defined only for insiders (words in the core), it is equivalent to twice the span of a standard word network. For any two insiders, find the minimum-length path that goes from the first word to the second and back to the first; the two-way span is the maximum of this quantity, taken over all possible insider pairs. For the Pocket Merriam-Webster, the two-way span is ten, achieved, for example, by APE and ANT in Figure 44a.

The *Official Scrabble Players Dictionary* contains 908 three-letter words, a substantial increase over the Pocket Merriam-Webster 539. The main network looks very different, consisting of 817 words, including 315 insiders (one large core of 308, plus satellite cores of 3 and 4 insiders), 259 starters, 139 enders, 27 preceders, 63 followers, 2 connectors, and 12 bypassers. Figure 44b shows the relationship among the three pieces of the core. Three of the words in the 308-word core (*emu, ask, obi*) are in parentheses; the words in the two smaller cores are bracketed; beginners and enders are capitalized.

Figure 44b also shows the two connectors, bit (joining *obi* in the large core to its in a small one) and *hit* (joining the follower *ghi* to *its*). Figure 44c depicts some of the twelve bypassers (*nun, our, ice, zoo, oaf, woe, hoe, roe, wax, rim, rid,* and *rin*).

Figure 44b Core Relations for Three-Letter Words in the *Official Scrabble Players Dictionary*

Words in brackets are in the secondary cores; words in parentheses are in the primary core

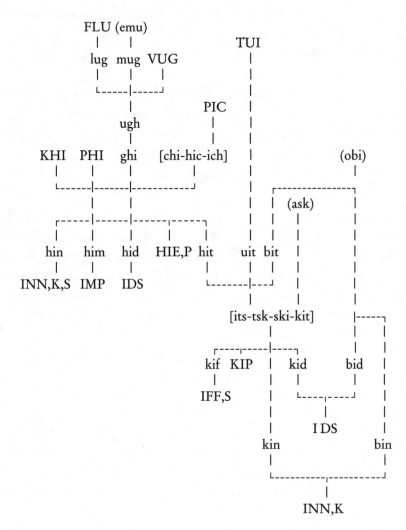

Figure 44c Bypass Relations for Three-Letter Words in the *Official Scrabble Players Dictionary*

Words in parentheses are in the primary core

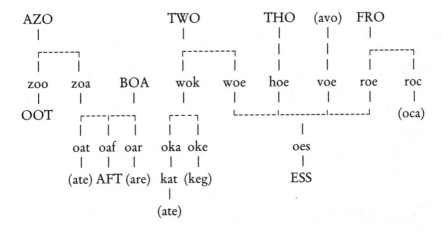

Neither the one-way nor the two-way span of this network is known. The ninety-one words not in the main network are all isolanos.

45 HALF-OVERLAPPING DIRECTED NETWORKS AND WORD FRAGS

Networks in which each word in a string half-overlaps the next are of special interest; these are (2n,n) directed networks, which can be studied by breaking the words into half-word pieces, or *frags*, and studying the directed network of frags instead. In the (4,2) directed network, each word consists of a frag joined by a directed link. An example of a frag network is given below:

$$
\begin{array}{l}
\text{IN} \leftarrow \text{SP} \leftarrow \text{WA} \qquad \text{DR} \rightarrow \text{UB} \\
\quad \downarrow \qquad \downarrow \qquad\qquad\qquad \downarrow \\
\text{TO} \quad \text{IT} \leftrightarrow \text{CH} \leftrightarrow \text{AR} \rightarrow \text{UM} \\
\quad | \qquad\qquad \uparrow \quad \downarrow \\
\quad | \qquad \text{FL} \rightarrow \text{EA} \leftarrow \text{ID} \leftarrow \text{SL} \\
\quad \downarrow \qquad\qquad\qquad \downarrow \\
\text{RI} \longrightarrow \text{SE} \rightarrow \text{ED}
\end{array}
$$

The full frag network, of course, is a far more tangled mass of fragments and links. The nomenclature introduced in Section 44 can be used: *CH, AR, ID, EA,* and *IT* are insiders, collectively forming the network core; *WA, SL, FL,* and *DR* are beginners; *UM, UB,* and *ED* are enders; *SP* is a preceder; *SE* is a follower; *IN, TO,* and *RI* are bypassers.

It is interesting to study the frag network of the 1,949 four-letter words from the two editions of the Pocket Merriam-Webster (1964, 1974). Of the 307 different frags found in these words, there are 133 insiders, 66 starters, 93 enders, 9 preceders, and 6 followers. There are no bypassers. All frags are found in a single network; there are no two-frag isolanos. Essentially, one has a densely packed core of insiders surrounded by starters and enders. Most of these are directly connected with the core, but a few are separated by preceders (*GL-IB-EX-, CR-IB-EX-, TU-BA-NE-, EC-RU-SE-, BR-AE-RO-, SL-AV-ER-, SI-GN-AT-, SL-OB-IT-, BL-OB-IT-, KN-OB-IT-, SN-OB-IT-, JE-HU-GE-, AC-HE-AD-*) or followers (*-AR-IA-MB, -AL-EE-RY, -CO-IF-FY, -SH-AH-OY, -AM-EN-VY, -EA-SY-NC*). In addition, many beginners connect directly with enders.

Complications arise when one translates the terminology of the frag network to the underlying (4,2) directed network. Each word consists of two frags and therefore must be identified by a hyphenated label such as starter-preceder (*tuba, sign*) or insider-insider (*core, tame*). By analogy with the (3,2) directed network, one can reassign single-word descriptors to words in the (4,2) network. It is evident that one should call a word an insider only if it consists of two insider frags, a preceder if it consists of a preceder frag and an insider frag, and a follower if it consists of an insider frag and a follower frag. However, one must distinguish between starters that lead to the core and starters that lead to a bypass of the core, a problem which did not arise before. Let us call a starter that leads to the core, such as *quad,* a starter as before, and one that does not lead to the core, such as *quiz,* a beginner; similarly, we distinguish between enders and finishers. Finally, we call a word consisting of a starter frag and an ender frag a *terminator.* To summarize, a starter-preceder-insider-insider-follower-ender frag string converts to a starter-preceder-insider-follower-ender string of overlapping words, and a starter-bypasser-

bypasser-ender frag string to a beginner-bypasser-finisher string of overlapping words.

The single connected network of two-letter frags from the Pocket Merriam-Webster converts to a multiplicity of (4,2) directed networks. There is a single large network of 1,730 words which has a dense core of 849 insiders surrounded by 749 starters and enders attached to it like barnacles to the hull of a ship, or sperm to the surface of an ovum. The largest barnacle consists of the starter *TUBA,* which has associated with it 15 preceders, from *babe* to *bath,* leading to the core, plus 17 finishers, from *baby* to *bawd.* The barnacle associated with the ender *ENVY* has 12 followers associated with it, from *amen* to *ween,* and 8 beginners, from *even* to *wren.* On the other hand, some barnacles consist only of a starter (such as *ajar*) or ender (such as *oleo*). There appear to be no bypassers. In addition to the 1,730-word main network, there are 219 terminators, from *bilk* to *zany,* unconnected with it.

The main network has a one-way span of nine, achieved by several different strings: *STEP-epic-icon-onto-tool-olio-iota-taka-kayo-YOYO, STEP-epic-iced-edge-gene-nevi-vita-taka-kayo-YOYO, STEP-epic-iced-edgy-gyve-veda-data-taka-kayo-YOYO,* and *ICKY-kyat-atop-opal-also-soda-data-taka-kayo-YOYO.* The two-way span is believed to be 13, from *ouzo* to *kayo* and return: *-OUZO-zone-near-arid-idol-olio-iota-taka-KAYO-yoke-kepi-pith-thou-OUZO-.*

It is not known what is the longest string of words with no repetitions in the main network; the theoretical maximum is 849, plus at most a starter, preceder, follower, and ender. It is unlikely that this maximum can be realized. A related problem is to find the largest string of words in the core, using no frags more than once. The theoretical maximum of 132 words (133 insider frags) cannot be achieved because of restrictions on rare frags; for example, the frag *KH* must be preceded and followed by *AN.* The following 111-word solution is probably close to the maximum achievable:

ki-wi-sp-ur-du-ma-gi-be-au-to-ok-ra-ja-il-ea-st-ye-ti-dy-
ke-pi-ne-vi-sa-ri-sk-id-ol-io-ta-ka-yo-ga-me-nu-ts-ar-ab-
et-ch-ap-ex-am-mo-no-un-do-pa-th-ou-zo-om-it-em-ir-is-
le-af-ro-de-li-my-na-zi-on-ce-di-va-se-ek-ed-gy-ve-ep-ic-

ky-at-op-us-er-go-od-or-al-so-lo-ci-ty-pe-as-hy-po-co-ho-
ax-es-py-re-ad-ze-bu-bo-la-cy-an-te-ak-in-ca-sh-ag-og

The study of trees and reverse trees is less interesting than it was for the three-letter Pocket Merriam-Webster directed network. The tree of any insider frag consists of all other insider frags plus all follower and ender frags for a total of 226; similarly, the reverse tree of any insider frag is 203. Beginners have slightly larger trees, of 227 or 228; enders, reverse trees of 204 or 205. Similar arguments apply to the (4,2) directed network; each insider has a tree of size 1,374 and a reverse tree of 1,252. The largest starter tree is the one for *TUBA*, with 1,407 words; the largest reverse tree is the one for *ENVY*, with 1,273.

A study has been made of the (8,4) directed network based on both editions of the unabridged Merriam-Webster, *Chambers Twentieth Century Dictionary*, and the *Official Scrabble Players Dictionary*. The main network of 2,813 words, a rather small fraction of the total corpus, contains 960 different frags, including 119 starters, 142 enders, 180 preceders, 12 followers, and 507 insiders. The frag *BARA* has a tree of 675 fragments associated with it, *THOU* 671, *SOUP* 669, and *ARRE* 667. The one-way span is 17, exemplified by *VIOL-ence-inte-grum-bles-buck-wash-down-turn-over-free-zing-anas-arca-dias-pine-cone-PATE*. The two-way span of the frag network is 23, from *BITS* to *CONE* and back to *BITS*: *BITS-talk-able-gate-ward-walk-over-free-zing-anas-arca-dias-pine-CONE-head-lock-outs-cold-cock-crow-foot-sore-hawk-BITS*. The two-way span of the (8,4) directed word network is, of course, the same.

The luxuriant tangle of core fragments can be combed out to reveal regular subsets, or meshes, in which words are formed by taking a frag and its right or down neighbor. For the (4,2) frag network, the largest mesh square is probably the one at the left; for the (8,4) frag network, the one at the right.

ha	sp	un	do	pa		fore	hand	line	side	long	wool	ball
lo	in	to	ne	st		hold	fast	back	bone	wood	rock	weed
co	ca	re	ar	ab		over	land	wash	tail	wind	fish	hook
ma	sh	am	id	ly		fire	lock	work	head	ship	worm	like
						plug	hole	able	gate	ward	less	ness

Substitutions are possible: *ve, le,* or *te* for *pa; da* or *la* for *ma; le* for *ly.* In the second, *cook book* and *shop life* can substitute for *fire lock* and *plug hole.* A six-by-six mesh could not be found, but a nine-by-four rectangle can be constructed.

46   TRANSPOSITIONS

A *transposition* (or transposal) is a word obtained from another word by a rearrangement of its letters. Any transposition can be decomposed into a succession of elementary operations, each consisting of the exchange in position of two letters—a metathesis. For example, *escort* is transformed via *cseort* and *coesrt* into *corset.*

The transposition of *prose* into *spore* is exactly the same as the transposition of *olive* into *voile:* both can be encoded by the numerical transformation 12345-41325, which says that the letter in first position is moved into the second position, the letter in second position is moved into the fourth position, and so on. To save space, the 12345 part is omitted and the transposition encoded 41325.

The inverse transposition of *spore* into *prose* is encoded by 24315. Not all transposition-pairs lead to two different numerical codes; *carol* to *coral* is represented by 14325, as is *coral* to *carol.* This occurs whenever each letter in the word remains fixed in its position (as C, R, L) or changes places with one other letter (as A, O).

The number of different n-letter transpositions is one less than the number of ways that n letters can be arranged: $n(n-1)(n-2)...(2)1$, denoted by the mathematical symbol $n!$ (factorial n). Because of the invariance of the *coral-carol* code, it is unnecessary to find $n!-1$ different transposition-pairs to illustrate all transposals; the number of transposition-pairs needed for words of two through six letters is 1, 4, 16, 72, and 397. A type collection of transposition-pairs of four-letter words from the Pocket Merriam-Webster is given in Figure 46a.

Figure 46a   A Type-Collection of Four-Letter Transpositions from the Pocket Merriam-Webster (*WW,* Feb. 1971, Aug. 1971)

1243 lien line	3214 bore robe	1342-1243 vein vine
1324 bolt blot	3412 chit itch	2314-3124 swap wasp

1432 spot stop	4231 dear read	2341-4123 evil vile
2134 able bale	4321 part trap	2413-3142 ante neat
2143 amen mane		2431-4132 alum maul
		3241-4213 rite tier
		3421-4312 pest step

Similarly, a type-collection of transposition-pairs of six-letter words from the unabridged Merriam-Webster is given in Figure 46b.

Figure 46b   A Type-Collection of Six-Letter Transpositions from the Unabridged Merriam-Webster (WW, Nov. 1977, May 1978)

123465	minuet	minute	213456	action	cation	432165	abides	dibase
123546	barely	barley	213465	lustre	Ulster	453126	insure	ursine
123654	warden	warned	213546	afield	failed	456123	German	manger
124356	united	untied	213654	Edison	deinos	463152	hestia	tashie
124365	stored	strode	214356	estrum	sertum	465132	blosmy	symbol
125436	incest	insect	214365	noised	onside	523416	course	source
125634	cretin	crinet	215436	nudity	untidy	523614	Cyrano	Nyroca
126453	wander	warden	215634	nautic	anicut	524316	conure	rounce
126543	pilots	pistol	216453	insoul	Nilous	526413	shirty	thyrsi
132456	farmed	framed	216543	lucite	uletic	532416	treads	derats
132465	bruise	buries	321456	marble	ramble	532614	orangs	garson
132546	crusty	curtsy	321465	merist	remits	543216	rebuts	tubers
132654	sander	snared	321546	derail	redial	546213	nigers	resing
143256	snatch	stanch	321654	stifle	itself	563412	anemic	iceman
143265	sorted	strode	341256	brumal	umbral	564312	almost	stomal
145236	barley	bleary	341265	feints	infest	623451	danger	ranged
146253	throes	tosher	351426	cartel	rectal	623541	daleth	halted
153426	sprite	stripe	351624	corset	rectos	624351	duties	suited
153624	pearly	player	361452	borate	rebato	625431	signal	liangs
154326	petals	plates	361542	restio	sortie	632451	dialer	railed
156423	rictus	rustic	423156	danger	gander	632541	coxite	exotic
163452	sprout	stroup	423165	airted	tirade	643251	drones	snored
163542	antres	astern	425136	unlist	insult	645231	creant	tanrec
164352	caudle	cedula	426153	danger	garden	653421	deltas	salted
165432	closer	cresol	432156	civets	evicts	654321	drawer	reward

123564-123645	retain	retina	136542-162543	Croats	costar
124536-125346	trades	treads	143526-153246	argues	augers
124563-126345	resign	reigns	143562-163245	orange	onager
124635-125364	steady	stayed	143625-153264	Romans	ransom
124653-126354	cheats	chaste	143652-163254	result	rustle
125463-126435	resing	renigs	145263-146235	strife	sifter
125643-126534	forest	foster	145326-154236	bleary	barely
132564-132645	breath	Bertha	145362-164235	cerous	course
134256-142356	stored	sorted	145623-156234	lupine	lineup

134265-142365	rouges	rugose		145632-165234	breath	bather
134526-152346	pearly	parley		146325-154263	petals	pastel
134562-162345	fringe	finger		146352-164253	canoer	cornea
134625-152364	purism	primus		146523-156243	merits	mister
134652-162354	claret	cartel		146532-165243	stupor	sprout
135246-142536	points	pitons		153462-163425	mental	mantle
135264-142635	thurse	tusher		153642-163524	unripe	uprein
135426-152436	pleats	petals		154362-164325	meatus	mutase
135462-162435	stinge	signet		154623-156324	medial	mailed
135624-152634	geodal	goaled		154632-165324	crones	censor
135642-162534	friend	finder		156342-164523	bather	Bertha
136245-142563	roamed	radome		156432-165423	detail	dilate
136254-142653	player	parley		164532-165342	presto	poster
136425-152463	glider	girdle		213564-213645	parson	aprons
136452-162453	plates	pastel		214536-215346	punted	uptend
136524-152643	points	piston		214563-216345	cinema	iceman
214635-216345	Danite	adient		236451-612453	routes	ouster
214653-216354	Abdiel	bailed		236514-512643	tinsel	inlets
215463-216435	ration	aroint		236541-612543	shamer	harems
215643-216534	ardent	ranted		241356-314256	grouse	rugose
231456-312456	smiled	misled		241365-314265	gluier	ligure
231465-312465	clouts	locust		241536-315246	hoaxed	oxhead
231546-312546	tholes	hotels		241563-316245	regain	earing
231564-312645	bridal	ribald		241635-315264	pleads	lapsed
231645-312564	presto	repost		241653-316254	orchid	rhodic
231654-312654	abides	biased		243156-413256	ascent	secant
234156-412356	plumed	lumped		243165-413265	aflush	Fulahs
234165-412365	ablest	bleats		243516-513246	signet	ingest
234516-512346	ranges	angers		243561-613245	throne	hornet
234561-612345	stable	tables		243615-513264	obtuse	buteos
234615-512364	sprite	priest		243651-613254	stared	trades
234651-612354	simple	impels		245136-415236	cleans	lances
235146-412536	others	throes		245163-416235	odeums	dumose
235164-412635	sterno	tensor		245316-514236	triune	runite
235416-512436	towels	owlets		245361-614235	stared	treads
235461-612435	tuners	unrest		245613-516234	uprose	poseur
235614-512634	ostler	sterol		245631-615234	scored	credos
235641-612534	cation	atonic		246135-415263	friend	redfin
236145-412563	pliers	lisper		246153-416253	ladies	aisled
236154-412653	spacer	parsec		246315-514263	spirea	praise
236415-512463	oleins	lesion		246351-614253	nomial	oilman
246513-516243	unleft	netful		256431-615423	filets	itself
246531-615243	shriek	hikers		261345-314562	boater	orbate
251346-314526	thread	hatred		261354-314652	German	engram
251364-314625	prates	repast		261435-315462	Daniel	aldine
251436-315426	virent	invert		261453-316452	cotise	oecist

251463-316425	ratios	aorist	261534-315642	ascent	stance
251634-315624	uredos	roused	261543-316542	listen	inlets
251643-316524	streak	tasker	263145-413562	famuli	aimful
253146-413526	crates	reacts	263154-413652	spinor	prison
253164-413625	albeit	libate	263415-513462	isotac	scotia
253416-513426	traces	reacts	263451-613452	spider	prides
253461-613425	silent	inlets	263514-513642	spiter	priest
253614-513624	arisen	reinas	263541-613542	soiler	oriels
253641-613524	lumina	unmail	264135-415362	pseudo	souped
254136-415326	stoner	tensor	264153-416352	unable	nebula
254163-416325	thenal	hantle	264315-514362	nailer	Arline
254316-514326	tholes	helots	264351-614352	sauger	argues
254361-614325	traces	recast	264513-516342	noetic	octine
254613-516324	hating	anight	264531-615342	dances	ascend
254631-615324	thoral	harlot	265134-415632	triose	Restio
256134-415623	plenum	lumpen	265143-416532	strone	tensor
256143-416523	scythe	chesty	265314-514632	moused	odeums
256314-514623	amides	mesiad	265341-614532	spinal	plains
256341-614523	scared	cedars	265413-516432	arkose	resoak
256413-516423	luting	ungilt	265431-615432	strone	tenors
321564-321645	listen	silent	342516-531246	insult	sunlit
324156-421356	halter	lather	342561-631245	slider	idlers
324165-421365	lustre	sutler	342615-531264	sprite	ripest
324516-521346	ulcers	Clerus	342651-631254	enfold	fondle
324561-621345	sample	maples	345126-451236	debris	brides
324615-521364	hamlet	Malthe	345162-461235	velour	louvre
324651-621354	Daniel	nailed	345216-541236	escort	corset
325146-421536	vowels	wolves	345261-641235	solemn	lemons
325164-421635	Lawrie	wailer	345612-561234	stable	ablest
325416-521436	raptly	paltry	345621-651234	depart	parted
325461-621435	dotage	togaed	346125-451263	camels	mescal
325614-521634	lament	mantle	346152-461253	Olenus	ensoul
325641-621534	slater	alerts	346215-541263	faster	strafe
326145-421563	timers	mister	346251-641253	coheir	heroic
326154-421653	gifted	fidget	346512-561243	deacon	acnode
326415-521463	rawest	waters	346521-651243	master	stream
326451-621453	sacred	cadres	351462-361425	median	damine
326514-521643	redtop	deport	351642-361524	domnei	medino
326541-621543	rugate	Guetar	352146-431526	tubers	brutes
341526-351246	ashore	hoarse	352164-431625	Teucri	uretic
341562-361245	goaled	algedo	352416-531426	dogies	geoids
341625-351264	medals	damsel	352461-631425	yogurt	grouty
341652-361254	spinet	instep	352614-531624	cashel	sealch
342156-431256	ruined	inured	352641-631524	ladies	deasil
342165-431265	pastel	staple	354126-451326	potman	tampon

354162-461325	unstar	Saturn		365214-541632	escrol	closer
354216-541326	triens	inerts		365241-641532	sailed	ideals
354261-641325	turbos	robust		365412-561432	aldine	denial
354612-561324	ambled	beldam		365421-651432	septal	plates
354621-651324	denial	nailed		423516-523146	insult	unslit
356124-451623	sector	corset		423561-623145	squeal	equals
356142-461523	escrow	cowers		423615-523164	linked	kindle
356214-541623	lapsed	pedals		423651-623154	ranged	gander
356241-641523	hustle	sleuth		425163-426135	tursio	suitor
356412-561423	daoine	Oneida		425316-524136	ethics	itches
356421-651423	starve	averts		425361-624135	snaily	inlays
362145-431562	lemony	myelon		425613-526134	thysel	shelty
362154-431652	Lesath	shelta		425631-625134	thecal	chalet
362415-531462	aldine	Delian		426315-524163	inputs	unspit
362451-631452	dispel	sliped		426351-624153	sailed	ladies
362514-531642	kitsch	thicks		426513-526143	masher	harems
362541-631542	septal	pleats		426531-625143	tinsel	silent
364125-451362	enacts	ascent		432516-532146	hidage	Adighe
364152-461352	usager	argues		432561-632145	erucin	curine
364215-541362	soaker	arkose		432615-532164	emodin	domnei
364251-641352	pretan	entrap		432651-632154	diaper	paired
364512-561342	insert	sterin		435126-452136	corban	Bracon
364521-651342	rebato	boater		435162-462135	trifle	filter
365124-451632	rectal	claret		435216-542136	things	nights
365142-461352	Tapiro	Portia		435261-642135	achtel	Thecla
435612-562134	staple	palest		462531-635142	santir	trains
435621-652134	deasil	sailed		463215-543162	gaiter	triage
436125-452163	quires	risque		463251-643152	miscue	cesium
436152-462153	traces	caster		463512-563142	Monday	dynamo
436215-542163	tailer	lirate		463521-653142	niters	estrin
436251-642153	sarong	organs		465213-546132	disbar	braids
436512-562143	region	ignore		465231-645132	shelta	lathes
436521-652143	reacts	caster		465312-564132	chapel	pleach
452316-534126	credit	direct		465321-654132	enigma	gamine
452361-634125	donate	atoned		523461-623415	rumble	lumber
452613-536124	gaskin	kiangs		523641-623514	manors	ransom
452631-635124	dietal	tailed		524361-624315	trepan	arpent
453162-463125	geison	soigne		524613-526314	Sherpa	phrase
453216-543126	tangue	gunate		524631-625314	dangle	lagend
453261-643125	staple	plates		526341-624513	snowed	endows
453612-563124	anthem	hetman		526431-625413	shrite	theirs
453621-653124	despot	posted		532461-632415	rialto	tailor
456132-465123	tribes	bestir		532641-632514	copied	epodic
456213-546123	lisper	perils		532416-542316	longed	engold
456231-645123	serang	angers		534261-642315	tinger	engirt

456312-564123	armful	fulmar	534612-562314	stride	driest
456321-654123	citrus	rustic	534621-652314	rental	antler
462315-534162	canter	trance	536214-524613	amends	desman
462351-634152	staple	petals	536241-642513	tinsel	enlist
462513-536142	mushla	haulms	536412-562413	chandu	daunch
536421-652413	tophus	upshot	563241-643512	snatch	chants
542361-634215	dilate	tailed	563421-653412	starch	charts
542631-635214	strove	voters	564231-645312	dearth	thread
543261-643215	solemn	melons	564321-654312	renish	shiner
543612-563214	result	lustre	624531-625341	turbeh	Hubert
543621-653214	result	luster	634251-642351	sarong	groans
546231-645213	tornus	unsort	634521-652341	relics	slicer
546312-564213	Leonid	indole	635241-642531	giants	sating
546321-654213	reluct	cutler	635421-652431	dearth	hatred
562341-634512	curine	neuric	643521-653241	stance	enacts
562431-635412	sealch	chelas	645321-654231	models	seldom

If a transformation is repeated a sufficient number of times on a given letter arrangement, one eventually returns to the original arrangement. This is most obvious in cyclic transpositions in which letters are transferred from head to tail, as in *tea-eat-ate-tea* or *mela-elam-lame-amel-mela*. For four-letter words, there exist nine transformations of two words, four of three words, and three of four words. These transformations have also been termed transposition rings. Three-word and four-word rings can be illustrated using words from the unabridged Merriam-Webster: *-doli-idol-lido-olid-*, *-ante-neat-etna-taen-*, *-arst-tsar-rats-stra-*, and *-peal-pale-plea-*, *-ales-elsa-slae-*, *-tsia-atis-sait-*, *-aryl-ryal-yarl-*. *Taen, arst,* and *sait* are found only in the first edition of the unabridged Merriam-Webster.

There are a wide variety of transposition rings of length two through six for five-letter words. However, there is no transposition ring that can be entirely illustrated by unabridged Merriam-Webster words. A cyclic transposition, often the easiest to construct, can be built out of words in the *Oxford English Dictionary,* or by using two placenames: *-ester-stere-teres-erest-reste-* and *-angor-Rango-orang-goran-Ngora-*. *Ngora* is a town in Uganda, and *Rango,* a town in Tibet. In his unpublished manuscript *Our Fabulous Language,* Murray Geller proposes *-erish-rishe-isher-sheri-heris-*. All but *sheri* (the body of formally established law in Islam) can be found in the *Oxford English Dictionary.* A near-miss for a six-word transposition ring: *-pales-sleap-peals-salep-pleas-sealp-* (*sealp* is not a word).

The subject of multiple transpositions of a single group of letters has been extensively explored. It is interesting to chart the most fecund letter-combinations for each word length, using words (or inferred words) found in (1) the Pocket Merriam-Webster or (2) the unabridged Merriam-Webster; the results are given in Figure 46c.

Figure 46c   The Most Transposable Letter-Combinations

Pocket Merriam-Webster

3 asp pas sap spa (4)
4 arts rats star tars tsar (5)
5 pares parse pears rapes reaps spare spear (7)
6 drapes padres parsed rasped spared spread (6)
7 detains instead sainted satined stained (5)
8 alerting altering integral relating triangle (5)
9 auctioned cautioned education (3)

Unabridged Merriam-Webster

3 aer are ear era rae rea (6)
4 aers Ares arse Aser ears eras raes rase sare sear sera (11) AELS,
   ABEL also
5 atles laets lates least leats salet setal slate sleat stale steal stela taels
   tales teals Tesla (coil) (16)
6 alerts alters artels estral laster lastre rastle ratels relast resalt salter
   slater staler stelar talers tarsel (16)
7 anestri asterin eranist nastier ratines resiant restain retains retinas
   retsina sainter stainer starnie stearin (14)
8 austrine instaure Itureans neutrias ruinates Sautrien seriaunt tau-
   rines unsatire uranites urinates (11)
9 actioners anoretics atroscine canotiers cerations certosina conar-
   ites creations ostracine reactions Tinoceras tricosane (12)

Interestingly, both dictionaries attain their transposition peak at five-letter words. However, the multiple-transposition production rate falls off more slowly with longer words in the unabridged Merriam-Webster.

If any English-language dictionary, gazetteer, or telephone directory is allowed, including inferred forms (plurals, past tenses, etc.), multiword phrases, and citation form plurals (abbreviated cfp in figure) ("there are many *Washingtons* in the United States"), Jeff Grant, updating a study by Dmitri Borgmann that began in *Language on Vacation* (Scribner's, 1965), has collected 157 transpositions of the letters *AEGINRST*. These are summarized in Figure 46d.

Figure 46d   The Great AEGINRST Machine (*WW*, Aug. 1976, Nov. 1976, Feb. 1994, May 1994)

AERTING'S cfp of *aerting*, pres. part. of *aert*, obs. form of *art* (*Web 1*)

AGINTERS enterprises named *aginter* (1989 Madrid TD, 1983 Lisbon TD)

ANGERIT'S cfp of *angerit*, old Scots past tense of *anger* (*DOST* quotes)

ANGRIEST superlative form of *angry* (*Random House*)

ANGRITES pl. of *angrite*, a meteoric stone (*Web 3*)

ARESTING Scots and ME form of verbal noun *arresting* (*DOST, MED*)

ARETING'S cfp of *areting*, ME pres. part. of *aret*, to reckon (*OED*)

ARGENTIS persons with surname *Argenti* (50 in Rome TD)

ARNESTIG surname of Ernest *Arnestig* (1989 Gotenburg TD)

ASTERING surname (4 in Stockholm TD); also pres. part. of *astere* (*OED*)

ASTINGER surname of Lene *Astinger* (1988 Copenhagen TD)

ASTRINGE to bind together, draw close, constrict, compress (*OED*)

ATERING'S cfp of *atering*, pres. part. of *ater*, obs. var. of *atter* (*Web 1*)

ATSINGER surname of Alisa *Atsinger* (1992 Houston TD); also Atlanta TD

EAST'RING poetic shortening of *eastering* (see *west'ring* in *OED* quote)

ENRAGIT'S cfp of *enragit*, old Scots past tense of *enrage* (*DOST* quote)

ENTIGARS persons with surname *Entigar*, as Robert (1992 Hartford TD)

ERIGANTS pl. of *erigant*, erron. form of *erigaut*, var. *herigaut* (*OED*)

ESTRINGA surname of Dolores *Estringa* (1983 Lisbon TD)

GAINTERS uses conceited airs and gestures (*SND*)

GAIRNEST poetic 2nd pers. form of *gairn*, N. England var. of *girn* (*EDD*)

GAIRTENS pl. of *gairten*, dial. var. of *garten*, a garter (*EDD*)

GAITNERS ones who set up corn in single sheaves (gaits) (*OED*)

GANISTER a fine-grained quartzite used in silica brick manufacture

GANTIERS persons with surname *Gantier* (14 in 1992 Paris TD) (*BMGC*)

GANTREIS old Scots term for a four-legged wooden barrel stand (*DOST*)

GANTRIES pl. of *gantry,* a four-footed wooden stand for barrels (*OED*)

GARENIST past part. of *garnishen,* ME word meaning to decorate (*MED*)

GARINETS persons with surname *Garinet* (5 in 1992 Paris TD) (*BMGC*)

GARNEIST var. of *garnist,* Scots word meaning properly equipped (*DOST*)

GARNESIT past tense of old Scots *garnis,* to embellish (*DOST* quotes)

GARNETIS old Scots pl. of *garnet,* a grenade (*DOST* quote)

GARNI-EST awkward or jocular superlative of *garni,* garnished (*CED*)

GARNITES enterprises named *Garnite* (1984 Melbourne TD)

GARSTEIN surname (2 in 1992 Oslo TD) (*BMGC*)

GASTERIN a preparation of the gastric juice of dogs (Gould)

GASTREIN surname of Jacqueline and Roger *Gastrein* (1990 Nice TD)

GASTRINE hormone made in the pyloric glands of the stomach (Gould)

GENITRAS ME term for the testicles; also the male genitals (*MED*)

GERAINTS males bearing the forename *Geraint* (*Oxford Dict. of Names*)

GERSAINT Edme François *Gersaint* (*Dict. of Universal Biog.*)

GERTINAS females bearing the forename *Gertina* (15 in *Förnammsboken*)

GE-STIRAN to guide or direct; to restrain (*Anglo-Saxon Dictionary*)

GIANTER'S cfp of *gianter,* awkward comparative of *giant* (*CED*)

GIERNATS persons with surname *Giernat,* as Chester (1990 Chicago TD)

GIERSTAN var. of *giestran,* yesterday (*Student's Dict. of Anglo-Saxon*)

GIESTRAN yesterday (*A Concise Anglo-Saxon Dictionary*)

GINESTAR town in Tarragona, Spain (*Columbia-Lippincott Gaz.*)

GINESTRA the broom, a shrub of Britain and western Europe (*OED*)

GIRANTES persons with surname *Girante* (3 in 1983 Lisbon TD)

GNASTIER comparative form of *gnaistie,* an old var. of *nasty* (*OED*)

GRAINEST poetic 2nd pers. form of *grain* ("thou *grainest*") (*OED*)

GRAINETS post offices such as *Grainet,* in Germany (*Inter. Regis. PO*)

GRANEIST surname of Andreas and Gisbert *Graneist* (1992 Hamburg TD)

GRANIEST superlative form of *grany*, Cornish var. of *grainy (EDD)*

GRANITES certain granular crystalline rocks

GRANTIES surname of Bryan *Grantie* of New Port Ritchey, Fla. (*PhoneDisc*)

GRANTISE obs. word for concession or permission (*OED*)

GRATIENS persons like Jean Baptiste *Gratien* (*Dict. of Universal Biog.*)

GRATINES bakes or broils food au gratin style (*Random House*)

GREATINS 2nd pers. sing. of *greatin*, ME var. of *greten*, to greaten (*MED*)

GREAT SIN mortal sin (*Cruden's Complete Concordance*)

GRETIANS pl. of *Gretian*, var. of *Grecian*, a native of Greece (*OED*)

GRETINAS persons with the surname *Gretina* (2 in *PhoneDisc*)

GRISANTE Saint *Grisante*, a name for St. Chrysanthus of Daria (*BMGC*)

GRITENAS surname (8 in *PhoneDisc*)

IGARNSET past part. of ME verb *garnishen*, to adorn, beautify (*MED*)

IGERANTS pl. of *igerant*, Oxfordshire var. of *ignorant (EDD)*

IGRANTE'S cfp of *igrante*, a ME past part. of *graunten*, to grant (*MED*)

IGRATEN'S cfp of *igraten*, a ME compound form of *greten*, to greet (*MED*)

INERT GAS one of the group of elements helium, neon, argon, etc.

INGARETS females bearing the forename *Ingaret* (*Oxford Dict. of Names*)

INGERTSA surname of Solveig *Ingertsa* (1989 Gotenburg TD)

INGESTAR large glass, bottle or measure of wine, used in Italy (*OED*)

INGRATES ungrateful people

INGREATS obs. term for makes great, magnifies (*OED*)

INRAGEST poetic 2nd pers. form of *inrage*, old var. of *enrage* (*OED*)

INTEGRAS pl. of *integra*, a model of the Honda automobile

INTERGAS name of a company (1989 Madrid TD)

NARGIEST superlative form of *nargie*, Scots for jeering (*Chamb. Scots*)

NEGARITS pl. of *negarit*, Amharic var. of *nagarit*, kettledrum (*Mus. Inst.*)

NEGRITAS pl. of *negrita*, serranoid fish of the West Indies (*Funk & Wag.*)

NEIGARTS pl. of *neigart*, Scots term for a miserly person (*DOST*)

NIGRATES certain asphalts mined at Soldier Summit, Utah (*Petroleum Dict.*)

RAGIN'EST awkward superlative of *ragin'* (*EDD* quote, ragin' mad)

RAIGNEST poetic 2nd pers. form of *raign*, var. of *reign* (*OED*)

RAINGEST poetic 2nd pers. form of *rainge*, var. of *range* (*OED*)

RANGIEST superlative form of *rangy* (*Random House*)

RASETING Scots var. of *resetting*, harboring a lawbreaker (*DOST*)

RATEINGS pl. of *rateing*, old var. of *rating*, a reproof (*OED* quote)

RATINGES pl. of *ratinge*, old var. of *rating*, fixing payment (*OED* quote)

REASTING dialect term meaning becoming rancid, as bacon (*EDD*)

REATING'S cfp of *reating*, pres. part. of *reat*, Scots var. of *write* (*DOST*)

REGAINST poetic 2nd pers. form of *regain* ("thou *regainst*") (*OED*)

REGAINTS pl. of *regaint*, a ME var. of *regent*, a ruler (*MED*)

REGANITS persons with the surname *Reganit* (3 in *PhoneDisc*)

REGIANTS pl. *regiant*, Scots var. of *regent* (*DOST*)

REGISTAN desert region in southern Afghanistan (*Times Concise Atlas*)

REIGNATS persons with the surname *Reignat* (3 in 1992 Paris TD)

RENAIGST poetic 2nd pers. form of *renaig*, Scots var. of *renegue* (*SND*)

RENIGATS pl. of *renigat*, old Scots var. of *renegade* (*DOST*)

RESATING pres. part. of *resate*, var. of Scots *resait* (*DOST*)

RESTAGIN' slang shortening of *restaging*, stage again (*Random House*)

RESTINGA town on the northern coast of Morocco (*TAW*)

RETANGIS to *tangi* is to lament, a Maori custom (*OED*, adding re-)

RIGANTES persons with the surname *Rigante* (3 in 1991 Montreal TD)

RINGATES persons with the surname *Ringate* (9 in *PhoneDisc*)

RING-SEAT a ringside seat, as in a boxing contest (*OED*)

RITENGAS small communities such as *Ritenga* in Angola (*TIG*)

SANTE GRI the full name of an individual (1992 Geneva TD)

SARGENTI surname (70 in 1983 Rome TD)

SATINGER awkward comparative of *sating*, meaning cloying (*OED*)

SEAT RING a replaceable ring that forms the seat of a valve (*Web 3*)

SERGANTI surname of Ruth *Serganti* of Clifton Heights, Penn. (*PhoneDisc*)

SERGIANT old var. of *sergeant* (*OED*)

SERIGNAT surname (3 in 1992 Geneva TD)

SIGNATER awkward comparative of *signate*, marked in some way (*OED*)

STAERING pres. part. of *staer*, Cheshire dial. form of *stare* (*EDD* quote)

STAINGER surname of John *Stainger* (1991 Calgary TD)

STAN GIRE short form of *Stan*ley W. *Gire* of Santa Clara, Calif. (*PhoneDisc*)

STANIGER surname (20 in *PhoneDisc*)

STARINGE pres. part. of ME verb *staren,* to stare (*MED*)

STEARING obs. word for a Newfoundland bird (*OED*)

STEINGAR surname of Rolf *Steingar* (1992 Oslo TD)

STIG ARNE full name of an individual (1992 Oslo TD)

STRAEING pres. part. of *strae,* a Scots form of *straw* (*OED*)

STRAIGNE obs. var. of *strain* (*OED*)

STRAINGE an old var. of *strange* (*OED*)

STRANGIE an old var. of *strangy,* strange (*OED*)

STREAING pres. part. of *strea,* a dial. var. of *straw* (*Web 2*)

STRIEGAN surname of Ulrich and Maria *Striegan* (1992 Munich TD)

TAERING'S cfp of *Taering,* Cornish dial. var. of *tearing,* violent (*EDD*)

TANGERIS persons with the surname *Tangeri* (3 in *PhoneDisc*)

TANGIERS var. of *Tangier,* of or from the city in Morocco (*Web 3*)

TANGIRES surname (5 in 1991 Baltimore TD)

TANGRIES var. of *Tangrys,* pl. of surname *Tangry* (4 in *PhoneDisc*)

TAREING'S cfp of *tareing,* in *taering-tub* (*EDD*)

TARGEIN'S cfp of *targein,* North Ireland dial. var. of *targing* (*EDD*)

TARGESIN trademark of an antiseptic and astringent (*Blakiston's*)

TARGINES river in Magna Grecia mentioned by Pliny (under *Tacina, Lempriere*)

TARIENGS pl. of *tareing,* old var. of *tarrying,* waiting (*OED* quote)

TASERING pres. part. of *taser,* using a Taser gun to stun (*3rd Barnhart*)

TEARINGS pl. of *tearing,* a fragment torn off something (*OED*)

TERAGNIS persons with the surname *Teragni* (3 in Buenos Aires TD)

TERANGIS persons with the surname *Terangi* (5 on *NZ Electoral Rolls*)

TE RINGAS persons with the surname *Te Ringa* (2 in 1992 Auckland TD)

TIERGAN'S cfp of *tiergan,* to irritate, annoy (*targe, EDD*)

TIGRANES name of several Armenian kings (*Webster's Bio. Dictionary*)

TIGREANS natives of the Tigre province of Ethiopia (*OED*)

TIRANGES town in Haute-Loire department, France (*TAW*)

TRAEING'S cfp of *traeing,* pres. part. of *trae,* Orkney var. of *thrae* (*SND*)

TRAGNIES communities such as *Tragny,* in France (*TIG*)

TRANGIES towns such as *Trangie,* in New South Wales (*TAW*)

TRASINGE old var. of *tracing,* the following of traces (*OED* quote)

TREGAINS persons with surname *Tregain,* as Count E. de *Tregain* (*BMGC*)

TREGIANS persons with surname *Tregian,* as Francis *Tregian* (*BMGC*)

TRENGIAS persons with surname *Trengia*, as Nicole (1991 Montreal TD)

An Anglo-Saxon Dictionary, Supplement, Bosworth and Toller, 1972

Blakiston's New Gould Medical Dictionary, 2nd Edition, 1956 (*Blakiston's*)

British Museum General Catalogue of Printed Works (*BMGC*)

Chambers English Dictionary, 1988 (*CED*)

Chambers Scots Dictionary, Alexander Warrack, 1911 (*Chamb. Scots*)

Columbia-Lippincott Gazetteer of the World, 1964

A Concise Anglo-Saxon Dictionary, John R. Clark Hall, 1962

Cruden's Complete Concordance of the Old and New Testaments, 1946

A Dictionary of the Older Scottish Tongue, Craigie (*DOST*)

A Dictionary of Universal Biography, Albert Hyamson, 2nd Edition, 1951

English Dialect Dictionary, Joseph Wright, 1905 (*EDD*)

Förnammsboken, Sture Allen, 1979

Funk & Wagnalls New Standard Dictionary of the English Language, 1974

Gould's Medical Dictionary, 5th Revised Edition, 1941 (Gould)

International Register of Post Offices, 1977

Lempriere's Classical Dictionary, 1826 (1894)

Middle English Dictionary, edited by Hans Kurath, 1959 (*MED*)

Musical Instruments: A Comprehensive Dictionary, Sibyl Marcuse 1964 (Mus. Inst.)

New Zealand Electoral Rolls, Southern Maori, 1991

Oxford English Dictionary, 2nd Edition, 1989 (*OED*)

Oxford Dictionary of English Christian Names, E. G. Withycombe, 1977

The Petroleum Dictionary, Lalia Phipps Boone, 1952

PhoneDisc, a CD database covering 4,000 U.S. telephone directories, 1991

Random House Dictionary of the English Language, 2nd Edition, 1987

Scottish National Dictionary, 1931–76 (*SND*)

The Student's Dictionary of Anglo-Saxon, Henry Sweet, 1967

3rd Barnhart Dictionary of New English, 1990

Times Atlas of the World, 1986 (*TAW*)

Times Concise Atlas of the World, 9th Edition, 1986

Times Index-Gazetteer, 1965 (*TIG*)

Webster's Biographical Dictionary, 1972

Webster's New International Dictionary, 1st Edition, 1924 (*Web 1*)

Webster's New International Dictionary, 2nd Edition, 1934 (*Web 2*)

Webster's Third New International Dictionary, 1976 (*Web 3*)

It is possible to find words for all twenty-four transpositions of the letters *AEST,* as demonstrated in Figure 46e.

Figure 46e   24 Rearrangements of *AEST* (WW, Nov. 1987)

AEST obs. form of "east" (*OED*)

AETS Shetland Islands dialectic form of "east" (*EDD*)

ASET an old word meaning "to set up, place" (*OED*)

ASTE a populated place in the *Off. Stand. Names Gaz.,* USSR

ATES the sweetsop tree (*Web 2*)

A-TSE a populated place in the *Off. Stand. Names Gaz.,* China

EAST to veer toward east; to orient (*Web 2*)

EATS things to eat; food (*Web 2*)

ESAT surname of Isac *Esat* (1982 Paris telephone directory)

ESTA a feminine given name (Evelyn Wells, *What to Name the Baby,* 1953)

ETAS pl. of *eta,* the seventh letter of the Greek alphabet (*Web 2*)

ETSA variant of *Itsa,* an Egyptian village (*Columbia-Lippincott Gaz.*)

SAET dialectic form of "saith," the mature coal-fish (*EDD*)

SATE to satisfy or gratify to the full (*Web 2*)

SEAT a chair (*Web 2*)

SETA a spinelike feather at the base of the bill (*Web 2*)

STAE a populated place in the *Off. Stand. Names Gaz.,* Sweden

STEA dialectic form of "sty," a ladder or stair (*EDD*)

TAES plural of "tae," Scots variant of 'toe' (*Web 2*)

TASE variant of "teise," to stretch or bend a bow (*OED*)

TEAS evening meals (*Web 2*)

TESA variant of "teesa," an Indian buzzard (*Funk & Wagnalls*)

TSAE Marquis *Tsae,* in 11th Edition of *Encyc. Britannica* (Vol. 5, p. 662)

TSE-A variant of "Sia," a New Mexico Keresan tribe (Hodge, *Handbook of American Indians North of Mexico,* 1907)

Long transpositions in the unabridged Merriam-Webster are usually rather uninteresting, being variant spellings of the same word such as *hydroxydesoxycorticosterone-hydroxydeoxycorticosterones,* noted by Kyle Corbin, or *duodenocholecystostomy-cholecystoduo- denostomy.* A transposition is well mixed if no more than three con- secutive letters in one word appear consecutively in the other. The longest unabridged Merriam-Webster well-mixed transposition is the seventeen-letter *basiparachromatin-Marsipobranchiata,* discov- ered by Charles Holding, which first appeared in the October 1971 issue of *The Enigma,* the monthly publication of the National

Puzzlers' League. Both words contain the trigram *SIP* and the bigrams *MA, RA, AR, CH,* and *AT.* The second longest, with sixteen letters, is *hematocrystallin-thermonastically,* which was discovered by John Edward Ogden in 1978; this contains only two repeated bigrams, *HE* and *ST.* It is worth noting that both transpositions were discovered before computers made this task far easier to accomplish.

There are four well-mixed transpositions of fifteen letters: *photoresistance-stenocrotaphies, cinematographer-megachiropteran, dechlorinations-ornithoscelidan,* and *romanticalities-recitationalism.* The longest perfectly mixed transpositions are fourteen letters long: *nitromagnesite-regimentations* and *rotundifoliate-titanofluoride.* Neither of these pairs has even a bigram in common.

Using a slightly more relaxed criterion than well-mixed, Kyle Corbin used a computer to find many previously unsuspected long transpositions of fifteen letters or more. His definition of a nontrivial transposition: (1) the words must not be reducible to shorter transposals by removing the same affix (*crates-reacts*), (2) they are not basically interchanged letter-sequences (*pterylographical calpetrographically*). His list is given in Figure 46f; it includes words from other dictionaries besides the unabridged Merriam-Webster, as well as hyphenated words and dictionary-sanctioned phrases.

Figure 46f Nontrivial Transpositions of Fifteen Letters or More (*WW,* May 1989)

All words are in the Second or Third Editions of the unabridged Merriam-Webster unless otherwise labeled

action regulators, congratulatories (Kyle Corbin, Alan Frank)
anthropomorphic, captorhinomorph (Corbin)
antiproteolysis, proselytisation [no dictionary] (Corbin)
apheliotropisms, omphalotripsies (Eric Albert, Corbin)
basiparachromatin, Marsipobranchiata (Charles Holding)
brain specialist, plebiscitarians (Albert, Corbin)
capture theories, serotherapeutic (Albert, Corbin)
centauromachias, marchantiaceous (Albert, Corbin)
cinematographer, megachiropteran (Howard McPherrin)
color sensations [*Century Dict.*], consolatoriness (McPherrin)
Continental code, delta connection (Corbin)
continuednesses, tendenciousness (Corbin)

contraction rules, reconstructional (Corbin, Frank)
correlativeness, overcentralises [no dictionary] (Corbin)
counterdoctrines, reconstructioned (Corbin)
counterreprisal, interoperculars (Albert, Corbin)
counterripostes, retrosusception (Corbin)
dechlorinations, ornithoscelidan (McPherrin)
decimalisations [*OED*], idiomaticalness (Corbin)
deprotestantise [no dictionary], predetestations (Corbin)
fraudlessnesses, self-assuredness (Corbin)
hematocrystallin, thermonastically (John Ogden)
inarticulatenesses, natural necessities (Holding)
inconsideration, nondictionaries (Corbin)
involuntariness, non-Universalist, unison intervals (Albert)
magisterialness, steamer sailings (Albert, Corbin)
mischaracterise [no dictionary], saccharimetries (Corbin)
nominalisations [no dictionary], nonassimilation (Corbin)
nondiscretionary, yarn conditioners (Albert, Corbin)
nonrealisations [no dictionary], siaresinotannol [*Century Dict.*]
   (Darryl Francis)
outside calipers, pseudorealistic (Albert, Corbin)
photoresistance, stenocrotaphies (Holding)
precivilisation [no dictionary], provincialities (Corbin)
pre-Raphaelitism, primal therapies (Corbin)
pretransmission, transimpression (Dennis Ritchie)
pro-Aristotelian, proletarisation [*OED*] (Corbin)
pronationalists, transpositional (Corbin)
recitationalism, romanticalities (Holding)
reclassification, sacrificial stone [*OED*] (McPherrin)
regionalisations [*Chambers 20th Cent.*], signal noise ratio (Corbin)
shortest-grained, straighter-nosed (Corbin)
skin resistances, train sicknesses (Albert, Corbin)

The transposability of a word is measured by the number of transpositions that exist for that word. This concept can be extended to words for which no transpositions exist, giving a clue concerning the likelihood that a transposition might be found if more sources were searched. Transposability can be approximately gauged by the transposition index: the number of letters that must be added to a word before it can be transposed. (For words having the same index value, relative transposability can be determined by the number of such augmented words.) This can be illustrated with the days of the week, allowing words from the Second Edition of the unabridged Merriam-Webster:

SUNDAY	1	unshady (unsad, Sudan, sandy, Dyaus, unsay)
MONDAY	0	dynamo
TUESDAY	1	day guest, unstayed, unsteady
WEDNESDAY	1	candyweeds (sandweed)
THURSDAY	2	hydraulist
FRIDAY	1	fair day (fiard, fraid, fairy)
SATURDAY	1	subdatary (daystar)

To break the tie among *Sunday, Wednesday, Friday,* and *Saturday,* count the number of words formable therefrom by removing a single letter; these are given in parentheses.

Long words often cannot be converted to others no matter how many letters are added. Again using the Second Edition of the unabridged Merriam-Webster, the shortest-known such word is *syzygy,* or *wuzzy* if cognates such as *fuzzy-wuzzy* are not allowed.

If dictionary phrases are allowed, Charles Holding has proposed the eighteen-letter transposition *natural necessities–inarticulateness-es.* This originally appeared in the September 1980 issue of *The Enigma.* Both words appear in the unabridged Merriam-Webster in singular form.

Howard McPherrin suggested in the June 1925 issue of *The Enigma* the seventeen-letter well-mixed transposition *intercosto-humeral-counterisothermal,* the latter a coinage.

For the record, one should note two Italian eighteen-letter transpositions in an article on wordplay in the *Encyclopedia Italiana*: *incartapecorimenti-ipercontaminatrice* and *interposizioncella-iperconstellazioni.* These sound like coinages. The first pair means "parchment-colored things" and "supercontaminating"; the second pair, "a small intermediate position" and "superconstellations."

47 SPECIAL TRANSPOSITIONS

There are a handful of eight-letter unabridged Merriam-Webster reversals: *desserts-stressed, samaroid-dioramas, detainal-laniated.* Going outside the unabridged Merriam-Webster, Dmitri Borgmann suggested several nine-letter examples:

DELESSERT-TRESSELED *Delessert* is the surname of a nineteenth-century French naturalist; *tresseled* is the past tense of *tressel,* a variant of *trestle*

DELIVERER-REREVILED *rereviled,* not in any dictionary, is formed by prefixing *re-* to the verb *revile*

NOSTREBOR-ROBERTSON *Nostrebor* is a community in Nottoway County, Virginia, presumably first settled by a Robertson

SEALCREST-TSERCLAES *Sealcrest* is a trademark listed in the *Trademark Register of the U.S.* (1977), and *Tserclaes* is part of the name of a Flemish nobleman in Hyamson's *A Dictionary of Universal Biography*

Darryl Francis and William Sunners argued for two additional *re-*entries:

STELLIFER-REFILLETS *refillets,* meaning to fillet [a fish] again, perhaps done by a chef repairing the handiwork of an incompetent assistant

DESSERTER-RETRESSED a *desserter* presumably prepares desserts in a restaurant kitchen; a woman whose hair has been braided or plaited again has had it *retressed*

The advent of national telephone directories on CD-ROMs has made it an easy task to search for persons whose first names transpose their last ones. In a list of some ninety million names, the following were found. Note that *Gary Gray* is more common than all others combined!

Gary Gray 544	Amy May 29	Marc Cram 9	Earl Lear 4
Ronald Arnold 147	Norma Moran 25	Albert Bartel 8	Romeo Moore 3
Edna Dean 57	Roland Arnold 23	Neal Lane 7	Leah Hale 2
Eric Rice 35	Lena Lane 17	Arnold Roland 6	Edna Dane 1
Ronald Roland 35	Dale Deal 10	Lewis Wiles 5	Albert Bartle 1
Debra Beard 31	Debra Bader 10	Erich Reich 5	Elsa Sale 1
Leon Noel 30			Lionel O'Neill 1

Ashley Halsey is listed in *Who's Who in America,* and *Leonardo Loredano* was a former doge of Venice. The New Zealand electoral rolls were scanned by Jeff Grant, who found *Gary Gray* 6, *Colin Nicol* 5, *Ronald Arnold* 5, *Jean Jane* 3, *Lionel O'Neill* 3, *Eric Rice* 1, *Norma Moran* 1, and *Kura Karu* (a Maori) 1.

The cyclic transposition, in which a letter is moved from the beginning of the word to the end to form a new word, is probably the commonest type of transposition. In a sample of 1,277 four-letter transpositions, the commonest five were 2341-4123 (*stop-tops*) with 167, 4312-3421 (*tsar-rats*) with 112, 1342-1423 (*peal-pale*) with 108, 3241-4213 (*ales-elsa*) with 107, and 3214-3214 (*tame-mate*) with 104. The rarest transposition was 2413-3142 (*ante-neat*) with only 29.

David Silverman called cyclic transpositions shift-words; this terminology should be avoided because of the similarity to letter-shifts, discussed in Section 56.

There are more cyclic transpositions involving the shift of the letter *S* from head to tail than all other letters combined. For unabridged Merriam-Webster words of six letters, one has 139 *S*-transpositions and 64 others; for seven letters, 157 and 34; for eight, 79 and 7; for nine, 30 and 3; for ten, 1 and 4; and for eleven, 2 and 2. Figure 47a gives the longest cyclic transpositions known from the unabridged Merriam-Webster for each letter of the alphabet. The longest one of all is the thirteen-letter *s-exarticu-late-s*.

Figure 47a Longest-Known Unabridged Merriam-Webster Cyclic Transpositions for Each Letter of the Alphabet

a-technic-a	g-elatin-g	m-elitis-m	s-exarticulate-s
b-Arne-b	h-eight-h	n-Eogaea-n	t-ringle-t
c-aribini-c	i-Waiwa-i	o-lived-o	w-ane-w
d-eviscerate-d	k-alac-k	p-unta-p	y-arrow-y
e-lectric-e	l-ethologica-l	r-enunciate-r	z-ad-z
f-lea-f			

Most of the cyclic transpositions involving the letter *S* are simply formed by plurals; a few, such as *s-cares-s, s-asses-s, s-packles-s,* and *s-trickles-s,* are formed by *-ess* words instead. One transposition, *S-Ansei-s,* falls into neither category; *Anseis* is the name of one of the twelve noble companies of Charlemagne, and a *Sansei* is the grand-child of a Japanese immigrant to the United States.

In Chapter 7 of his book *Wheels, Life and Other Mathematical Amusements* (Freeman, 1983), Martin Gardner discusses the number of different ways of folding various rectangular road maps. He points out an interesting logological problem: if one writes down the letters of a word on the unfolded segments of a road map, can it be folded in such a way that another word can be read off from the top down on the folded map? The simplest, and perhaps most natural, version, is an *n*-segment strip such as the one formed by a roll of postage stamps. Martin Gardner points out that all possible permutations of two and three segments are foldable, but eight of the twenty-four possible permutations of four segments are unfoldable, corresponding to transpositions such as *bolt-blot* and *ante-neat*. In certain cases, a transposition is foldable in one direction but not the other; for example, *vein* can be folded to *vine*, but not *vine* to *vein*. The fraction of foldable permutations decreases rapidly as the number of segments increases: for five segments, seven out of twelve are unfoldable, and for six segments, four out of five.

The mathematics of map-folding becomes much more complicated in two dimensions. For example, there are 1,368 ways that a three-by-three map can be folded. Gardner identifies as "difficult" the problem of folding the three-by-three road map into the permutation 463129785, which can be characterized by the mnemonic "fold *TON, PEA, FLU* into *PANTOUFLE.*"

48 TRANSPOSITIONS OF PHRASES AND TEXT

Phrases or sentences can be transposed into other phrases and sentences. Unless the phrase contains a number of rare letters, it is generally quite easy to construct another phrase out of it. To make phrase transposition more challenging, the additional requirement has often been imposed that the transposed phrase be, in some sense, a synonym or descriptor of the original. If this has been achieved, the transposed phrase is called by members of the National Puzzlers' League an anagram of the first.

Anagrams have been a part of wordplay for more than two millennia, dating back to the ancient Greeks. The usual objective was to take a person's name and convert it into some phrase that characterized its owner, such as *Florence Nightingale* into *Flit on, cheering angel, Piet Mondrian* into *I paint modern;* or *Dante Gabriel Rossetti* into *greatest born idealist*. A collection of United States presidential examples ranging from good to dreadful is presented in Figure 48a.

Figure 48a Presidential Anagrams from Lincoln to Bush (*WW*, Feb. 1977)

ABRAHAM LINCOLN oh, call man "brain"
ANDREW JOHNSON
ULYSSES SIMPSON GRANT surpassingness my lot
RUTHERFORD BIRCHARD HAYES hard cry bothers fraud heir
CHESTER ARTHUR truth searcher
JAMES A. GARFIELD lead far, sage Jim
GROVER CLEVELAND govern, clever lad
WILLIAM MCKINLEY wily mice kill man
BENJAMIN HARRISON Irish banjo manner
THEODORE ROOSEVELT he overrode loot set
WILLIAM HOWARD TAFT a word with all: I'm fat
WOODROW WILSON woos lorn widow
WARREN GAMALIEL HARDING him laggard? a real winner!
CALVIN COOLIDGE naive cold logic
HERBERT CLARK HOOVER the ever-black horror
FRANKLIN DELANO ROOSEVELT Eleanor kin, last fond lover
HARRY S TRUMAN rash army runt
DWIGHT DAVID EISENHOWER he did view the war doings
JOHN FITZGERALD KENNEDY zing! joy darken, then fled
LYNDON BAINES JOHNSON no ninny, he's on job, lads
RICHARD MILHOUS NIXON hush! nix criminal odor
GERALD RUDOLPH FORD hard pull for "red dog"
JAMES EARL CARTER a rare calm jester
RONALD WILSON REAGAN no, darlings, no ERA law; insane Anglo
warlord
GEORGE HERBERT WALKER BUSH huge berserk rebel warthog

During the past one hundred years, the National Puzzlers' League has published approximately ten thousand anagrams in *The Enigma,* its monthly magazine. Although the quality of an anagram is a subjective matter, some of those generally recognized as superior are cited in Figure 48b. Anagrams depending on one's political point of view, such as A LIBERAL (able liar) or REAGANOMICS (a con game, Sir) are not included. Short high-quality anagrams are harder to find than long ones; all the examples are eighteen letters or fewer.

Figure 48b A Collection of Fifty High-Quality Anagrams

PITTANCE a cent tip (The Duke, June 1913 *Enigma*)
DORMITORY dirty room! (TH, 2 May 1899, "Complications," in
Inter-Ocean)

GREYHOUND hey, dog, run! (King Carnival, Dec. 1898 *Enigma*)

ASTRONOMERS moon starers (*Farmers Almanac*, 1821)

H.M.S. *PINAFORE* name for ship (Mangie, Sept. 1975 *Enigma*)

THE EYES they see (Anonyme, 15 Jan. 1896, *The Oracle*)

PRESBYTERIAN best in prayer (*The Masquerade*, 1797–1802)

NEGATION get a "no" in (Yercas, Dec. 1926 *Enigma*)

OLD MASTERS art's models (Traddles, Dec. 1898 *Enigma*)

MOTHER-IN-LAW woman Hitler (Nypho, Apr. 1936 *Enigma*)

A GENTLEMAN elegant man (Nypho, Aug. 1911 *Enigma*)

ENDEARMENT tender name (Jo Mullins, 23 Sept. 1899, *The Ardmore Puzzler*)

ANGERED enraged (Kenneth, 3 Jan. 1899, *The Ardmore Puzzler*)

DESEGREGATION Negroes get aid (Pacifico, July 1956 *Enigma*)

CABARET a bar, etc. (Hoho, Dec. 1941 *Enigma*)

CONVERSATION voices rant on (Sam Weller, Dec. 1898)

BLANDISHMENT blinds the man (Kee Pon, Dec. 1917 *Enigma*)

APT pat (King Carnival, 1905, "Telegraph Twisters" in Philadelphia *Telegraph*)

DIPLOMACY mad policy (Jemand, Jan. 1916 *Enigma*)

RECEIVED PAYMENT every cent paid me (D.C.Ver, 14 July 1897 *Golden Days*)

CHRISTIANITY charity's in it (ALS, 1 Aug. 1905, *The Ardmore Puzzler*)

THE NUDIST COLONY no untidy clothes (Ellsworth, Oct. 1933)

DELICATESSEN ensliced eats (Anonyme, Oct. 1921 *Enigma*)

FRAGILE e.g., frail (Hi Kerr, June 1926 *Enigma*)

DECIMAL POINT I'm a dot in place (A. Chem, Aug. 1928 *Enigma*)

ARMAGEDDON mad god near (Fanacro, Oct. 1973 *Enigma*)

WAITRESS a stew, Sir? (Osaple, July 1948 *Enigma*)

INCOMPREHENSIBLE problem in Chinese (Gemini, July 1929 *Enigma*)

INCONSISTENT n is, n is not, etc. (Wrong Font, Dec. 1943 *Enigma*)

HYPOCHONDRIAC cry "ohh, Doc...pain" (Wabbit, Feb. 1990 *Enigma*)

STORMY WEATHER showery matter (Baful, July 1964 *Enigma*)

SEXUAL INTERCOURSE relax, enjoy coitus (Dmitri Borgmann, May 1974 *WW*)

SERAGLIOS girl oases (Ab Struse, Apr. 1979 *Enigma*)

PROGNOSIS signs: poor (Hap, June 1975 *Enigma*)

RAMSHACKLE charm? leaks (Hap, Dec. 1975 *Enigma*)

THE RELIEF PITCHER fierce hitter? help! (Larry, Nov. 1974 *Enigma*)

ROCKY MOUNTAINS o, man—ski country (Ruthless, Nov. 1985 *Enigma*)

WILD OATS sow it, lad (Remardo, Mar. 1917 *Enigma*)

PROTECTIONISM nice to imports (Hercules, Feb. 1928 *Enigma*)

HIBERNATED bear hit den (Viking, Mar. 1934 *Enigma*)
THE PIANO BENCH beneath Chopin (Manx, Sept. 1985 *Enigma*)
SUNBATHE heat buns (Double-H, Jan. 1984 *Enigma*)
DEBIT CARD bad credit (Te-Zir-Man, Nov. 1993 *Enigma*)
THE CAFETERIA fact: I eat here (Travv, Sept. 1976 *Enigma*)
FALSEHOOD has fooled (Ab Struse, Apr. 1993 *Enigma*)
PAST DUE date's up (Beacon, Sept. 1993 *Enigma*)
PASTORSHIP parish post (Kea, Oct. 1994 *Enigma*)
THE STUTTERER utters "t-there" (Ulk, June 1992 *Enigma*)
A STEWARD draws tea (Panache, July 1994 *Enigma*)
IN FLAGRANTE DELICTO Ted, Ella fornicating (Shrdlu, Mar. 1989
Enigma)

Transpositional poetry—poetry in which each line is a rearrangement of letters—has been composed by many people; it is seldom memorable. One of the best examples is given in Figure 48c, a sonnet using the letters of its title, written largely by David Shulman and published in *The Enigma* in June 1936 and again in December 1980.

Figure 48c Washington Crossing the Delaware (*The Enigma*, June 1936, Dec. 1980)

A hard, howling, tossing, water scene:
Strong tide was washing hero clean.
"How cold!" Weather stings as in anger.
O silent night shows war ace danger!

The cold waters swashing on in rage.
Redcoats warn slow his hint engage.
When general's star action wish'd "Go!"
He saw his ragged continentals row.

Ah, he stands—sailor crew went going,
And so this general watches rowing.
He hastens—Winter again grows cold;
A wet crew gain Hessian stronghold.

George can't lose war with 's hands in;
He's astern—so, go alight, crew, and win!

Sonnet composed by Ab Struse (David Shulman) and published in the June 1936 *Enigma* (corrected in Dec. 1980). Four lines were published previously: 1 Jim Jam (James B. Kirk), in "Knit Knots" in the *Norristown Herald and Free Press* of 9 Sept. 1879; 5 Percy Vere (Alvah S. Pendleton) in *Harper's Young People*, 11 July 1882, and in an unnamed source in 1880; 8 Skeeziks (William L. Ougheltree) in 10 Nov. 1890

Thedom (Conundrum Club of New York); 12 Hercules (Howard B. McPherrin) in the May 1932 *Enigma.*

Letter-by-letter transpositions seldom, if ever, are applied to longer phrases than single lines of poetry. The transposition of poems is usually carried out on a word-by-word basis instead. Two cases can be distinguished: a person takes a well-known poem and attempts to rearrange its words into a new set of thoughts, or a person is presented with a list of words (the disassembled poem) and asked to create a poem out of it. Long poems (at least two hundred words) are usually rearrangeable into a different story line, although the mood of the original is usually captured by the word choices; an example by Wayne Carlson of Idaho State University, created on 6 May 1973, is given in Figure 48d.

Figure 48d   A Reconstructed Poem

Composed upon Westminster Bridge, September 3, 1802
(Wordsworth)

Earth has not anything to show more fair:
Dull would he be of soul who could pass by
A sight so touching in its majesty:
This City now doth, like a garment, wear
The beauty of the morning; silent, bare
Ships, towers, domes, theatres, and temples lie
Open unto the fields, and to the sky;
All bright and glittering in the smokeless air.
Never did sun more beautifully steep
In his first splendour, valley, rock, or hill;
Ne'er saw I, never felt, a calm so deep!
The river glideth at his own sweet will:
Dear God! the very houses seem asleep;
And all that mighty heart is lying still!

Decomposed upon Buddy's Bar, May 6, 1973 (Wayne Carlson)

A city is lying still, asleep in the dull morning;
A steep hill towers more unto the smokeless sky,
Touching the heart and soul of God.
Bare fields doth lie in the valley,

Like ships that glideth, all silent in the river.
I saw all His own houses, now temples to the sun;
Sight at first has never felt more dear.
Who would not wear His garment, open to the calm air?
Could anything be so beautifully bright and glittering?
He will never show its theatres and domes;
Or pass by this fair Earth; a mighty rock,
Of very deep beauty, splendour, and majesty
Ne'er did seem so sweet!

Short poems usually converge on the original, even when this is unknown to the constructor; an example is given in Figure 48e. Can the reader pick out the original? (The answer is the first cardinal number in the second paragraph of Section 48.)

Figure 48e   Crazy California: Three Reconstructions (*WW*, May 1975)

California's hanging on somehow.
But it wouldn't matter if it fell off
   Into the ocean.
Everyone's crazy there, anyway.
Wet or dry, they'd go on living underwater.
   So who cares? (A. Ross Eckler)

California's hanging on somehow
But it wouldn't matter anyway if it fell off
   Into the ocean.
Everyone's so crazy there,
They'd go on living underwater.
   Wet or dry, who cares? (Margaret Eckler)

California's so crazy
It wouldn't matter if somehow
It fell off into the ocean.
Wet or dry—who cares…
Everyone's hanging on underwater,
But they'd go on living there anyhow. (Murray Pearce)

California's hanging on somehow,
But if it fell off into the ocean
   It wouldn't matter.
Wet or dry, everyone's crazy there anyway—
They'd go on living underwater.
   So who cares? (Mary J. Hazard)

A chapter in Howard Bergerson's *Palindromes and Anagrams* (Dover, 1973) is devoted to the mathematics of poetic reconstruction; he christens it Vocabularyclept Poetry.

49   TRANSDELETIONS AND TRANSADDITIONS

The transdeletion combines two operations previously discussed, a deletion followed by a transposition (*dower* to *word,* or *Olympic* to *policy*). The transaddition is the inverse operation, a letter addition followed by a transposition.

What is the longest word that can be transdeleted down to a single letter? For the Pocket Merriam-Webster, the answer appears to be the twelve-letter *reactivation;* for the unabridged Merriam-Webster, the sixteen-letter *representational.* The transdeletions are given in Figure 49a.

Figure 49a   The Longest Pocket Merriam-Webster and Unabridged Merriam-Webster Words Transdeletable Down to One Letter
(*WW*, Aug. 1979, Aug. 1982)

reactivation, ratiocinate, recitation, intricate, interact, nitrate, attire, irate, rate, art, at, a

representational, transperitoneal, presentational, septentrional, steprelation, interseptal, eternalist, reinstate, interest, entries, insert, reins, rise, sir, is, I

It is possible to construct a transdeletion chain on a seventeen-letter word if one nondictionary word is allowed: *reclamationist,* found in a 19 January 1946 *Saturday Evening Post* article; this is given in Figure 49b.

Figure 49b Two Seventeen-Letter Transdeletion Pyramids Based on Inferred Words in Unabridged Merriam-Webster and One Non-Dictionary Word (*Reclamationist*) (WW, Aug. 1979, May 1988)

ANTICEREMONIALIST	ANTICEREMONIALIST
NONMATERIALISTIC	NONMATERIALITIES
RECITATIONALISM	ORNAMENTALITIES
RECLAMATIONIST	INTERLAMINATES
REMASTICATION	MATERNALITIES
CREMATIONIST	MATRILINEATE
CREATIONISM	TRILAMINATE
REMICATION	TERMINALIA
MANTICORE	LATIMERIA
REACTION	MATERIAL
CERTAIN	TALIERA
RETAIN	RETAIL
TRAIN	ALTER
RANT	RATE
TAN	TEA
AT	AT
A	A

Alternatively, Kyle Corbin demonstrated that it is possible to construct a seventeen-letter transdeletion chain if inferred forms not explicitly spelled out in the unabridged Merriam-Webster are permitted; this is also given in Figure 49b.

Will Shortz cited a nineteen-letter transdeletion chain in German from *Buch der Ratsel* (1972) by Karl Heinz Paraquin; however, the longer words seem to be coined, such as *Gutsarbeiterzeugnis* (farm worker's report), *Gratisuebersetzung* (a translation made for free), *Uebertragungszeit* (communication transmission-time), and *Arbeitsunterzeug* (work underwear).

Long transdeletions often involve only minor rearrangements of the original word. In fact, less than half of the known seventeen-letter transdeletions in the unabridged Merriam-Webster can be considered genuinely interesting:

anticeremonialist-nonmaterialistic
chromotypographic-microphotography
untrigonometrical-countermigration
peritoneomuscular-ultraceremonious
antistreptococcin-contraceptionist
anthropophagistic-anopisthographic
preterintentional-interpenetration

Of the three known eighteen-letter unabridged Merriam-Webster transdeletions, the best-mixed one is *thermoelectrically-electrometrically.* If hyphenated words or dictionary phrases are allowed, Kyle Corbin has found the following of eighteen letters or more: *confidentialities–self-identification, spherical geometry–electromyographies, unmercenarinesses–insurance messenger, discharge potential–indicator telegraphs, ultraconscientious–contribution clauses,* and the champion, *theoreticopractical–poetico–architectural.*

In general, there are many ways that a word can be transdeleted; if all are diagrammed, the result is an intertwining tangle that is collectively called the *roots* of a word (by analogy with the roots of a tree). The successive transadditions of a word, called the *branches,* can be equally complex. A relatively simple picture of the roots and branches of a word, *Olympic,* is given in Figure 49c.

There is no generally recognized term for the set of all words that can be formed out of the letters of a master word. These words include but are not limited to the roots of a word; some of the words in the set may not be connectable to the master word by an unbroken transdeletion chain. Finding such word sets is a very common newspaper puzzle, and many years ago prize contests were based on it. It is rather surprising that no one has tried to popularize the corresponding transaddition puzzle—that of finding all words containing the letters of the master word.

Among all words of a given length from a specified dictionary, which one is most fecund as a master word? Experimentation with the Pocket Merriam-Webster suggests that they are *sap 6, pate 14, spate 42, repast 96,* and *piaster 169.* Alan Frank used a computer to assess a large number of likely words of lengths three through nine (with all letters different) in the *Official Scrabble Players Dictionary.* The best ones he found were *tea 9, east 24, stare 62, repast 149, plaster 273, pilaster 526, triplanes 917.* As might be expected, there were a number of other words that closely approached these in fecundity. Furthermore, long words with repeated letters are often in the running. Master words yield about 1.6 as many words in the *OSPD* as they do in the Pocket Merriam-Webster. It is conjectured that the unabridged Merriam-Webster outscores the Pocket Merriam-Webster by a factor of 2.6. However, there seems to be a law of diminishing returns in opera-

Figure 49c   Roots and Branches of *Olympic* (*WW*, Aug. 1984)

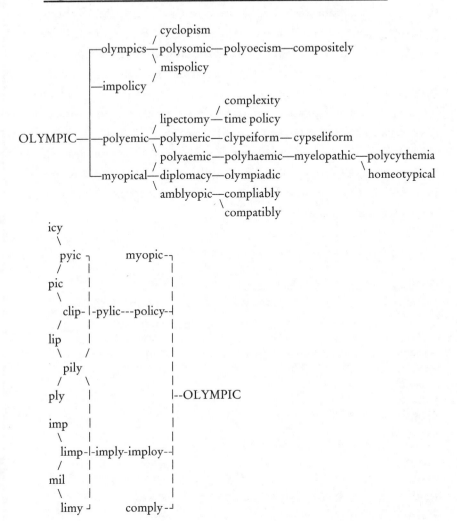

tion; a master word of four letters is 2.7 times as prolific as a master word of three letters, but this ratio shrinks to 1.7 for master words of nine versus eight letters

It has been said that a picture is worth a thousand words, but this is not linguistically true: the word *picture* yields only 46 Pocket Merriam-Webster words, or 173 unabridged Merriam-Webster words, or 273 words if the *Oxford English Dictionary* and the *Times Index-Gazetteer* are also searched. It is just possible that a combination of ten letters such as *AEILNOPRST* or *ADEILO-*

PRST might generate a thousand Pocket Merriam-Webster words; similarly, a combination of eight letters such as *AEILPRST* ought to easily generate a thousand unabridged Merriam-Webster words. Jeff Grant searched a variety of unabridged dictionaries and gazetteers to find a little more than one thousand words in the seven-letter *piaster.*

To perform an alphabetic transaddition, one takes a group of letters, adds in turn the letters from *A* through *Z*, and attempts to rearrange the letters to form twenty-six words. A list of twenty-six unabridged Merriam-Webster transadditions on *at* is presented in Figure 49d, together with Jeff Grant's *Oxford English Dictionary* alphabetic transaddition on *eorstu.*

Figure 49d   Some Alphabetic Transadditions (*WW*, May 1980)

Oxford English Dictionary	Unabridged Merriam-Webster	*Official Scrabble Players Dictionary*
soutAre	tAa	Areas
Bouters	Bat	Bares
strouCe	Cat	sCare
rousteD	taD	reaDs
estourE	Eat	Erase
Foutres	Fat	Fears
Gestour	taG	Gears
soutHer	Hat	sHare
stuorIe	aIt	raIse
Jouster	taJ	raJes
stouKer	Kat	raKes
outLers	aLt	Laser
Moustre	Mat	sMear
uNstore	taN	earNs
stOouer	oaT	arOse
Posture	aPt	sPare
Quoters	Qat	————
Rouster	aRt	Rears
Sourest	Sat	Sears
sTouter	Tat	raTes
sUtoure	taU	Urase
Vouster	Vat	raVes
Wourtes	taW	sWear
seXtour	taX	raXes
Youster	taY	Years
trouZes	Zat	raZes

Stoouer is not listed in boldface in the *OED*, but is found in a 1557 quotation under *Stover*. A near-alphabetic transaddition is possible using the *Official Scrabble Players Dictionary;* only *AEQRS* is lacking. Alan Frank has used a computer to search for the most transaddable sets from this dictionary, for words from three through eight letters. He found that *AT* lacked *aqyz*, *EST* lacked *kq*, *AERS* lacked *q*, *EORST* lacked *jq*, *AEINST* lacked *jqy*, *AEINRST* lacked *jqvxyz*, and *AEGINRST* lacked *afjnqxz*. These data suggest that several alphabetic transadditions based on the unabridged Merriam-Webster remain to be discovered.

Substitute-letter transpositions, introduced by Dmitri Borgmann in *Language on Vacation* (Scribner's, 1965), are a slight variation on transdeletions and transadditions. In a substitute-letter transposition, one letter of a word is replaced with another and the letters rearranged to form a new word. Kyle Corbin has found the largest nontrivial example, the twenty-one-letter *enterobacteriologists-gastroenterocolitises* (*S* substituted for *B*). Word-pairs can be found in quite small word-sets: *Thursday* can be rearranged to *Saturday* if the *H* is replaced with *A,* and *Saturn* to *Uranus* if the *T* is replaced by *U.*

The December 1984/January 1985 issue of *Games* magazine featured a contest with considerable logological interest: Construct a chain of substitute-letter transpositions in which each step substituted a different letter of the alphabet, for a theoretical maximum of twenty-six steps (twenty-seven words). To ensure long-word chains, each was scored by the product of the number of steps and the word-length. A twenty-six-step chain of twelve-letter words was found by Michael Wolfberg after the contest ended:

> meliorations-iConolatries-Viscerotonia-eXorcisation-
> craniotoMies-Gastrocnemii-romanticiZes-cremaTionist-
> iNteractions-increPations-incineRators-contrariWise-
> rHetoricians-orcheStrinas-cEratorhines-secretionarY-reFect
> orians-serOreaction-intercooLers-interlocKers-
> necrolAtries-celeBrations-neUroblastic-subJectional-
> Discountable-elucIdations-eQuinoctials

Using thirteen-letter words, Kyle Corbin won the contest with a total of twenty-three substitutions (no *J*, *Q*, or *F*):

capitalnesses-sKepticalness-tYpicalnesses-plicatEnesses-
ceLestialness-Delicatessens-deatHlinesses-ethiCalnesses-
Wealthinesses-eaRthlinesses-Versatileness-Preessentials-
prOlatenesses-potaBlenesses-blastoGenesis-Notablenesses-
tUnablenesses-Mutablenesses-tAmablenesses-
amIablenesses-miXablenesses-esTimableness-beaStlinesses-
siZablenesses

Can a twenty-six-word set of twelve letters be found in which the
last word joins the first one in a substitute-letter transposition?

FIVE
ALPHABETICAL ORDER AND SCORING

NOT ONLY DOES the alphabet have twenty-six letters, but these letters have a conventional order: *A, B, C,* on through *Z.* This chapter examines various types of wordplay dependent on the order. The mathematically inclined logologist can go a step further, assigning numerical values to the letters and manipulating those values in various ways. Although isolated discoveries in alphabetical wordplay date back many decades, no one seems to have recognized it as a topic in its own right. In *Language on Vacation* (Scribner's, 1965), Dmitri Borgmann devoted three sections of Chapter 6 (Halving the Alphabet, Letter Sequences, Alphabetical Words) to it. He returned to the subject in *Beyond Language* (Scribner's, 1967) with sections entitled Aces and Kings, The New Chemistry, and Balance and Beauty.

Many results in this chapter are incomplete, and could be easily extended by the patient logologist armed with the unabridged Merriam-Webster and a computer.

51 THE LAST WORD

Unabridged dictionaries do not agree on the last word in the English language. Among current dictionaries, the *Oxford English Dictionary* is the most conservative, listing *zyxt,* an obsolete form of *see.* Next in line, the unabridged Funk & Wagnalls gives *zyzzle,* meaning "to make a sputtering or hissing sound, as meat being fried." The first edition of the unabridged Merriam-Webster printed *zythum,* a kind of ancient malt beverage; this was bettered in 1934 when the second edition recorded *Zyzzogeton,* the name of a genus of large South American leafhoppers. Although one would not expect a college dictionary to upstage an unabridged one, this happened in 1969 when the *American Heritage Dictionary* elected to end with *Zyzzva,* the name of a genus of tropical American weevils. (Are taxonomists competing with each other in coining last words?) The last word, at least in major dictionaries, is *zzz,* appearing in the unabridged Random House in 1966. Language purists may be unwilling to admit this onomatopoeic imitation of a person sleeping, even though it has appeared in print in countless comic strips.

The two-Z barrier was breached many years ago in a specialized dictionary, Rupert Hughes's *The Musical Guide* (later, *Music-Lovers Encyclopedia*), published in various editions between 1905 and 1956. Its final entry, *ZZXJOANW* (shaw) <u>Maori</u> 1.Drum 2.Fife 3.Conclusion, remained unchallenged for more than seventy years until Philip Cohen pointed out various oddities: the strange pronunciation, the odd diversity of meanings (including "conclusion") and the non-Maori appearance of the word. (In English transliteration, Maori uses the fourteen letters *AEGHIKMNOPRTUW,* and all words end in a vowel.) A hoax clearly entered somewhere; no doubt Hughes expected it to be obvious, but he did not take into account the credulity of logologists, sensitized by dictionary-sanctioned outlandish words such as *mlechchha* or *qaraqalpaq.*

Names have always offered more fertile ground than dictionaries in searching for the last word. In the second supplement to *The American Language,* H. L. Mencken cites the existence of the female given name *Zzelle.* Last names beginning with two or more Zs have flourished in American telephone directories. Archimedes I.

Zzzyandottie appeared in the Manhattan telephone directory in the 1960s; he is cited by John G. Fuller in *Games for Insomniacs* (Doubleday, 1966). By 1973 nearly fifty names with two or more Zs could be located in telephone directories; though the names often change, examples can be found even today. The champion name for many years was Zachary *Zzzzra* of San Francisco, cited in several editions of the *Guinness Book of World Records*. When in the late 1970s he was nudged out of last place by Zelda *Zzzzwramp*, he quickly changed his surname to ZZZZZZZZZRA.

Are these names real? Though no one has ever made a systematic study of the matter, it seems likely that these testimonials to human vanity exist only in the telephone book, and that their owners otherwise go through life bearing more conventional names. A 29 October 1979 article in *Time* magazine related that Zachary Zzzzra was in reality a painting contractor named Bill Holland who uses his telephone name as an advertising gimmick. However, there are disadvantages: he has received phone calls in the middle of the night from Australia, and people illegally charge calls to his number.

What is the last legitimate surname in the United States, one that is used by a family over several generations? The last family genealogy in the Library of Congress is *Zwingly*. One can assume that the commitment to a surname is fairly solid if its bearer is willing to apply for a Social Security account which will pay him a pension ten to forty years in the future. In the 1960s, the last surname in Social Security records was *Zyzo*, borne by four registrants. In the early 1990s the records of some forty-seven million deceased Social Security recipients became available on CD-ROM. This source listed three two-Z individuals: Peter *Zzgac* (1893–1963), Charles *Zzlstra* (1896–1973), and Margaret *Zzng* (1908–1980). However, these are quite possibly keypunch errors for Zygac, Zylstra, and Zyng. There were four people surnamed *Zyzys,* Stella (1889–1964) of Massachusetts; Stanley (1889–1982) of Florida; Alex (1893–1971) of Illinois; and Anna (1904–1971) of Illinois. There were also four people surnamed *Zyzyk.* There are no *Zyzys* entries in telephone directories, but Kenneth *Zyzyk* is listed in Utica, Michigan, and Patricia *Zyzyk* is in El Paso, Texas. Two of the *Zyzo* clan of Wallingford, Connecticut, have died: Frank (1931–1987) and Mary

(1903–1991). Working backward, one finds nineteen deceased *Zyzniewski*s and nine *Zyznar*s, the commonest names starting with *Zyzn*.

The last placename, at least in the United States, appears to be *Zzyzx* (pronounced "Zeye-zix"), approved 14 June 1984 by the United States Board on Geographic Names as a locality between the Soda Mountains and Soda Lake, 12.1 kilometers northeast of Crucero, San Bernardino County, California. *Zzyzx Springs* is the similarly sanctioned name of a nearby spring. At the end of the Second World War, Curtis Howe Springer illegally built a health spa on this Mojave Desert site which he operated (along with a radio station) for some thirty years. He was evicted by federal marshals in 1976 for alleged violations of food and drug laws, as well as unauthorized use of federal land; since then it has been the Desert Studies Center administered by the California State University system. Springer claimed that he made up the name. There is a highway sign on Interstate 15 about one hundred miles southwest of Las Vegas, pointing to an exit for *Zzyzx Road.*

52   WORDS CONTAINING ADJACENT ALPHABETICAL LETTERS

Three cases of interest can be distinguished: words in which the letters are adjacent and in alphabetic order (as in *ABCoulomb*), words in which the letters are not necessarily adjacent (as in *ABsConDEd*), and words in which the letters are neither adjacent nor in alphabetic order (as in *FEeDBACk*).

This problem has been frequently discussed. An alphabetic sequence in a word is said to be undominated if a word can be found containing all the letters in that sequence, but no word can be found containing a longer sequence including the letters of the original one. Thus, *RSTU* is an undominated sequence for words with letters adjacent and in order, for there are no words containing the pentagrams *QRSTU* or *RSTUV*, the hexagrams *PQRSTU*, *QRSTUV*, or *RSTU-VW*, etc. On the other hand, *RSTU* is not an undominated sequence for words with letters neither in alphabetic order nor adjacent;

VenTRiloQUiSt, for example, contains the more inclusive sequence *QRSTUV.*

A list of undominated words with respect to the Pocket Merriam-Webster is given in Figure 52a, followed by similar ones for the unabridged Merriam-Webster.

Figure 52a Undominated Alphabetic Sequences, Pocket Merriam-Webster (*WW*, May 1982)

Consecutive Letters of the Alphabet

Adjacent in Order	Not Necessarily Adjacent but in Order	Not Necessarily Adjacent, Not Necessarily in Order
BC bobcat	ABCDE ambuscade	ABCDEF feedback
CD anecdote	DEFG defog	CDEFGHI lightfaced
DEF deft	EFGHI prizefighting	GHIJK straightjacket
FGH afghan	HIJK hijack	IJKL jailbreak
GHI sighing	JKL jackal	JKLM lumberjack
HIJ hijack	KLMN kleptomania	KLMNOP kleptomania
KL ankle	LMNO luminous	NOPQRSTU quadruplications
LMN calmness	MNOP monopoly	QRSTUV ventriloquist
MNO somnolent	OPQ opaque	RSTUVW liverwurst
NOP nope	PQRS parquetries	WXY waxy
Q quit	QRST quartermaster	YZABC recognizably
RSTU understudy	RSTU rostrum	
UV mauve	STUV destructive	
W we	UVW purview	
XY waxy	WXY waxy	
YZA coryza	YZAB hypnotizable	
ZAB sizable		

Undominated Alphabetic Sequences, Unabridged Merriam-Webster (*WW*, May 1982)

Adjacent and in Order	Not Necessarily Adjacent but in Order	Not Necessarily Adjacent, Not Necessarily in Order
ABC dabchick	ABCDE ambuscade	CDEFGHI lightfaced
CDE ecdemic	CDEF campodeiform	GHIJK straightjacket
DEF deft	DEFGH underfreight	HIJKL kjeldahlize

EFG trefgordd	EFGHI prizefighting	IJKLM jamlike
FGH afghan	HIJK hijack	JKLMNO Koggelmannetje
GHI sighing	JKL jacklight	KLMNOP kleptomania
HIJ hijack	KLMNO Kilmarnock	LMNOPQR quadripul-monary
IJK satlijk	LMNOP limnophile	NOPQRSTU quadru-plications
KL ankle	NOPQ unopaque	PQRSTUV supraquanti-valent
LMN calmness	PQRS parquetries	RSTUVW liverwurst
MNOP limnophile	QRST quartermaster	WXY waxy
OPQ popquiz	RSTUV interdestructive	XYZABC benzoxycam-phor
QR miqra	UVW purview	YZABCDEF brazen-facedly
RSTU understudy	WXY waxy	
UV mauve	XYZAB oxygenizable	
W we	ZABC Mozambican	
XYZ hydroxyzine		
YZAB analyzable		

OveRSTUffed and *undeRSTUdy* are the only Pocket Merriam-Webster words with alphabetical tetragrams. The word *lIGHt-FaCED* is the only Pocket Merriam-Webster word with seven consecutive letters neither adjacent nor in order; words with six such letters include *BACkFiElD, FIGurEHeaD, PRereQUiSiTe, PicTUReSQue, BArEFaCeD, tIGHtFistED, PhaNtOMLiKe, ForE-sIGHteD, FarsIGHtED, BioFEeDbACk,* and *FrIGHtEneD,* all found by Tom Pulliam.

If hyphenated words or phrases are allowed, the sequence *ABCDEFGHI* can be found in three Merriam-Webster entries: *BrIGHt-FACED, BlACk-FaCED HiGhland,* and *BlEACHInG FielD.* For *FGHIJKL,* there is *HaLF-JoKInG.* The well-known proper name *KILiMaNJarO* contains the sequence *IJKLMNO.* No Merriam-Webster word contains more than nine consecutive letters, but the unabridged Random House word *QUaSi-cOMPLe-meNTaRy* contains ten: *LMNOPQRSTU.* This sequence is also found in the Merriam-Webster phrase *aziMUThaL eQuidiStaNt PROjection.*

Figure 52b lists all known Merriam-Webster words containing alphabetical tetragrams *MNOP* and *RSTU.*

Figure 52b All Unabridged Merriam-Webster Words with Alphabetic Tetragrams (WW, May 1982)

---

gyMNOPa(e)dia, gyMNOPedic, GyMNOPhilona, GyMNOP-
aedes
liMNOPhil(e), liMNOPhilous, LimMNOPhilidae, liMNOPhilid,
LiMNOPithecus, liMNOPlankton(ic)
soMNOPathy, soMNOPathist
SeMNOPithec(e), seMNOPithecine, seMNOPitheque, SeMNO-
Pithecinae, SeMNOPithecus
ThaMNOPhilus, ThaMNOPhis, thaMNOPhile, thaMNOPhiline,
ThaMNOPhilinae
oveRSTUff(ed), oveRSTUdy, oveRSTUdied, oveRSTUd, oveR-
STUdious(ly), oveRSTUdiousness
undeRSTUff(ing), undeRSTUmble, undeRSTUdy
supeRSTUff

Corresponding lists of undominated words can be made for letters in reverse alphabetical sequence. Figure 52c gives lists for letters adjacent and in reverse order for unabridged and for Pocket Merriam-Webster words; the corresponding lists for nonadjacent letters have not been assembled.

Figure 52c Undominated Alphabetic Sequences, Reversed Alphabet
(WW, May 1982)

Pocket Merriam-Webster: BAn, bEDClothes, FED, wronGFul,
churcHGoer, JIHad, blacKJack, eLK, firMLy, cantONMent,
uPON, toRQue, miSRead, nUTS, oVUm, We, pYX, lAZY
Unabridged Merriam-Webster: carBAZYlic, baCBAkiri, bED-
Clothes, FED, sonGFEst, churcHGoer, JIHad, stoLKJaerre,
firMLy, tamPONMent, toRQue, miSRead, nUTS, keVUTzah,
hoWVe, boXWeed, asphYXiate

Figure 52d is an amusing fictional account containing the letters *A* through *Q* in order, translated from the Dutch; the original can be found in Battus's *Opperlandse taal- & letterkunde* (Querido, 1981).

Figure 52d Who Says *A* Must Say *B* (WW, Aug. 1985)

It is not well-known that an airline once played a role in the draining of the Noordoostpolder (1). The Department of Water Management (2) divided the N.O.P. into quadrants and borrowed from KLM (3) the PH-OEI (4) to fly all day over the imaginary lines in order for the workers on the ground to orient themselves properly. For the pilots this was boring work—especially so for the legendary exRussian pilot Smirnoff (5) who detested flying around in little square patterns. He would, in fact, much rather have flown on the Goudkust (6) of South Carolina, or, as he himself would say "Gdkust en Sth Carolina" because he could not pronounce the diphthong OU.

Flip Gortzak, who in those years was the Financial Genius of KLM at the Eelde airport, the home base of the N.O.P. pilots, told me an amusing story about Smirnoff. F.G., as everyone called him because of his initials, his occupation, and his love of Florins and Guilders, told Smirnoff that Plesman (7) intended to provide the same alignment service for the work then being carried out on the Amsterdam-Rhine canal near Abcoude (8). Smirnoff reacted to this with the outburst "Als boven *Abcde, F.G., hij KLM N.O.P. q*uadranten laat vliegen, dan ga ik terug naar Mosk!" (9)

(1) The Noordoostpolder, or Northeast Polder (N.O.P.), is part of the long-range reclamation of the inland Zuyder Zee for agriculture.
(2) This is a Dutch government agency charged with the oversight of the canal system.
(3) The acronym of the Dutch national airline.
(4) The identification letters for a particular plane, no doubt selected because of its homonymy with *phooey.*
(5) Smirnoff was a well-known KLM pilot in the 1930s, who helped develop the airline route between the Netherlands and Indonesia. This had some of the glamour of the early Pan-American clipper route across the Pacific about the same time, or of the earlier Orient Express.
(6) *Goudkust* means "gold coast," located in South Carolina rather than Florida so the author could introduce a second word with the *OU* diphthong.
(7) Plesman was the director-general of KLM from the 1930s through the 1950s.
(8) Abcoude is a Dutch town near the Amsterdam-Rhine canal.
(9) This translates as "If he [Plesman] makes me fly KLM Northeast Polder quadrants above Abcoude, F.G., I'm going back to Moscow." As usual, Smirnoff is unable to pronounce either Abcoude or Moscow (*Moskou* in Dutch) correctly.

53 *A-TO-Z* WORD LISTS

This topic of alphabetic wordplay has not been extensively explored. In April 1976, a subscriber to the British magazine *Games & Puzzles* posed this problem: What is the shortest list of words containing the letters of the alphabet in order? There is, in general, a trade off between the number of words and number of extra letters needed, as illustrated by three mixed-dictionary examples due to Jeff Grant:

> ABC, DEFoG, HIJacK, LiMNOPhil, QueRiST, UVroW, XYZ (7,38)
> ABC, DEFoG, HIJ, KLaM, NOP, QueRiST, UVroW, XYZ (8,33)
> ABC, DEFoG, HIJ, KLaM, NOP, QRS, TU, VoW, XYZ (9,29)

His words have been drawn from the unabridged Merriam-Webster and the *Oxford English Dictionary* (*QRS* appears in the third edition of the former as part of the phrase *QRS complex*).

Language purists may wish to impose more stringent rules: no single-letter words allowed (other than *A* or *I*), and no abbreviations (all words must be pronounceable, not spelled out as *ABC* and *XYZ*). Under these rules, the minimum-letter Pocket Merriam-Webster list for *A* to *Z* and for *Z* to *A* appear to be

> nAB, CoDE, FiG, HIJacK, LiMN, OP, QuRSh, TUrVes, WaXY, Zip (10,40)
> haZY, oX, WaVe, oUT, SiR, QuiP, ON, MiLK, JIg, HoG, FED, CuB, A (13,39)

Corresponding lists for the unabridged Merriam-Webster have not been devised. The minimum-word Pocket Merriam-Webster *A-to-Z* and *Z-to-A* word lists are derivable from Section 52; these appear to be:

> AmBusCaDE, FiG, HIJacK, LuMiNOus, ParQuetRy, deSTrUctiVe, WaXY, feZ (8,53)
> laZY, oXboW, oVUlaTionS, toRQue, POlyNoMiaL, sKyJackIng, tHouGhtFulnEss, DisComBobulAte (8,73)

Figure 53a is Howard Bergerson's literary version of an *A-to-Z* word list.

Figure 53a The Panalphabetic Window (*WW*, Aug. 1980)

Several years ago at a noisy nightclub a male friend invited me to join him at his table, and introduced me to a girl who was with him, named Xan Xu, with the information that she had made TV commercials for the 7-Up Company.

"My friend Howard knows things about words," he assured her.

"Like what?"

Within seconds I had irretrievably committed one of my great social blunders. "Oh, for example, I know something about THE UNCOLA which is, uh, interesting."

"What is it?"

"It's not *really* interesting," I said, sweating profusely and trying to beat a hasty retreat.

"Oh, come on!" she insisted.

"Okay," I gulped. "If you number the letters of THE UNCOLA from one to nine, you can rearrange them to 9 6451 2783." I waited miserably while the two of them counted on their fingers and marked on a napkin with a pen. Xan Xu figured it out ahead of him and crumpled the napkin, leaving my friend—who will remain anonymous—mystified.

"What are you going to do with this item?" she asked.

"I thought I'd send it to some girlie book."

"Oh." She stared at me and her eyes smoldered.

"Yeah. You know, like *Playboy*..." I squirmed and mopped my brow. Then a strange thing happened. Xan Xu, I realized, was most justifiably unfriendly—but I hardly noticed the meaning of her words as she spoke, though I listened aghast:

"Well, ABout porn, I Can say DEFinitely that althouGH I loathe JunK Like that Myself, I doN't prOPose to Question otheR people'S righT to it, becaUse, in my VieW, if seXY magaZines and X-rated movies are what they want instead of the real thing, more power to them!" And with that she betook herself and him from my presence, out to the dance floor.

"My God!" I shouted inwardly as I walked home through a midnight thunderstorm, "the panalphabetic window!—the narrowest panalphabetic window freely occurring in nature that I have ever seen or ever hope to see! The probability of such a freely occurring event must be infinitesimal...."

54 HOMONYMS OF THE ALPHABET

Many of the letters of the alphabet are homonymic to English words (*B* bee, *C* sea, *DK* decay). In *La Littérature Potentielle* (1979), Georges Perec exploited this idea by writing, in French, a playlet, "The Horrors of War," in which the entire dialogue is a recital of the alphabet in order. An English-language analogue, "Nixon and the Bee," is given in Figure 54a.

Figure 54a Nixon and the Bee (*WW*, Aug. 1976)

Ivan held up the short piece of magnetic tape with scepticism. "You say that this is the missing ten seconds of the notorious Watergate tape?"

Boris stared at his chief in surprise. "Of course...didn't I tell you how KGB agent Nikolai Ripoff stole it from the office of Professor Esty of the Cornell Linguistics Department? And isn't it well known that Professor Esty was one of the blue-ribbon panel that investigated the original White House tape, using highly sophisticated techniques of noise suppression and message enhancement to recover the missing words?"

"But why," asked Ivan, reaching for an empty tape reel, "was there never any public report of the recovered message?"

"That's obvious," replied Boris. "The message was so sensational in import that political pressure was brought to bear on Esty and his colleagues to keep it quiet—to pretend, in fact, that they were unable to decipher the tape at all. I'll bet the U.S. Government will pay us a pretty kopek not to reveal its contents."

By now, Ivan had expertly spooled the tape on the reel and was placing the reel on the Ampex. "That remains to be seen," he said dryly. He flipped the switch on, and both men leaned forward expectantly.

A BEE...Ivan turned the machine off to ponder the import of this phrase. "A bee? But of course—there must have been a bee brought in with the vase of flowers that always sits in the Oval Office, and Nixon has interrupted the meeting to warn the others of its presence." Satisfied with this interpretation, Ivan turned the machine back on.

...SEEDY...This demanded a second halt for assessment.

"Hmmm," mused Boris, "no doubt the bouquet was picked and arranged many hours earlier. By now, the bee had exhausted the nectar and is slowly starving—reflected in his debilitated appearance and sluggish movements."

...EEEE!....The sudden scream caught both men by surprise; clearly someone, lulled into a false sense of security by the bee's torpidity, has tried to remove the bee from the room and has been stung.

...IF, GEE, A CHI-...The two Russians looked at each other in bewilderment. If this were Nixon speaking, clearly his mind had been affected by the bee sting. This slurred, rambling phrase was not Nixon's usual crisp, incisive style. Had he gone into anaphylactic shock? Was he starting to say that the china vase holding the bouquet had concealed the bee, and it would be better to use a cut-glass vase in the future?

...JAKE, A YELL!...Someone in the next room heard Nixon's scream and was telling his associate, Jacob, about it.

...AMEN. O, PEEK...By now both men were somewhat perplexed. "Could the others believe that Nixon had been killed by the sting, and they are praying over his inert body?" asked Ivan. "And why should they have to peek at him? I'll never understand the American way of death."

...(YOU ARE ESTY)...Since it is most unlikely that Professor Esty was present at the time of the bee sting, this tape must have been inadvertently overwritten during the reconstruction experiments in Professor Esty's laboratory, perhaps at a time when he was distracted by the entrance of a visitor verifying the professor's identity.

...YOU'VE—EEEE!...Back on the original tape, it is appearent that a second bee in the bouquet, heretofore unnoticed, has stung another Oval Office conferee in the middle of a sentence.

...DOUBLE, YOU!...This cryptic exhortation was apparently directed at Nixon's doctor, as he prepared an anti-venom shot, alerting him to the fact that two doses would now be needed.

...EGGS..."I must confess," said Boris, "bafflement at this one-word statement. Was it a breakfast conference in the Oval Office? Or was that an oblique reference to the anti-venom serum being administered to the President? Our virologists tell us that many vaccines are grown in unfertilized chicken eggs..."

...WHY'S HE The tape ended abruptly at this point, in the middle of a sentence. Still, Ivan was able to reconstruct the situation: "His secretary, attracted by the commotion, entered the Oval Office. Seeing Nixon on the floor with a doctor bent over him, she cried in a startled voice 'Why's he lying there?' but we heard only the first half."

"So," mused Boris, "the reason for suppressing the tape is clear. The men around Nixon couldn't let the country know that the President had been crippled by a bee sting and was temporarily unable to govern, so they attempted, as part of the cover-up, to erase the relevant part of the tape. Remember, Ivan, that the American people have been unusually skittish about presidential health ever since Woodrow Wilson lay paralyzed for many months after World War I. Secrecy must be maintained for the good of the country—a principle which we Russians have honed to perfection, but which the Americans are still learning to apply."

If near-homonyms are allowed as well, the bare recital of the alphabet without interpolative material can make a weird sort of sense. Various literary examples of this genre are presented in Figure 54b.

Figure 54b Alphabetic Recitals (WW, May 1981, Aug. 1981)

Eh! Be seedy, ye effigy, at shy Jake.
A lemon, opaque. You are a stew—
Feed a bull, you ex! Why said?   —ALLAN SIMMONS

Abby seized Dee's effigy, hijacked Elle's minnow,
Piqued curest tease. "You've double-used," ex-wised Zee.
                                                  —LOUIS PHILLIPS

A beast's sea-deaf. Gee! High jockey elm, an O.
Pease cue arrest you. V double-U ex-wide Z.
                                                  —LOUIS PHILLIPS

Abie see de eel elf. Gee! Etch high Jake.
Hey! Element toe pique you? Arrest tea. You've eel.
Double you eggs. Why zeal?   —BORIS RANDOLPH

Hay, be seedy! He-effigy, hate-shy jaky yellow man, O peek!
You are rusty, you've edible, you ex-wise he!
                                                  —HARRY MATHEWS

Hay Bee! Is he deaf? Gee!
Hey Chi! D'ya kill 'em? Nope.
Curious to you, Vita?
But you ask, "Why is he?"   —SCOTT MACGREGOR,
                                                  MINNIE JARDINE

55   WORDS CLASSIFIED BY ALPHABETIC PROPERTIES

There are a handful of unabridged Merriam-Webster words of six letters or more in which the letters appear in alphabetic order without repetition:

> abdest, Achior, acknow, acorsy, adempt, adipsy, agnosy, almost, befist, begirt, behint, beknow, bijoux, biopsy, cestuy, chintz, deflux, dehors, dehort, Deimos, deinos, diluvy, dimpsy, ghosty

> Adelops, egilops, aegilops

If repeated letters are allowed, one can add *beefily, begorry,* and *billowy* to the seven-letter list. Suppose that the alphabet is written in a circle, with *A* following *Z;* what words can be spelled out in less than one cycle? In addition to the seven-letter words above, *begorra, belotta, glossae,* and *subcell* qualify. Two more eight-letter words, *mortbell* and *subfloor,* have also been identified.

Curiously, it is harder to find long words with letters in reverse alphabetical order.

> ponica, sonica, spolia, Spolie, sponge, tromba, uronic, vomica, yolked
> sponged, wronged

With repeated letters allowed, one can add *spiffed, spoofed, spooked, spooled, spooned, trigged, trolled,* and *zyxomma.* With hyphens allowed, *spoon-feed* is the longest reverse alphabetical word known.

Six-letter words with all letters different can be sorted into 720 different categories according to the alphabetic positioning of their letters. To illustrate this concept, consider the analogous problem for three-letter words which can be sorted in exactly six ways:

123	for, hit, beg
132	dig, jug, are
213	can, six, pay
231	nub, run, two
312	you, tip, ten
321	the, one, led

Observe in the first row that *F* comes before *O*, and *O* before *R* in the alphabet; the same is true for *H, I, T,* and *B, E, G.* Figure 55a consists of a type-collection of 720 six-letter words, all from the unabridged Merriam-Webster. It is extremely unlikely that a full type-collection of 5,040 seven-letter words could be similarly assembled.

Figure 55a A Type-Collection of the 720 Letter-Orders of Six-Letter Words (*WW*, Nov. 1978)

Words in this table have the alphabetical order of their letters numerically encoded: ALMOST 123456, ZEPHYR 613254. To find a word corresponding to a code, change the last three digits to the appropriate -0+ symbol: 123456 to 123-0+, 613254 to 613-+0. Numbers are listed by row and symbols by column.

	- 0 +	- + 0	0 - +	0 + -	+ - 0	+ 0 -
123	almost	chorus	deputy	deform	adjust	acetol
124	import	corpus	beings	aching	amount	belong
125	absent	detour	firmly	active	acnode	absurd
126	actors	action	design	acting	abuser	citron
132	flimsy	agents	injury	coitus	albums	becurl
134	direst	dingus	chores	behind	closer	behold
135	county	afresh	dourly	bisque	answer	birsle
136	covers	fruits	glyphs	course	advice	beyond
142	anchor	fights	clergy	alcove	groups	ambush
143	client	fronts	agency	consul	argues	growth
145	blocks	artful	copies	borize	enough	closed
146	bought	asylum	bother	boyish	cousin	couple
152	guilty	areito	bodies	elfish	column	cresol
153	credit	folium	brings	ariose	driven	engulf
154	bright	brogue	aspect	bronze	crotin	around
156	buyers	astern	anthem	buying	bounce	copied
162	exhort	awhirl	budget	buckle	aweigh	arched
163	export	bugdom	builds	ashore	douser	ethnic
164	curios	bridle	avoids	coming	avouch	custom
165	author	bridge	broken	during	bolide	atomic
213	minors	famous	fairly	bagwyn	editor	backed
214	barest	genius	gently	galosh	liquor	hansom
215	family	litmus	danger	baking	caster	carved
216	caught	candle	catkin	eating	heroin	caused

231	chairs	giants	beauty	dictum	flavor	blazon
234	forest	delays	mostly	coryza	flower	impute
235	insert	behalf	dismay	mosque	foster	insure
236	detail	doubts	denial	disorb	dismal	chroma
241	claims	grants	boards	coarse	chapel	clause
243	honest	inlets	climax	cherub	months	injure
245	botany	dilate	direct	cornua	dorsal	copula
246	hotels	coward	fluids	cinema	gospel	invoke
251	grains	erbium	brakes	braise	brazen	change
253	dreams	breath	gripes	engird	engram	enfold
254	homely	donate	honker	enigma	frozen	ground
256	entail	double	bowman	hoping	formal	formic
261	cubist	braced	dwarfs	cyanol	branch	craned
263	junior	exodus	ethics	guimpe	guitar	ethnic
264	domain	curate	junket	dolina	oyster	fringe
265	mythos	combed	burial	futile	furoin	frolic
312	cabins	habits	penury	facing	factor	cabled
314	gaiety	merits	partly	galore	result	manure
315	hardly	markup	hamlet	masque	master	nature
316	layers	carbon	father	having	hawser	garlic
321	hearty	hearts	poetry	lignum	robust	plexus
324	miners	lineup	portly	ignore	minuet	minute
325	misery	poseur	jitney	hemina	listen	gerund
326	powers	leucon	genial	Edwina	routes	heroic
341	modest	prints	flames	opaque	graves	incuse
342	priest	decays	fields	fiesta	proves	infuse
345	forces	noteum	sturdy	motive	mortal	hinted
346	novels	inward	mother	nowise	inroad	housed
351	nudity	modern	frames	glaive	gravel	income
352	surety	embark	quires	embira	molten	inhume
354	golden	inmate	longer	lomita	isotac	jolted
356	hoyden	intake	morgen	moving	jounce	formed
361	nudist	exacts	guards	mycose	ovates	fucoid
362	others	quoits	syntax	mucosa	quotes	hydric
364	lumber	island	hunger	friend	munshi	jumped
365	lutein	itself	muslin	jungle	putsch	gushed
412	gadfly	paints	jacket	facile	lactim	fabric
413	safety	remits	magnet	septum	palter	salute
415	savory	length	native	market	marvel	person
416	garden	handle	revolt	marine	launch	paused
421	plenty	plants	neatly	rectum	phasor	rebush
423	ideals	sprout	melody	hegira	plover	Nimrod
425	resalt	octave	sourly	risque	mental	perula
426	petals	rewash	ocular	method	sexual	metric

431	mighty	points	nearby	plaque	player	sleuth
432	recast	sleazy	midway	fedora	nectar	pleura
435	mincer	phrase	linear	lingua	postal	listed
436	sought	herald	pounds	jingle	smutch	poured
451	models	ophism	inches	praise	glance	prison
452	organs	locate	stormy	ophite	induce	noetic
453	prices	strewn	turkey	strive	proven	proved
456	studio	forced	oxygen	motile	normal	stupid
461	quaint	nudism	judges	swarth	suitor	subtle
462	sugent	typhus	suclat	muckma	swivel	luetic
463	number	jugate	sunlit	owlish	switch	joined
465	murage	myself	orphan	outing	myriad	pushed
512	radios	radium	ladies	radish	salvor	fabled
513	safety	throws	simply	ramose	salver	ransom
514	panels	tergum	object	making	sequin	raised
516	thumps	marble	sauger	saying	paunch	marked
521	theory	tedium	thinly	signum	sector	scathe
523	silent	tophus	worthy	shinza	silver	refund
524	timely	scrawl	phones	torque	rental	should
526	obtain	retalk	thumbs	period	unwrap	thymic
531	widely	teacup	planes	trisul	slayer	phasic
532	uneasy	todays	signet	plinth	sliver	nebula
534	legacy	sprawl	pilfer	shrewd	spruce	showed
536	trucks	toward	trunks	squire	source	linked
541	places	sodium	pocket	plague	travel	played
542	pokily	libate	trophy	tropyl	sketch	poetic
543	slight	solate	policy	tongue	trowel	lifted
546	unveil	voyage	squeal	trying	trough	posing
561	tubers	stable	stamen	mobile	nuclei	public
562	ordain	subage	ordeal	xylose	stench	myelic
563	preach	symbol	sypher	ruling	prince	stored
564	strain	strand	stream	strike	stride	turned
612	wagons	region	tables	racing	tensor	sacred
613	senior	zephyr	tamper	talose	values	Salome
614	weight	random	walker	taking	unstop	wanted
615	waters	sermon	vermin	waving	malice	walked
621	theirs	reckon	thanks	wealth	victor	weapon
623	unrest	seldom	things	virtue	winter	thorpe
624	remain	rehang	violet	remind	visual	simple
625	pencil	wisdom	scream	shrine	scribe	throne
631	widest	whefts	shaken	tickle	search	second
632	vicars	pigeon	yields	vedika	signal	vicuna
634	timber	silane	singer	shield	worsen	wilted
635	virago	repaid	verbal	single	thrice	winked

641	trails	viable	uncles	wraith	tocsin	picked
642	trials	wreath	trends	ungird	spiral	volume
643	wonder	zonate	wrongs	thecia	unload	united
645	unpack	sprang	unreal	spring	thread	worked
651	urchin	placed	soaken	tragic	trance	rocked
652	solemn	urbane	social	ungild	spinal	uphold
653	pleach	upland	vulgar	trifle	zodiac	smiled
654	solace	voiced	spoken	unlike	police	sponge

Words can be classified by alphabetic properties in other ways. For example, consider the alphabet circle introduced earlier. Any word can be characterized by the positions of its letters on the circle. In particular, there always exists a longest gap of consecutive unused letters in the circle. For example, the word *animal* does not use the twelve consecutive letters O through Z, and the word *tooth* does not use the thirteen consecutive letters U through Z followed by A through G. The larger this number, the more concentrated the word is in a single part of the alphabet; *deeded* has a gap of twenty-four, as do *noon* and *tutu*.

Eugene Ulrich sorts words into three groups according to another alphabetical property of the letters. He christens a word a *vicinal* if all its letters have alphabetic neighbors; for example, *hedonist* is a vicinal because D and E, H and I, N and O, and S and T are all alphabetic neighbors, and there are no letters that do not have this property. Similarly, *actively* is a nonvicinal because no letter in it is alphabetically adjacent to another letter in it. Not surprisingly, most words fall into a third group. In *suture*, R, S, T, and U are neighbors but E is isolated. One can write stories consisting purely of vicinals or of nonvicinals, as given in Figure 55b.

Figure 55b Vicinals (*WW*, Aug. 1983)

> Bedfast hedonist fights hoiden, foments bedlam; sport done, this undermost bighead sighted Jacobin post tabu documents on chipboards. Unsought, high-minded sponsors meddled—becalmed, chided combatants, condemned cohabitations, requested support, stressed antidisestablishmentarianism.

Non-Vicinals (*WW*, Aug. 1983)

> Unlyric alto (howler!) vocalizes actively, squealing, squawking and squeaking morceaux in upward octave, as peculiar,

drunk clarinet player, certainly reacting, privately quickens, plunges uneasily twice, wrecking carpeting. Whereat uncaring Mississippi mortgage receiver did cogitate officially, tyrannically disqualify drinking Pennsylvanian categorically, thereby aggravating souse incapacitatingly.

What is the longest nonvicinal with no repeated letters? The theoretical maximum is thirteen since the alphabet has twenty-six letters. The longest ones known are the ten-letter examples *anticlergy, caperingly, escapingly, kerygmatic, taperingly, trivalency,* and *wateringly.* If repeated letters are allowed, the longest known nonvicinal is *interpenetratively.* If hyphens are allowed, these records increase to *parcel-tying* and *nievie-nievie-nick-nack.*

The longest Merriam-Webster vicinal is the twenty-seven-letter *hydroxydesoxycorticosterone;* the twenty-eight-letter *antidisestablishmentarianism* is not in this dictionary.

Philip Cohen has suggested another way to classify words alphabetically. As noted earlier, *almost* and *billowy* have all letters in alphabetical order and can thus be termed *monoalphabetical. Femininity* contains the interwoven alphabetical sequences *EMNN* and *FIIITY,* and can be called *bialphabetical.* (Note that these sequences are not unique; *FMNN* and *EIIITY* serve equally well.) Words can be classified according to the smallest number of alphabetical sequences they contain.

A rule that invariably constructs a minimum set of alphabetical sequences has yet to be formulated. However, one can determine a lower limit to the number of sequences required by searching for the longest possible descending alphabetical sequence. For example, in *femininity* it is two: *fe, mi,* or *ni.* The word *antidisestablishmentarianism* contains the descending alphabetical set *TSLIHEA,* so that it must have at least seven interwoven ascending sequences:

```
A----I------------------I-----M-N----R-----------
--NT-----------T------------------T----------------
--------DIS---S----------S----------------------S---
------------E--------L------------------------M
------------------A------------------A---AN-----
--------------------B------H------------I----I----
--------------------------------E-----------------
```

An open question: what are the longest bi-, tri-, ... alphabetical words in the unabridged Merriam-Webster? (The corresponding question for the shortest such words is trivial; look for words such as *sponge* or *wronged.*) The Merriam-Webster word *anthropomorphologically* contains a descending alphabetical sequence of nine, *TRPOMHG-CA*, the longest such known; it can be dissected into nine interwoven sequences. Do words exist in which the minimum number of interwoven sequences exceeds the descending alphabetical sequence?

A related word classification scheme makes use of the idea of invariance. A letter in a word is invariant if it appears in the same place in the word as its position in the alphabet; thus, *A, B, D,* and *E* are invariant in the words *ABiDE* and *ABoDE*. Figure 55c exhibits unabridged Merriam-Webster words containing various invariant letters of the alphabet.

Figure 55c Invariant Alphabetical Letters

> A, eBb, baCk, banD, writE, relieF, restinG, retrencH, personalIty, counterobJection, quarterbacK, hierarchicaL, parallelograM, sesquipedaliaN, pronunciamientO, acquaintanceshiP, thermogalvanometeR, interchangeablenesS, noninterventionalisT, pseudomonocotyledonoUs, immunoelectrophoreticallY

There exist Merriam-Webster words with five invariant letters: *ABaDEnGo, ABuDEFduf, AgammaGlobuLiNemiaS, AntiantHropoMorPhiSm, ApoDEictIcaL, ArChEncephaLoN, ArChErsHIp, ArChEtypIcaL, nonDEFeasibLeNess, nonDEFensibLeNess, non-DEFinIteLy, nonDEFinItiveNess,* and *syngEnesIotraNsPlanTation.* Invariant sentences can also be constructed: *A BaD EgG HIt KLM wiPeRS Two WaYs* (no doubt blocking the view of the pilot).

If the idea of invariance is generalized, it provides yet another way to classify words by their alphabetical properties. A group of letters is said to be locally invariant if they match the alphabet when appropriately shifted, as in *DEFicIt* or *imPulSe*. One can classify each word by the number of alphabet shifts it exhibits. For example, *wretch* contains four such shifts: *Wretch, wReTch, wrEtcH,* and *wretCh.* One can label each alphabet shift by the letter matching the first letter of the word; thus *wretch* is characterized by the alphabet shifts *W, Q, C,* and *Y,* and one can replace *wretch* with the pattern *WQCQYC.* Patterns such as *WQCQYC* and *PNDNXD* are placed in the same group; the different patterns of a group can be labeled using the earliest pattern in the alphabet (*ABCBDC*). Figure 55d exhibits the different patterns corresponding to four-letter Pocket Merriam-Webster words.

Figure 55d A Type-Collection of Alphabetic Patterns for Four-Letter and Five-Letter Words (*WW*, Feb. 1993)

Pattern	Pocket Merriam-Webster Words
abcd	adze, aeon, aero, aery, afar, afro…
aabc	ABbe, ABet, ABle, ABly, ABut, DEad…
abac	ArCh, BoDy, ChEw, ClEw, CrEw, DoFf…
abca	AciD, AmiD, AriD, AviD, AulD, AweD…
abbc	aLMs, aNOn, bABy, cHIc, cHId, cHIn…
abcb	aChE, aCmE, aCnE, aCrE, aMmO, aWaY…
abcc	aiDE, arAB, atOP, baLM, baST, beST…
aaab	DEFt, DEFy, NOPe, STUb, STUd, STUn
abaa	BAdE, BiDE, BoDE, ChEF, ClEF
aaba	ABeD, HIcK
abbb	eRST
aabb	HIDE, HIGH, NODE, STAB, STOP
abab	GRIT, SPUR
abba	BABE, SHIV, WHIZ
abcde	acorn, acrid, actor, adapt, adieu, adios…
aabcd	ABack, ABaft, ABash, ABbey, ABbot, ABeam…
abacd	AsCot, BaDge, BaDly, BuDdy, BuDge, ChEap…
abcad	BakEr, BalEr, BasEs, BesEt, BetEl, BevEl…
abcda	AcutE, AdagE, AdobE, AddlE, AdorE, AeriE…
abbcd	aDEpt, aRSon, aSTer, aSTir, bEFit, bEFog…
abcbd	aGaIn, aLoNg, aPaRt, aPoRt, bEiGe, bLaNd…
abcdb	aLthO, aZteC, bEacH, bEecH, bElcH, bEncH…
abccd	adDEr, adOPt, anNOy, apHId, auGHt, baLMy…
abcdc	baWdY, brIcK, brInK, brIsK, buRnT, caChE…
abcdd	angST, avaST, banTU, beaNO, beaST, blaDE…
aaabc	DEFer, STUck, STUdy, STUff, STUmp, STUng, STUnk, STUnt
abaac	BeDEw, BiDEd, ClEFt, EiGHt, PaRSe, PuRSe
aabca	ABasE, ABatE, ABovE, ABusE, DEatH, DEptH, STraW, STreW
aabac	DEiGn, OPeRa, STaVe, SToVe
abaca	SqUaW

abcaa	AsiDE, BriEF, DouGH
abbbc	
abbcb	cHIcK, cHInK, rABiD, sHIrK, tHIcK, tHInK, tOPeR, wHIsK
abcbb	lLaNO, nEiGH, wEiGH
abccc	buRST, fiRST, veRST, woRST, wuRST
aabbc	NORSe
ababc	GLINt, GRITs, LANCe, LINKs, PARCh, SLUNg, SLUNk, SPURn
abbac	BABEl, LABOr
aabcb	NOWaY, STIcK, STInK
abacb	CHEcK, CHEeK, RETcH, ROToR, SHUcK, SQUaT
abbca	
aacbb	DEiST, GHoST, SToOP, STrOP
abcab	BOnER, BOrER, BOwER, BOxER, OVaRY
abcba	ALiNE, ALoNE, CLaNG, CLiNG, CLuNG, PLaNT, SCrEW
acabb	ChEST, GrIEF, GrIST, GuIDE, SqUAB, SoUGH
acbab	BeRET
acbba	AnKLE, LeTUP
abbcc	cHIDE, cHIEF, cHINO, eTUDE, sNOOP, tHIEF, tHIGH, wHIST
abcbc	bYWAY, bLINK, cLINK, sLINK
abccb	aPHIS, dONOR, hONOR
aabaa	ABiDE, ABoDE
abbaa	ANODE

Certain patterns are of particular interest to logologists. For example, what is the longest word in which each letter has its own unique alphabet shift (pattern *ABCDEF...*)? Leonard Gordon used a computer to identify the eighteen-letter *quantificationally*. Similarly, what is the longest word containing nothing but doubly crashing alphabets? Leonard Gordon identified the twelve-letter *humistratous* with the pattern *ABCDEEFBFDCA*, followed by *redividing* and *stretchers*. What word has the most letters in a single alphabet shift? Chris Cole identified many unabridged Merriam-Webster words with six: *OPeRaTiVelY* (and relatives such as *coOPeRaTiVelY* or *OPeRaTiVitY*), *iNOPeRaTiVe*, *iNOPporTUnelY*, *noNsPiRiTUallY*, *DauGHterLiNesseS*, *DEFinItiveNesseS*, *gyMNOPlaST*, *nEiGHborLiNesseS*, *unDEFendabLeNesseS*, *baLaNOPlaSTy*, and *NOnfeSTiVelY*.

Alphabetical patterns are analogous to word patterns, discussed in Chapter Two. Any question asked about a word pattern can be rephrased as a question about an alphabetical pattern by visualizing the alphabetical pattern as a "word":

(1) *quantificationally* is analogous to *dermatolglyphics,* the longest word with no repeated letters (Section 26)
(2) *humistratous* is analogous to *scintillescent,* the longest pair isogram (Section 29)
(3) *coOPeRaTiVelY* is analogous to *hUmUhUmUnUkUnUk-UapUaa,* a word with the most repeated letters (Section 34)
(4) *undeRSTUdy* is analogous to *waLLLess,* a word with three consecutive identical letters (Section 32)

The concept of invariance can be extended to the reverse alphabet. The words *oVerpRoPOrtionInG* and *anThRoPOteLeoloGy* have locally invariant groups of six letters, and an invariant sentence is: *mY oWl? iT is uPON My aginG FEDorA.*

Finally, a word can be compared letter-by-letter with its own letters in alphabetic order; for example, *thing* alphabetizes to *ghint,* in which *H*, *I*, and *N* are in the same position in both letter-sequences. The longer the word, the more likely it is that such a match occurs. Among words with no repeated letters, the longest one with no self-invariance is *benzhydroxamic;* among all Merriam-Webster words, the longest is *trinitrophenylmethylnitramine.*

56 LETTER-SHIFTS, SHIFTGRAMS, COLLINEAR WORDS

It has been known at least since *Language on Vacation* (Scribner's, 1965) that certain words can be transmuted into other words by shifting each letter the same number of steps in the alphabet. For example, the letters of *cheer* shifted forward seven steps yield *jolly,* and the letters of *irk* shifted thirteen steps, *vex.* One assumes that the alphabet is arranged in a circle with *A* following *Z* to accommodate the middle letter of the latter example.

Not surprisingly, it is easiest to find shift-pairs for short words. A sampling of the 185 shift-pairs of three-letter words in the Pocket Merriam-Webster is given in Figure 56a, arranged by the thirteen different step sizes.

Figure 56a Three-Letter Shift-Pairs in the Pocket Merriam-Webster
(WW, Nov. 1979)

1   add-bee, nee-off, nos-opt, ohm-pin, dud-ere, its-jut, end-foe...
2   ice-keg, rye-tag, lye-nag, eye-gag, dye-fag, rum-two, asp-cur...
3   elm-hop, lab-ode, box-era, orb-rue, lob-ore, fob-ire, pry-sub...
4   woo-ass, lap-pet, pep-tit, bet-fix, sap-wet, owl-sap, paw-tea...
5   not-sty, ado-fit, adz-fie, don-its
6   fin-lot, sue-yak, boy-hue, bug-ham, mix-sod, gun-mat, via-bog...
7   bee-ill, him-opt, hot-ova, gnu-nub, yen-flu, par-why, lax-she...
8   egg-moo, oaf-win, sow-awe, god-owl, log-two, bat-jib, law-tie...
9   tip-cry, sir-bra, ire-ran, irk-rat, rib-ark, lie-urn, elk-nut...
10 her-rob, buy-lei, wet-god, hut-red, wee-goo, emu-owe, hem-row...
11 odd-zoo, tab-elm, axe-lip, hen-spy, pit-ate, ant-lye, hep-spa...
12 hop-tab, cot-oaf, hip-tub, air-mud, coy-oak, job-van, awl-mix...
13 bin-ova, ant-nag, tnt-gag, bar-one, vex-irk, she-fur

The Pocket Merriam-Webster yields shift-pairs of four-letter words for all step sizes but two; one must go to the *Official Scrabble Players Dictionary* to obtain a full set. A selection of *OSPD* shift-pairs of four-letter and five-letter words is given in Figure 56b.

Figure 56b Four-Letter and Five-Letter Shift-Pairs in the Official
Scrabble Players Dictionary (WW, Feb. 1990)

1   ohms-pint, adds-beet, czar-dabs, inks-jolt, star-tubs, ants-bout...
2   slam-unco, wyle-yang, slag-unci, typy-vara, caps-ecru, pyic-rake
3   crop-furs, molt-prow, folk-iron, perk-shun, dolt-grow, cord-frug...
4   fang-jerk, dawn-hear, punk-tyro, open-stir, pelt-show, lawn-pear...
5   fizz-knee, ordo-twit, azon-fets, djin-ions, fido-knit, nidi-snin
6   wits-cozy, limy-rose, hymn-nest, loam-rugs, buff-hall, lion-rout...
7   link-spur, whee-doll, ibex-pile, yeti-flap, whir-dopy, whit-dopa...
8   loaf-twin, weal-emit, hawk-pies, task-bias, talk-bits, vans-diva...
9   drib-mark, slip-bury, trig-carp, sire-bran, crib-lark, trek-cant...
10 deed-noon, semi-cows, tout-dyed, redo-bony, jehu-tore, byte-lido...
11 spot-daze, path-ales, clad-raps, spit-date, itch-tens, paid-alto...
12 road-damp, jogs-vase, figs-ruse, cuss-ogee, dodo-papa, ribs-dune...
13 gnat-tang, reef-errs, crag-pent, ebbs-roof, balk-onyx, rail-envy...

1 sneer-toffs, adder-beefs, steer-tuffs, sheer-tiffs
2 osmic-quoke
3 teloi-whorl
4 banjo-ferns, pecan-tiger, alkyd-epoch, lutea-pyxie, bejan-finer...
5 fizzy-kneed
6 wolfs-curly, jimmy-posse, chain-ingot, munch-satin, muffs-sally...
7 latex-shale, wheel-dolls, later-shaly, cheer-jolly, timer-aptly...
8 tsars-baiza, setal-ambit
9 jerky-snath, sleep-bunny, xeric-gnarl, river-arena, wiver-frena
10 uredo-ebony, secco-commy, sewed-cogon, ruddi-benny, cubed-melon
11 hints-styed, spots-dazed, spits-dated, drips-octad, raphe-clasp...
12 touch-fagot, dirum-podgy, gassy-smeek, hoggs-tasse, didos-pupae...
13 frere-serer, craal-penny, green-terra, creel-perry

There are twenty-four shift-triples of Pocket Merriam-Webster three-letter words, listed in Figure 56c, but only one shift-quadruple: *God(8)owl(4)sap(4) wet.*

Figure 56c Pocket Merriam-Webster Shift-Triples (*WW*, Nov. 1979)

add(1)bee(7)ill	him(6)nos(1)opt	elm(3)hop(12)tab	bin(6)hot(7)ova
mud(10)wen(4)air	oaf(8)win(6)cot	ant(11)lye(2)nag	tnt(11)eye(2)gag
fad(8)nil(6)tor	hep(4)lit(7)spa	log(6)rum(2)two	bed(7)ilk(9)rut
nun(6)tat(8)bib	fob(3)ire(9)ran	irk(9)rat(4)vex	don(5)its(1)jut
via(6)bog(6)hum	ape(11)lap(4)pet	law(4)pea(4)tie	fur(6)lax(7)she
rib(9)ark(3)dun	haw(4)lea(4)pie	bus(6)hay(8)pig	mix(6)sod(8)awl

For four-letter words, no shift-triples could be found in the Pocket Merriam-Webster, but there are several in the *OSPD: lane(7)-shul(23)peri, dodo(6)juju(6)papa, flap(13)sync(6)yeti, aped(5)fuji(10)-pets, eaux(10)okeh(4)soil,* and *beef(10)loop(4)psst.* For five-letter words, one unabridged Merriam-Webster shift-triple is known: *Gobbo(12)sanna(4)werre;* others undoubtedly exist.

For words of six letters or more, shift-pairs are quite rare. In *Language on Vacation,* Dmitri Borgmann noted the Pocket Merriam-Webster examples *fusion(6)layout* and *abjurer(13)nowhere.* All known six-letter shift-pairs in the unabridged Merriam-Webster are listed in Figure 56d; the seven-letter examples are *unfiber(7)-bumpily, primero(3)sulphur,* and *Chechen(13)purpura.*

Figure 56d Six-Letter Shift-Pairs in the Unabridged Merriam-Webster

(*WW*, Nov. 1979, Feb. 1990, Aug. 1993)

1   anteed-bouffe, steeds-tuffet
2   pyrryl-rattan
3
4   hazzan-ledder, cazzan-gedder, banian-fermer, lallan-pepper, sap-pan-wetter
5
6   biffin-hallot, Tillim-Zorros, wiggin-commot, jigjig-pompom, alohas-grungy, munchy-satine, bombyx-hushed, fusion-layout
7   manful-thumbs, lateen-shallu, panfil-whumps, inkier-purply
8   caddaw-killie
9   prieve-yarnen, reefer-annona, verity-enarch
10 muumuu-weewee
11 splits-dawted
12
13 greeny-terral, becuna-orphan

There appears to be only one eight-letter shift-pair: *wiliwili(6)coro-coro.* This was found by identifying pattern words of this nature as by far the most likely place to find a shift-pair, and searching through Levine's lists of pattern words; nowadays the job is a trivial one for a computer to perform.

In the movie *2001: A Space Odyssey* the computer was nicknamed *HAL;* various people have noted that a single letter-shift yields *IBM.* The letter-shift *errs(13)reef* is a comment on the *Exxon Valdez* disaster (note the unlucky step size). Perhaps the most remarkable letter-shift of all is an interlingual one: *yes* transmutes to *oui!*

Contrarily, one can search for word pairs in which there are no matching shifts between corresponding letters. For short words such pairs are almost trivial to find; in *word pair,* W to P shifts 19, O to A shifts 12, R to I shifts 17, and D to R shifts 14. A nine-letter example is *interpret* to *statesman* with shifts of 10, 6, 7, 15, 13, 3, 21, 22, and 20. Longer examples should be easy for a computer to discover.

Letter-shift multiples such as *God(8)owl(4)sap(4)wet* have a geometric interpretation. They can be viewed as irregularly spaced points on a straight line in three-dimensional space: *God* is plotted with coordinates (7,15,4), *owl* with coordinates (15,23,12), *sap* with coordinates (19,27,16), and *wet* with coordinates (23,31,20). The difference between *God* and *owl* is (8,8,8), between *owl* and *sap* is (4,4,4), and between *sap* and *wet* is also (4,4,4); all coordinates are equal and multiples of four. Collinear words need not be so restricted; one requires only that the differences between successive pairs be proportional, as (a,b,c) and (na,nb,nc), where a, b, and c are positive or negative integers. For example, *GYP-HUM-KID-LEA,* with coordinates (7, 25,16), (8,21,13), (11,9,4), and (12,5,1), generate successive differences (1,-4,-3), (3,-12,-9), and (1,-4,-3), in which $a = 1$, $b = -4$, and $c = -3$. Most word lines have twenty-six different potential letter-combinations along them, a few of which will actually form words. Some word lines (those for which a, b, and c are even numbers) have only thirteen possibilities. Leonard Gordon suggested the nomenclature *skewed, slanted,* and *normal* word lines for those alignments in which none, one, or two of the successive differences is zero.

How many of the twenty-six letter-combinations on a word line actually form words? Robert L. Ward once claimed that there were thirty-one sets of four collinear three-letter words in the second edition of the unabridged Merriam-Webster. However, he tacitly restricted himself to skewed word lines, and overtly restricted himself to words with coordinates less than or equal to twenty-six (no circular alphabets). If one looks at normal word lines such as *BAT-CAT-EAT-FAT-HAT-KAT-MAT-PAT-RAT-SAT-TAT-VAT,* very large scores can be attained; in fact, going beyond the unabridged Merriam-Webster dictionaries, it is possible to find all twenty-six letter-combinations forming words (see Figure 21b). For skewed word lines, a database of 1,680 three-letter words from the Second and Third editions of the unabridged Merriam-Webster, *Chambers Twentieth Century,* the *Official Scrabble Players Dictionary,* and the *Oxford English Dictionary* produced one with eleven entries: *EWK-GUL-ISM-MOO-SIR-UGS-WET-GUY-MOB-SIE-WEG* (2,-2,-1). The word line *DIM-ELK-FOH-GRE-HUB* is one of five with no gaps. For four-letter words, a database of 7,273 words from the same dictionaries produced a skewed word line with five entries: *JAUN-KETO-LISP-OUPS-PYOT* (1,4,-1,-1). The word line *JAZZ-MESS-PILL-SMEE* is one of nineteen that have no gaps.

None of these skewed word lines has any differences of thirteen steps. When a difference of thirteen appears, the corresponding letter in the word oscillates between two alternatives. If these are common letters such as *E* and *R* or *A* and *N,* the chances for collinear words are greatly enhanced. This is demonstrated by the following three-letter word line: *RAA-ENG-RAM-ENS-RAY-ENE-RAK-RAW-RAG-RAS-ENY-RAE-ENK-RAU-RAC* (13,13,6). The four-letter word line is equally long: *BRAG-VENT-PRAG-JENT-DRAG-LENT-FRAG-NENT-BENT-PENT-DENT-RENT-FENT-TENT-HENT* (−6,13,13,13).

Halfway words, so christened by Christopher McManus, are trios in which every letter in the middle word is equidistant in the alphabet between the corresponding letters in the end words. For example, *jig* is a halfway word with respect to *age* and *ski* because *J* is halfway in the alphabet between *A* and *S, I* is halfway between *G* and *K,* and *G* is halfway between *E* and *I.* These are special examples of collinear words. In the word line, the words *age* and *ski* repeat infinitely often; *age* has coordinates (1,7,5), (27,33,31), (53,59,57), and so on. By picking properly spaced *age-ski* pairs, one can identify the midway words *wig* and *wit,* as well as the nonsense combinations *jvg, jit, jvt, wvg,* and *wvt.* Halfway words of three, four, or five letters are easy to find; Figure 56e lists all six-letter and seven-letter halfway words in the *Official Scrabble Players Dictionary.*

Figure 56e Halfway Words of Six Letters (WW, Feb. 1992)

bulbar-kopeck-tithed
dipped-mensch-valval
fusile-googol-hikers
living-nereid-panada
misfit-renigs-wailer
moulin-pirogi-scored
octavo-repent-uglify
pulped-smooch-vernal
rawest-skulls-tusser
tactic-weewee-zigzag

capote-merino-witchy
faunae-kelped-picric
glebae-nocked-uratic
luffas-pommel-tittle
mopper-prongs-sunlit
mullas-propel-sortie
papyri-sermon-vitals
purist-smolts-velour
rental-scorch-tapped

caveat-heughs-mitior
fulham-kronen-portio
ickier-knolls-mysost
mental-scorch-yapped
moulin-phloem-sacral
nuchae-trined-zootic
pavise-scroll-venues
raphae-termed-vitric
senior-timers-umlaut

auxetic-grumped-morulae
ballast-kennels-tippier

miltier-pommels-sunfast

The related concept of a *shiftgram* was devised by Howard Bergerson. One is allowed to transpose the letters after the alphabetic letter-shift, as *music(8)ucaqk* to *quack*. Not surprisingly, shiftgrams can be constructed out of considerably longer words. The longest known unabridged Merriam-Webster shiftgram, discovered by Dmitri Borgmann, is *overleaned(4)szivpierih* to *viziership;* a computer search should turn up eleven-letter or possibly twelve-letter examples (*esogastritis* to *cyclammonium* is a near-miss). It is easier to locate shiftgrams that move thirteen steps in the alphabet and reproduce the original word; ten-letter examples of this are *reprobance, emblazonry, intergrave,* and *viverrinae.* The twelve-letter *tangantangan* and the hyphenated *tear-reviving* also reproduce themselves.

57   SCRAMBLED ALPHABETS

Many of the results presented in this chapter would look very different if one were allowed to rearrange the alphabet as one pleased. In general, one asks the following question: Which rearrangement would maximize some wordplay property? Since there are 26! = 403 septillion possible arrangements to consider, it is evident that, even using a computer, one is unlikely to come up with the "best" arrangement. However, one can often find a "good" arrangement that is very near the optimum one.

To illustrate this genre, there are only sixty Pocket Merriam-Webster four-letter words with no repeated letters that can be read off from the alphabet in order: *abet, ably, aery, . . . lost, most, nosy.* What alphabetic rearrangement would maximize the number of Pocket Merriam-Webster words? David Robinson of Los Angeles asked this question in a "Search for Gold" puzzle contest in the early 1970s; the winner found 398 words, a more than sixfold improvement. It would be interesting to see how much a computer could improve on this. The rearranged alphabet was *BSFPWCHJQ-MOAVUIRNGLKTDZEXY.*

In contrast, it is easy to construct a scrambled alphabet that contains no four-letter words with no repeated letters from the Pocket Merriam-Webster: *HLMNRWBCDFGJKPQTVXZSYEIUAO.* In fact, it is very nearly possible to ban all three-letter words with no repeated letters by a different rearrangement: *UAOEYJQXVG-MHKTPSZDBFCNRLWI* admits only the word *obi*. Is it possible to find a scramble that admits no three-letter words? Darryl Francis conjectured that *iaos* is the only unabridged Merriam-Webster word for four or more different letters that appears in order in *UIAOEYS-DBPMHTGNLRKCFWVJQXZ*.

Another reason for rearranging the alphabet is to ensure that it contains nothing but trigrams found in Pocket Merriam-Webster words. As noted in Section 52, the standard alphabet performs badly in this respect; the only alphabetic trigrams appearing in words are *DEFt, aFGHan, siGHIng, HIJack, caLMNess, soMNOlent, caN-OPy, undeRSTudy, underSTUdy, corYZA,* and *siZABle* out of the twenty-six theoretically possible in a circular alphabet. Figure 57a demonstrates that the rearrangement of the alphabet to ... *QURGH-FICKJAWNTZVOMSPLYBDEX* ... contains twenty-six trigrams found in Pocket Merriam-Webster words. The trigrams are contained in nineteen words rather than the maximum of twenty-six; is it possible to find eighteen or fewer words that do the job?

Figure 57a A Trigram–Friendly Alphabet (WW, Aug 1977)

```
Q U R G H F I C K J A W N T Z V O M S P L Y B D E X
Q U R sh
 b U R G h
thorou G H F are
     pat H F I nder
         F I C K le
          lo C K J A W
                A W N ing
             do W N T own
                chi N T Z
              bar mi T Z V ah
               rende Z V O us
                     V O M it
                 bro O M S tick
                 circu M S P ect
                       S P L een
                       P L Y
                  mo L Y B D E num
                     in D E X
                          E X Q U isite
```

The same problem can be proposed for tetragrams found in unabridged Merriam-Webster words; the best solution, given in Figure 57b, lacks *J* and *Q* and furthermore does not close the circle. It seems doubtful that a Merriam-Webster solution can be found, but a multidictionary one may be possible.

Figure 57b A Tetragram-Friendly Alphabet (*WW*, Aug. 1977)

```
        G H P O L V S B E C K W A N D U R M I X T Y F Z
    bou G H P O t
      cath H P O L e
            P O L V erine
           s O L V S B E rgite
              mi S B E C oming
                 B E C K on
                 n E C K W A rd
                hai K W A N
                      W A N D er
                     g A N D U l
                        e N D U R e
                           D U R M ast
                           t U R M I t
                         ove R M I X T ure
                              s I X T Y F old
                                 s T Y F Z iekte
```

The inverse problem, rearranging the alphabet so that no trigram in it is found in an unabridged Merriam-Webster word, is easier to solve; Philip Cohen proposed the circular alphabet ... *CVSGZY-EJXAQOIUFNMRBTKDLHPW*...which apparently does the job.

Alan Frank used the computer to find a circular rearrangement of the alphabet so that any six adjacent letters can be found in an unabridged Merriam-Webster word. In the existing alphabet, this occurs for sequences like *KLMNOP KLePtOMaNia* or *RSTUVW liVeRWUrST* as well as twelve others. Figure 57c demonstrates that the circular alphabet ... *M CVITLBZQUXFRNEDHWYJKA-SOPG*...works. Can a circular alphabet that works for any seven adjacent letters be found?

David Silverman issued a logological challenge: Rearrange the alphabet so that the sum of the letters in the longest word read in order from left to right, and the longest word read in order from right to left, is maximized. Mary J. Hazard proposed *JKMQVWXZSUNCOPYRIGHTABLFED,* which accommodates the words *uncopyrightable* (fifteen letters) in one direction and *deflations* (ten letters) in the other. It seems likely that computer matching of long words with no repeated letters could increase this slightly. In the Collegiate Merriam-Webster, the words *questionably* and *anchorite* work.

Figure 57c A Hexagram-Friendly Alphabet (WW, May 1983)

MCVITLBZ victimizable
   ITLBZQU quizzability
      LBZQUXFRN benzofuroquinoxaline
         UXFRNE refluxing
           XFRNED transfixed
             FRNEDH friendship
               RNEDHW underweigh
                 NEDHWY honeydew
                   EDHWYJKA jayhawked
                     WYJKAS jayhawks
                       YJKASO jackboys
                         JKASOP jackpuddinghoods
                           KASOPG kampongs
                             ASOPGMC campgrounds
                               OPGMCVIT overcompensating

Suppose that one constructs a list of words collectively containing a specified arrangement of the letters of the alphabet, using as few total letters as possible. If the arrangement is alphabetic, this problem was discussed in Section 53, where a forty-letter solution was exhibited for Pocket Merriam-Webster words; if any arrangement is allowable, this problem was discussed in Section 27, where it was demonstrated that it is impossible to generate a pangram out of Pocket Merriam-Webster words. This being so, the fewest number of letters in the alphabetic list is twenty-seven, as in *LAMB,SQUaWK,FJORD,CHINTZ,VEX, GYP.*

For what letter-arrangement is the corresponding minimum letter-total as large as possible? This is a much more difficult question to answer. The following list of words has fifty-three letters: *Is,Up,AgO,bEY,aCQuit,JaDe,oR,oX,GoWn,PoeM,SaFe,HeLm,*

NaZi,BacK,To,Vie. Can it be reduced to fifty-two or fewer, or is there another alphabetic rearrangement that yields a minimum list of words totaling more than fifty-three letters? To avoid trivialities, note that one-letter words such as *A* and *I* are not allowed.

58 LETTER-SCORING

If *A* is assigned the numerical value 1, *B* is assigned 2, and so on through *Z* assigned 26, many numerical games can be played with words. Perhaps most important, words can be classified into groups according to either the sum or the product of the numerical values of the letters.

Words having the same product have been termed *subtranspositions* of each other by Howard Bergerson; simple examples are *and* (1×14×4 = 56) and *hag* (8×1×7 = 56) or *five* (6×9×22×5 = 5940) and *lock* (12×15×3×11 = 5940). Naturally, all transpositions are subtranspositions as well. Two interesting questions arise: (1) What is the most common product? (2) What is the largest product shared by at least two words? For a small dictionary such as the Pocket Merriam-Webster, it is conjectured that 300 is the most fecund product, with words *alee, beef, cabby, cede, dace, doe, eel, job, lay, lee, ode,* and *to.* The two words *haematospectrophotometer* and *hematospectrophotometer* have the same product, 258,875,854,848,000,000,000,000, because they differ only in the single letter *A.* Eliminating trivial cases such as these, the longest known subtransposition pair from the unabridged Merriam-Webster is *preceptor-dillydally,* with a common product of 1,866,240,000; note that they have no letters in common.

Obviously, there are a large number of different groups into which subtranspositions can fall. These can be reduced to only nine groups, each labeled by a single digit, by the simple expedient of repeatedly summing the digits in the product. The number 258,875,854,848,000,000,000,000, for example, reduces successively to 72 and 9. Most words end up in the 9-group. In the Pocket Merriam-Webster, 36 percent of three-letter words are thus classified; this rapidly increases to 75 percent of five-letter words and 98 percent of ten-letter ones. It is easy to prove that a word will end up in the 9-group if it contains either an *I* or an *R*, or if there at least two occurrences of the letters *C, F, L, O, U,* or *X*. In short, if the product contains 9 as a factor, it will always reduce to 9. In the days before hand-held calculators, this property was used in elementary-school arithmetic classes to check the accuracy of multiplication. Since few people recognize this test in linguistic guise, one can win bar bets and the like by offering to "guess" in which group an unknown stranger's surname or given name lies.

If words are classified into groups according to the sum of the numerical values of their letters, the smallest and largest scores for unabridged unhyphenated dictionary words of length one through twenty-four are presented in Figure 58a.

Figure 58a Lightweight and Heavyweight Words (*WW*, Nov. 1972 Nov. 1995)

a (1.00), aa (1.00), baa (1.33), abba (1.50), caaba (1.60), bacaba (1.67), abebaea (2.43), Fabaceae (3.00), beccaccra (3.33), Galacaceae ((3.90), cabbagehead (3.55), elaeagnaceae (5.00), cabbageheaded (3.69), Hamamelidaceae (5.79), Flagellari-aceae (6.53), lactobacillaceae (6.56), brachiocephalicae (7.00), achromobacteraceae (7.61), palaeacanthocephala (7.53), chlamydobacteriaceae (7.70), chemicopharmaceutical (8.90), historicocabbalistical (9.55), scientificogeographical (9.30), pseudosaccharomycetaceae (9.54)

z (26.0), zy (25.5), zuz (24.33), zyxt (23.75), wuzzy (24.20), xystus (21.33), Zyzomys (21.29), untrusty (19.75), Zorotypus (19.44), topsyturvy (20.10), trustworthy (18.82), topsyturvily (18.50), untrustworthy (18.61), untumultuously (18.21), untrustworthily (17.53), unpresumptuously (17.25), hydrox-yisobutyryl (16.77), typhloureterostomy (16.11), hypophy-seoprivously (16.26), ureteroneocystostomy (15.50), coun-terrevolutionists (14.95), dacryocystosyringotomy (14.91), ureteropyelonephrostomy (14.91), transureteroureterosto-my (15.33)

Gematria is the study of words as classified by letter sums. Its practitioners attach much significance to the fact that related words have the same score, such as *Jesus* and *messiah* (74), *madonna* and *Magdalene* (62), or *immoral* and *sinful* (81). There are many secular examples as well: *genius* and *madness* (75). In his book *English Is Gematria* (Jerusalem: Apocalypse Press, 1988), Peter K. Peterson avers that the formation of English words was governed by an unconscious need for balance and order in written and spoken communication, leading to such pairings as *death* and *decay, odds* and *ends,* or *thick* and *thin.* However, it seems highly likely that coincidences like these arise merely because a large number of words have been sorted into a relatively small number of different categories.

In *Beyond Language* (Scribner's, 1967), Dmitri Borgmann introduced the concept of a *difference word* (Problem 45, The New Chemistry): Replace each letter in a word with its numerical value, subtract this value from its successor (canceling any negative signs that occur), and translate the resultant numbers back into letters. For example, *form* is scored (6,15,18,13); the successive differences are (9,3,-5); the corresponding word is *ice. Urn* is the difference word for *vase.* Most difference words are quite short. One can construct small networks in which each word of length *n*-1 is the difference word of one or more words of length *n*.

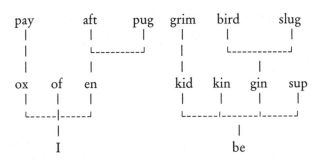

Longer examples include *eldest-Ghana, Fritos-liked,* and *bedroom-canchi.* Tom Pulliam constructed the difference word pyramid *boxty-mide-dea-ad.*

There are other ways to form difference words. For instance, one can make sure that each numerical value is greater than its predecessor by adding 26 (or a multiple thereof) to the original value. *Form* becomes (6,15,18,39), and the successive differences (9,3,21) lead to the nonword *icu.*

Charles Bostick proposed sum words as an interesting counterpart to difference words. He christened them "can do" words, since *do* is the sum word for *can:* convert *can* to (3,1,14); add successive pairs to obtain (4,15), subtracting 26 if necessary to make sure all sum values are 26 or less; reconvert (4,15) to obtain *do*. Three six-letter specimens are *affine-slows, arpent-shush,* and *sanded-torii.* Tom Pulliam found the seven-letter *canfuls-dotage.*

59   WORD BALANCE

A balanced word is one in which the sum of the numerical values of the letters, divided by the number of letters in the word, equals 13.5, the average numerical value of the alphabet. Dmitri Borgmann exhibited a number of balanced words in *Language on Vacation,* including the word *logology,* resurrected from obscurity to mean recreational linguistics. To illustrate, *logology* = 12+15+7+15+12+15+7+25 = 108, and 108/8 = 13.5. The longest unabridged Merriam-Webster balanced words, discovered by Susan Thorpe, are *intercrystallization* and *uncontrovertibleness.* Balanced words can be regarded as one-dimensional versions of Ouroboros worms, discussed in Section 82.

Most balanced words show a preponderance of letters from the second half of the alphabet, not surprising when one notices that the seven commonest letters in the last half, *NOPRSTU,* are on the average closer to the *M-N* balance point than the seven commonest letters in the first half, *ACDEIHL.* An extreme example of this is *NONION,* with only one letter out of six from the first half of the alphabet.

Some balanced words, like *expiator,* are truly balanced: the score of the first half (5+24+16+9) is equal to the score of the second half (1+20+15+18). A few consist wholly of balanced letter-pairs; *over-slight* contains the balanced pairs *V* and *E, O* and *L, I* and *R, S* and *H,* and *G* and *T.* One can sort out balanced pairs into different words, such as *groovy* and *billet;* these are called balanced partners. Many other properties of balanced words can be formulated.

The centrally balanced beam word, introduced by J. A. Lindon, is a more sophisticated version of the balanced word. In a centrally balanced beam word the position of the letter in the word as well as its numerical value plays a role. Visualize a word as a series of weights evenly spaced along a beam, with each weight proportional to the letter value; where must the beam be supported by a fulcrum to achieve balance? If the balance point is at the center of the word (under the third letter of a five-letter word, or midway between the third and fourth letters of a six-letter word), then it is called a centrally balanced beam word. A simple example is *chimed,* for which the balance is $(3 \times 5) + (8 \times 3) + (9 \times 1) = 48 = (13 \times 1) + (5 \times 3) + (4 \times 5)$. The longest known centrally balanced beam word is *anidiomatical,* in the unabridged Merriam-Webster. Not surprisingly, palindromes are centrally balanced beam words.

A different type of word balance is provided by the numerical tautonym. In a numerical tautonym (which must always contain an even number of letters) the sum of the numerical values of the first half of the word equals the sum of the numerical values of the last half. Thus, for *ass/ent, ass* $(1+19+19) = 39 = ent$ $(5+14+20)$. Short examples are not too difficult to find; the longest such word known in the unabridged Merriam-Webster is *biobiblio/graphical.* Word tautonyms are always numerical tautonyms.

The numerical tautonym can be generalized to words of length *mn,* in which each part of length n has the same numerical sum. For *m* equal to three, examples include *no/ti/on* and *tra/nsf/und,* and for *m* equal to four, *ta/ng/li/ng* and *ove/rse/cur/ely.* For *m* equal to five, no dictionary example is known, but the placename *Gl/en/do/ra/do,* a town in Minnesota, works.

WORD GROUPS
SIX

In the preceding chapters, the letter-properties of individual words were analyzed in a variety of ways. In contrast, this chapter exhibits words that are individually quite ordinary in appearance, but derive their unusualness in combination with other words. The classic example of this type of wordplay, and for many years the only one, is the word square. Even in a field as thoroughly exploited as the word square, however, it is possible to make new discoveries, such as the transposition word square and the compound word square.

Other word group patterns have been studied very little, and offer considerable opportunity for computer generation of larger examples than shown here.

61 WORD SQUARES

It can be argued that more effort has been put into the construction of large word squares than any other logological activity. Word squares are very old. The palindromic one shown below was constructed early in the second century A.D., on a tile found in the debris of the *villa publica* of the Roman governor of Budapest. However, the modern history of the word square can be said to start with the publication of the six-square below in the 2 July 1859 issue of the British magazine *Notes & Queries*.

```
S A T O R        C I R C L E
A R E P O        I C A R U S
T E N E T        R A R E S T
O P E R A        C R E A T E
R O T A S        L U S T R E
                 E S T E E M
```

Much of the construction of large squares was carried out between 1875 and 1940 by members of the National Puzzlers' League and related organizations. It was recognized quite early that squares were most conveniently built from the bottom up. Vast amounts of labor were poured into the assembling of reverse word lists: lists of words alphabetized from last letter to first (i.e., written in reverse and then alphabetized). Lists of hundreds of thousands of eight-letter and nine-letter words were extracted from dozens of specialized dictionaries and gazetteers, and published in editions of twenty or less. Even with the aid of such books, the construction of a single nine-square typically involved several days of trial-and-error labor; about one thousand have been constructed since the first in 1897 by Arthur F. Holt.

In the word squares illustrated above, the same words appear in both the horizontal and the vertical directions. Double word squares, in which the horizontal words and the vertical words are entirely different, are also possible. As a rule of thumb, a double word square of a given size has proven to be as difficult to construct as a single word square of the next larger size. In general, far less work has been done on double squares.

Because of the immense labor on word squares, quite a lot is known about what is possible to construct. A computer search by Douglas McIlroy revealed 52 examples of seven-squares constructible from the Collegiate Merriam-Webster, excluding inferred forms such as plurals, past tenses, participles, and the like. A similar computer search found 112 double six-squares in the Collegiate. None of these six-squares or seven-squares uses words entirely in the Pocket Merriam-Webster, although the two below come close, lacking only *Avesta,* the second book of Zoroastrianism, and *layered.*

It seems likely that Pocket Merriam-Webster squares of these sizes can be constructed using inferred forms, as is the case for the seven-square. In 1987 and 1988 Dmitri Borgmann presented in *Word Ways* his nominees for the finest six-squares, seven-squares, and eight-squares.

```
RACISM          WASSAIL
EVINCE          ANTENNA
PERSON          STRINGY
ASCENT          SEIZURE
STUCCO          ANNULAR
TASTER          INGRATE
                LAYERED
```

Only one single-dictionary eight-square was ever discovered by hand: the *agaricus* one below, found by Mrs. A. H. Burkholder, appeared in the November 1926 *Enigma,* the monthly publication of the National Puzzlers' League. More than sixty years later, Eric Albert and Chris Long used the computer to find forty-seven eight-squares containing only boldface entries from the Second Edition of the unabridged Merriam-Webster. Twenty more squares can be added by substituting derived forms, principally *-S* or *-D*. The *agaricus* square below is one of a set of twelve closely related squares obtained by replacing *A* with *E* in *recanter, N* with *R* in *cantonal,* or *D* with *S* or *R* in *startled.* Murray Pearce nominates the second square below as the finest one of its size ever constructed. Although it contains one non-dictionary entry, *East Eden* (a small town in New York), the other words are quite common, all but *Viennese* appearing in the Collegiate Merriam-Webster. The square was originally published in 1902 by Charles B. Stewart. Jeff Grant suggested the substitution of *eastered* (*easter* is a verb in the Second Edition of the unabridged Merriam-Webster).

```
AGARICUS        DECISIVE
GENERANT        EGOMANIA
ANACONDA        COMPUTES
RECANTER        IMPOTENT
IRONWORT        SAUTERNE
CANTONAL        INTERNED
UNDERAGE        VIENNESE
STARTLED        EASTEDEN
```

The first nine-square below, constructed by Wayne M. Good-win, was published in the July 1928 *Enigma*. For many years it was regarded as the finest nine-square ever discovered; it contains eight dictionary words and only one placename, *Eavestone* (a town in Yorkshire, England). The first nine-square consisting entirely of words from a single dictionary, the Second Edition of the unabridged Merriam-Webster, was found using a computer by Eric Albert, and was originally published in the October 1989 *Enigma*. It is also presented below.

```
FRATERIES        NECESSISM
REGIMENAL        EXISTENCE
AGITATIVE        CIRCUMFER
TITANITES        ESCARPING
EMANATIST        STURNIDAE
RETITRATE        SEMPITERN
INITIATOR        INFIDELIC
EAVESTONE        SCENARIZE
SLESTERED        MERGENCES
```

Albert began running his nine-square program on his computer both at home and at work at the start of June 1989. The work computer performed flawlessly, but his home computer failed more nights than not, sometimes only an hour after he had gone to bed:

> I spent many hours patching together the data files that resulted from these crashes, files that kept track of what work had been completed in the computer's increasingly brief moments of sanity. I began to threaten the machine with physical violence, but to no avail.

But on 27 June 1989, when he returned home from work, he found the nine-square shown above on his computer screen:

> Adrenaline coursing in my veins, I plowed through the three volumes of my *Web 2* book until I had no doubts: all the words were there! A passage from a book by Nobel prize–winning physicist Richard Feynman ran through my thoughts: 'I went on and checked some other things, which fit, and new things fit, and I was very excited. It was the first time, and the only time, in my career that I knew a law of nature that nobody else knew.'
>
> Two years have passed, and that personal computer has long since gone to the great hardware museum in the sky. I don't lament its passing, but I find I retain some affection toward the old thing….Technology marches on, making pioneering efforts seem crude and faintly amusing. My current home computer can do the complete 9×9 search in one weekend.

Chris Long subsequently found two nine-squares with all words in the *Oxford English Dictionary;* the first appeared in the October 1993 *Enigma.*

```
WORCESTER      BESTRIDES
OVERLARGE      ECPHONEMA
RECOINAGE      SPERGULIN
CROSSTIED      THREERING
ELISIONAL      ROGERENES
SANTONATE      INUREMENT
TRAINAGES      DELINEATE
EGGEATERS      EMINENTER
REEDLESSE      SANGSTERE
```

Eminenter can be found in the text illustrating words ending in *-er.*

Relatively few double eight-squares have ever been constructed. Palmer Peterson of the National Puzzlers' League produced at least twenty-four, and Figure 61a gives, with definitions of the words, one produced by Jeff Grant.

Figure 61a A Double Eight-Square (WW, Feb. 1992)

```
T R A T T L E D
H E M E R I N E
A P O T O M E S
M E T A P O R E
N A I L I N G S
A L O I S I A S
T E N T M A T E
A S S E S S E D
```

TRATTLED past tense of *trattle:* a Scottish term meaning to prattle, chatter, or gossip (*Web* 2)

HEMERINE of or belonging to a day, a medical expression sometimes used of a fever that recurs daily (*OED*)

APOTOMES in Greek music, intervals of a semitone in the Pythagorean scale (*Web* 3)

METAPORE the foramen of Magendie, a passage through the midline of the roof of the fourth ventricle (*Web* 2)

NAILINGS plural of *nailing,* a fastening with nails, nail-making; also slang for an act of nailing or catching someone (*OED*)

ALOISIAS individuals named Aloisia, a feminine form of Aloysius occurring in the sixteenth and seventeenth centuries in parish registers of Hinton Charterhouse, England (*The Oxford Dictionary of English Christian Names,* 3rd Edition, E. G. Withycombe, 1977)

TENTMATE an associate in a tent (*Web* 2)

ASSESSED fixed or determined the rate or amount of (*Web* 2)

THAMNATA a city assigned Joshua as an inheritance and burial place, referred to in 1st Maccabees 9:50 in the Apocryphal Old Testament, and appearing in the Douay Bible (*Web* 2)

REPEALES an early form of *repeals:* revokes, rescinds, annuls (*OED,* 1625 quotation)

AMOTIONS plural of *amotion:* removal of a specified object from a place or position (*Web* 3)

TETALITE a variety of calcite near spartaite, containing about 9 percent of carbonate of manganese (*Dictionary of the Names of Minerals,* A. H. Chester, 1896)

TROPISMS natural inborn inclinations (*Web* 3)

LIMONIAS an old name for either of the small long-leaved orchids *Serapias longifolia* or *Cephalanthera longifolia* (*A Dictionary of the Flowering Plants and Ferns,* 8th Edition, J. C. Willis, revised by H. K. Airy Shaw, 1973)

ENERGATE an obsolete term meaning to energize or give energy to
(*OED*)

DESESSED past tense of *desesse,* a sixteenth-century form of the verb
disease: to deprive of ease (*OED*)

The search for a ten-square has been far less successful. A single-
dictionary ten-square is an impossible dream, but it seems that one
might exist using words appearing in English-language texts. Arthur
F. Holt constructed a considerable number of tautonymic ten-
squares (consisting of words such as *chimachima* or *kerrikerri*) in the
1920s, but these invariably used words from one or more foreign-
language sources. The best of the tautonymic ten-squares was constructed by Dmitri Borgmann and Darryl Francis; it consists entirely
of hyphenated words. In a tautonymic ten-square, each word must
appear twice horizontally and twice vertically. However the word
algal-algal is used four times in each direction. Another word,
ogung-ogung bulu, appears only as part of a dictionary-scanctioned
phrase. All four words can be found in one or more of three contemporary dictionaries: *Webster's Third New International Dictionary
of the English Language; The International Atlas* (published by Rand
McNally in 1969); *Musical Instruments: A Comprehensive
Dictionary* (1964), by Sibyl Marcuse. It is shown below.

Can a nontautonymic ten-square be found? Jeff Grant has constructed several of varying degrees of acceptability, the best of which
is given below.

The definitions for the words of the latter square are:

ASTRALISED past tense of the verb *astralise,* a British variant of
astralize, to interpret myth as of a significance relative to the
stars. Although not found in dictionaries, the word can be located in J. Puhvel's *Comparative Mythology* (1987), p. 104:
"...Anahid, the planet Venus in astralized Iranian myth."

SCHOLARITY schooling, instruction, training (*Funk & Wagnalls*).

THYLACINES Tasmanian wolves, formerly common in Australia
(*Web 3*).

ROLY NADERS persons such as Roly Nader, who, although listed
as Roland Scott Nader in the 1988 Houston telephone directory, confirmed by letter that he goes by the nickname
"Roly."

ALAN BROWNE there are seven men with this name on the New
Zealand electoral rolls. *Who's Who in America* (1988–89) also lists

an Alan Browne, an American bank consultant born in 1909.

LA CAROLINA a commune on the southern slopes of the Sierra Morena in Spain (*Webster's New Geographical Dictionary*, 1972).

IRIDOLINES *iridoline* is an oily liquid compound derived from coal-tar (*Funk & Wagnalls*). Chemists say that the plural form, though not attested by dictionaries, is possible.

SINEWINESS the state or quality of being sinewy (*Web 3*).

ETERNNESSE variant of *eternness,* a rare and obsolete synonym for "eternity" (*OED*, 1608 quote).

DYSSEASSES plural of *dysseasse,* a sixteenth-century variant of *disease* (*OED*).

```
DAOLADAOLA          ASTRALISED
ALGALALGAL          SCHOLARITY
OGUNGOGUNG          THYLACINES
LANGALANGA          ROLYNADERS
ALGALALGAL          ALANBROWNE
DAOLADAOLA          LACAROLINA
ALGALALGAL          IRIDOLINES
OGUNGOGUNG          SINEWINESS
LANGALANGA          ETERNNESSE
ALGALALGAL          DYSSEASSES
```

With the advent of the computer, it has at last become possible to discover all of the squares that can be constructed from a stockpile of words. This has led to the concept of the support of a square, defined as the number of words needed, on the average, to produce a single square.

The following gedankenexperiment may help the nonstatistician. Suppose that from a much larger set of words, one repeatedly draws random subsets, each equal to the support in number. If for each of these subsets one determines the number of squares that can be formed, and takes the average of these numbers over many such drawings, it will tend toward the number one.

The support of an *n*-square can be calculated from the following scaling formula:

Support = (number of words)/(number of squares found)$^{1/n}$

Douglas McIlroy used the computer to form 54 seven-squares from 9,663 seven-letter words and names in the Collegiate Merriam-Webster; substituting these numbers into the formula, one obtains 9663/541/7 = 5459. It is likely a dictionary only a little over half the size of the Collegiate could have produced a seven-square. Especially for large squares, the number of squares found increases rapidly with respect to the number of words in the stockpile. Calculations by Chris Long of the number of squares found from various stockpile sizes of four-letter words (726 to 3,718) confirms that for large lists the number of squares rapidly becomes astronomical. For four-squares the calculated support is typically 90; however, 7,364 four-letter words could be expected to produce 45 million four-squares.

The real usefulness of the support comes when it is extrapolated from small squares, where statistics like the ones above are easy to obtain, to much larger ones, where only a few squares have ever been found. In particular, a relatively crude extrapolation revealed why the ten-square has been so hard to find; its support is approximately 220,000 words, not likely to be achieved unless one admits place-names, personal names, obsolete words, and plausible variants as Jeff Grant did. More to the point, it suggests that any computer-based search is likely to fail unless a stockpile nearly this large is generated. (But if the stockpile is only a few percent larger, solutions should be easy for the computer to find.)

Chris Long developed a theoretical support model which can be applied to either single or double word squares. In his model, he assumed a hypothetical universe of "words" constructed by drawing letters independently and at random from the alphabet using English-language text probabilities ($E = .13$, $T = .10...$, $Q = .0010$, $Z = .0008$).

$$\text{Support} = (15.8)^{(n-1)/2} \text{ for a single n-square}$$
$$\text{Support} = (15.8)^{n/2} \text{ for a double n-square}$$

Interestingly, these formulas verify the conjecture of National Puzzlers' League form-constructors reported earlier in this section—the single square is as hard to construct as the double square of the next smaller size. For single squares of size 3 through 10, the theoretical supports are 16, 63, 250, 992, 3,944, 15,678, 62,320, and 247,718.

The experimental support generally exceeds the theoretical one by 50 percent; Long found experimental supports of 90 and 350 for four-squares and five-squares, respectively, and Leonard Gordon found an experimental support of 1,300 to 1,700 for six-squares. If this bias persists for larger squares, it is indeed bad news for finding a ten-square; perhaps 350,000 words are needed to do the job.

On the other hand, work by Leonard Gordon suggests that the

support depends strongly on the nature of the word stockpile. In particular, stockpiles in which vowel-starting words are as common as consonant-starting ones have markedly lower support values than more typical mixtures, which overwhelmingly contain consonant-starting words. While adding any word to a stockpile will (marginally) increase the chance that a ten-square can be produced from it, vowel-starting words are more valuable additions. This becomes important if one runs up against the ability of the computer to process large numbers of words; as the stockpile size increases, the number of possible squares that can be formed from it increases far faster. (For the moment, one is more limited by the meager stockpiles available.)

A surprising prediction of the theoretical model, confirmed by experimental results, is that for sufficiently large stockpiles of words the number of double squares exceeds the number of single squares. For four-squares the crossover comes at a stockpile size of 1,850, or thirty times the support; for five-squares, it comes at a sample size of 5,870. The theoretical prediction of the crossover size for an n-square is the support size for an $(n+2)$-square.

What are the commonest word squares of various sizes? This can be answered by a minimax criterion: Add words of length n one at a time to the stockpile, in decreasing order of their frequency in English-language text as documented by Kucera and Francis in *Computational Analysis of Present-Day American English* (Brown University, 1967), and stop when a word square is produced For three-squares through six-squares, the commonest squares are believed to be the ones given below. The numbers indicate the frequency of the word in the Kucera and Francis million-word corpus:

1772 CAN	686 SAME	130 MONTH	12 CEASED
4395 ARE	456 AWAY	47 OPERA	50 ENGINE
1635 NEW	1125 MADE	698 NEVER	5 AGENDA
	401 EYES	46 TREND	3 SINFUL
		42 HARDY	8 ENDURE
			25 DEALER

The first three of these squares required stockpiles of 21, 68, and 455, respectively; compare this with the theoretical supports of 16, 63, and 250. The six-square, found by Dmitri Borgmann, may not be the commonest; it may be possible to find a square in which every word has five or more occurrences.

62 VARIATIONS ON THE SQUARE

The word square admits many variations. Perhaps the most obvious is to extend it to three dimensions, forming word cubes (the same set of words in three orthogonal directions) or triple word cubes (a different set of words in each direction). An n-cube contains n words repeated three times apiece, and $n(n-1)/2$ words used six times apiece, for a total of $3n^2$ words. A triple n-cube contains $3n^2$ different words.

An early, but imperfect, six-cube can be found in Dmitri Borgmann's *Beyond Language* (Scribner's, 1967) in Problem 61: Three-Dimensional Thinking. Jeff Grant constructed a six-cube and a triple five-cube, both based on words in the *Oxford English Dictionary;* details are given in Figure 62a.

Figure 62a A Six-Cube and a Triple Five-Cube Based on the *Oxford English Dictionary* (WW, Aug. 1978)

1	REMADE	2	ENAMEL	3	MACULA
	ENAMEL		NARINE		ARENAS
	MACULA		ARENAS		CERITE
	AMULET		MINIME		UNITER
	DELETE		ENAMOR		LATERE
	ELATER		LESERE		ASERED

4	AMULET	5	DELETE	6	ELATER
	MINIME		ENAMOR		LESERE
	UNITER		LATERE		ASERED
	LITOTE		EMETIN		TERENE
	EMETIN		TORIED		ERENDE
	TERENE		ERENDE		REDEEM

1 STRAP	2 ARECA	3 TAMAL	4 ESILE	5 DETER
ARENA	GAVOT	OVATE	REDEN	ALENE
LAVAL	ANELE	NITON	AMESE	RASEE
AMENE	MINAL	ELEMI	RENED	ETTLE
SALAD	ASERE	RESEN	ENTRE	DESES

ASENE listed as *asen(e)*, past part. of the archaic verb *asee*

ATELE a form of *atel*, an obs. adjective meaning terrible (1230 quote)

ATOME sixteenth- to eighteenth-century form of *atom*

COLAR fifteenth- to sixteenth-century form of *collar*

ENEDE an early variant of *ende*: a duck

ENELE a fifteenth-century spelling of *anele*

ERARE fourteenth- to sixteenth-century Scottish form of *erer: sooner*

GAVOT an early variant of *gavotte*

LENIN mentioned in the meaning of *Leninist*

NOTEN thirteenth-century form of *note:* to use or make use of something

RENED fifteenth- to sixteenth-century spelling of *reined*

SARED an early Northern and Scottish form of *sored*

He also constructed a triple six-cube containing ninety-one dictionary words, two foreign words, three placenames, and twelve plausible coinages. The seven-cube proved somewhat easier to construct, but still required such outré words such as *Sssssss* (the title of a movie), *steinin'* (slang form of *steining,* a variant of *steening,* the lining of a well), and *tintily* (the adverb corresponding to *tinty,* full of tints).

One can define "cubes" in four or more dimensions. In Figure 62b, Darryl Francis exhibits a quadruple three-hypercube in four dimensions based entirely on unabridged Merriam-Webster words. J. A. Lindon constructed a three-hypercube which appeared in the October 1961 *Recreational Mathematics Magazine,* privately published by Joseph Madachy of Kettering, Ohio. Darryl Francis has also constructed a quintuple two-hyperhypercube: a cube in five dimensions containing eighty two-letter words, seventy-eight from the unabridged Merriam-Webster and two from the *Times Index-Gazetteer.*

A second variation on the word square consists of using as many different letters as possible. A double four-square is easy to construct with words from the unabridged Merriam-Webster, as shown by George H. Ropes below. The second four-square, by Jeremy Morse, is restricted to words in the *Chambers Twentieth Century Dictionary.* The third square, by Jeff Grant, uses Pocket Merriam-Webster words with the exception of *ruly;* note that the upper left *B* can be replaced with *G.*

```
C Y S T        G O W F        B A S H
O P A H        U D A L        R U L Y
R I M U        M I R E        I T E M
F L E D        P N Y X        G O W N
```

Figure 62b   A Quadruple Three-Hypercube in the Unabridged
Merriam-Webster (WW, Aug. 1971)

A L A	R O B	T W O
A E N	T E U	A R N
R A A	A R M	E Y E
E A N	I B A	E A R
S R I	Y A S	R I E
E A S	O Y E	S A W
S O N	A E A	T S T
H A E	E T H	O I I
A M P	R E U	S L E

27 words in rows: ala, rob, two, aen, teu, arn,...
27 words in columns: aar, ese, sha, lea, ara, oam,...
27 words in same position (row): art, low, abo, ata, eer, nun,...
27 words in same position (column): aes, ash, rea, lao, era, asp,...

It is theoretically possible to construct a five-square with all letters different. The nearest approach is the following twenty-two-different-letter square by Jeff Grant, using *Oxford English Dictionary* words.

WH I C K	to squeak like a pig
R O B Y N	14th–15th century var of *robin*
A F I V E	in five (parts)
MU Z E D	past tense of early form of *muse*
P L A T S	plans or diagrams
WR A M P	a twist or strain
HO F U L	an old word meaning "careful"
I B I Z A	a breed of dog found on Ibiza
C Y V E T	seventeenth-century var of *civet*
K N E D S	an early dialectical form of *kneads*

A square that uses every letter of the alphabet at least once appears to be impossible to construct. The closest approach, by Jeff Grant, based on three different dictionaries, is exhibited in Figure 62c, which follows.

Figure 62c A Six-Square Using Twenty-three Different Letters (*WW*, Feb. 1980)

```
F  J  O  R  C  K
L  U  V  I  A  N
A  D  E  P  T  I
G  E  R  M  A  L
H  O  B  A  L  L
T  W  Y  N  E  S
```

FJORCK	jocular name for a very small person (*Eng. Dial. Dict. Supp.*)
LUVIAN	variant of *Luian*, a language of the Hittite Empire (*Web 2*)
ADEPTI	adepts (proficient persons) (*OED*, 1704 quote under *adept*)
GERMAL	a rare synonym of *germinal* (*Web 2*)
HOBALL	a clown, fool, idiot (*OED*)
TWYNES	early spelling of *twins* or *twines* (*OED*)
FLAGHT	variant of *flaught:* a sudden flight (*Eng. Dial. Dict.*)
JUDEOW	variant of *Judew*, an old word for Jew (*OED*)
OVERBY	across the way (*Web 2*)
RIPMAN	early variant of *reapman:* a reaper (*OED*)
CATALE	fifteenth-century spelling of *cattle* (*OED*)
KNILLS	early form of *knells* (*Web 2*)

A cyclic square is one in which each successive word is formed by beheading the previous one and adding the letter to the tail, as *tea-eat-ate*. The largest cyclic square in the unabridged Merriam-Webster is *lame-amel-mela-Elam;* the largest in the *Oxford English Dictionary* is *ester-stere-teres-erest-reste.* If the letter placed at the tail does not have to be the one removed at the head, it is a progressive square. Progressive five-squares can be formed from Collegiate Merriam-Webster words, as demonstrated by a National Public Radio contest directed by Will Shortz in February 1994. The winner generated the sequence *scrap-crape-rapes-apest-pesto-estop-stope-toper-opera.* This is, of course, part of a (5,4) word chain network; these are discussed in Section 44.

A transposition square is a square array of letters in which each row and column can be rearranged to form a word. The two largest known transposition squares based on unabridged Merriam-Webster words are an eleven-square and a double twelve-square; oddly, the hierarchy of difficulty encountered in regular word squares does not pertain to these. These squares are presented below. Both are constructed in a highly symmetric manner, relying on the structure of a Latin square (a two-dimensional layout used in statistically designed experiments). The second square is slightly defective, using one two-word dictionary term, *goliath crane*. No doubt a computer could find larger examples.

C A C E I L N O R T U	corniculate	S P A A C E I L N O R T	psiloceratan
U D A C E I L N O R T	radiolucent	T L O A A C E I L N O R	reallocation
T U E A C E I L N O R	reinoculate	R T G I A A C E I L N O	Italo-Grecian
R T U G A C E I L N O	out-clearing	O R T D P A A C E I L N	leptocardian
O R T U K A C E I L N	unactorlike	N O R T U A A A C E I L	aeronautical
N O R T U N A C E I L	crenulation	L N O R T D S A A C E I	declarations
L N O R T U O A C E I	unicolorate	I L N O R T F R A A C E	refractional
I L N O R T U R A C E	interocular	E I L N O R T E C A A C	acceleration
E I L N O R T U S A C	ulcerations	C E I L N O R T M G A A	metalorganic
C E I L N O R T U T A	countertail	A C E I L N O R T V C A	clavicornate
A C E I L N O R T U V	countervail	A A C E I L N O R T H G	goliath crane
		N A A C E I L N O R T B	nonbacterial

column words: stenocranial, parcellation, angelica-root, dilaceration, precautional, cordaitalean, sternofacial, recreational, melanocratic, rectovaginal, anchoretical, carbogelatin

The compound word square, devised by Harry Partridge, is perhaps the most intricate generalization of the word square. It is illustrated by the simple example below.

	toe	own	bib
ATE	At	To	bE
SET	So	wE	iT
MAY	Me	An	bY

The letters in each word bounding the square are distributed in order in the row or column adjacent to that word; the two letters in each box of the square are then rearranged to form a word. For greatest elegance, all words both inside and outside the square should be different; in fact, even the same two letters in two different boxes should be eschewed.

These can be generalized to double compound word squares, in which two words are distributed horizontally in each row and column to form four-letter words in the boxes. Note that the words to the right of the square are read into the square right to left, and the words below the square are read in bottom to top.

	load	rank	oven	aeon	
STEM	loST	TOry	soLE	MapS	SLOT
VEIL	VioL	hEaL	vAIn	WeLl	WALL
PERT	raPT	cAnE	PuRe	ToeS	SPAT
INCH	EdIt	TaNk	COrn	HyMn	MOTE
	trio	achy	runs	yelp	

A three-dimensional compound word square is presented in Figure 62d.

Figure 62d   A Three-Dimensional Compound Word Square (*WW*, May 1981)

Top Layer			Middle Layer			Bottom Layer		
LOT	ICY	AGE	THY	WOO	ION	RED	HIT	ONE
GAS	APE	RAP	RIG	ERA	AYE	MAT	YES	TAG
PER	NOD	SEW	DIM	ADO	PAN	SON	OAT	BAR

Words Bounding the Square on

Top Face			Left Face			Front Face		
THE	COT	GIN	LIE	SEA	ROE	EGO	DAY	SPA
AIM	PRY	RAT	TOO	GAY	MAN	DRY	DEW	PEN
PIN	NOT	WAR	DIE	TEA	SOB	OAR	ASH	AGO

THE in top face is in loT, tHy, rEd; COT is in iCy, wOo, hiT,...
LIE in left face is in Lot, Icy, agE; SEA is in gaS, apE, rAp,...
EGO in front face is in pEr, Gas, lOt; DAY is in noD, Ape, icY,...

63 PARTIALLY OVERLAPPING WORD GROUPS

Consider the seven three-letter words *ado, ore, bar, boy, yea, bed,* and *dry*. Individually these are very ordinary, but together they form a group with extraordinarily interesting properties:

```
ADO   A   D   O
ORE           E O R
BAR   A B       R
BOY     B     O   Y
YEA   A     E     Y
BED       B D E
DRY       D     R Y
```

These seven words consist of a total of seven letters, each used three times. Each word contains three different letters. Any word has exactly one letter in common with any other word (the partial overlap property); for example, *ado* shares an *A* with *bar* and *yea*, a *D* with *bed* and *dry*, and an *O* with *ore* and *boy*. Furthermore, each possible letter-pair drawn from *ABDEORY* appears in exactly one word (the letter-pair property); for example, *AB* is only in *bar*, *AD* is only in *ado*, and so on.

This pattern was noted by Ronald C. Read in the February 1963 *Recreational Mathematics Magazine,* privately published by Joseph Madachy of Kettering, Ohio; it subsequently appeared in Dmitri Borgmann's *Beyond Language.*

These word groups are known as finite projective geometries in mathematics, and are closely related to balanced incomplete block designs used in statistical experimentation. The four-letter analogue, using words in the unabridged Merriam-Webster, was constructed by Mary J. Hazard:

```
CITY    C   I           T Y
CLAD  A C D   L
CONE    C   E     N O
CWMS    C       M   S W
DIME      D E I M
DOTS      D       O S T
IOWA  A     I     O   W
MANT  A         M N   T
MOLY          L M O     Y
NILS        I L N S
WELT        E L     T W
WYND      D     N   W Y
YEAS  A   E         S Y
```

The five-letter analogue was attempted, but only sixteen of the required twenty-one words could be found, even using a wide variety of dictionaries. It is unlikely that a complete set can be found, even with the aid of a computer.

Further word groups of this nature can be constructed if one relaxes the partial overlap property to allow words to have *m* letters in common (not just one), and the letter-pair property to allow pairs of letters to appear together in *n* words, not just one. In fact, one can construct a word group known as a *Baltimore transdeletion* (a name coined by Charles N. Crowder in 1904, according to *A Key to Puzzledom* [1906]), in which one drops letters one at a time in turn from a letter-set and rearranges the others to form words.

> 3-letter words (AEST) eat, sat, sea, set
> 4-letter words (AENST) neat, sane, nest, tans, seat
> 5-letter words (ACERST) rates, caste, crest, carts, cares, crate
> 6-letter words (AILNPST) splint, plants, pliant, paints, plains, instal, plaits
> 7-letter words (AEGINRST) stinger, gaiters, retains, seating, strange, ratings, granite, erasing
> 8-letter words (ADEINORST) trinodes, notaries, intrados, tornades, asteroid, strained, sedation, rationed, donaries
> 9-letter words (ACEILNORST) stercolin, relations, contrails, consertal, creations, sectorial, larcenist, sectional, crotaline, censorial

All words are in the unabridged Merriam-Webster. If one is dealing with *n*-letter words, each word has *n*-1 letters in common with every other word, and each letter-pair appears together in *n*-1 words.

Can word groups be constructed that are neither finite projective geometries nor Baltimore transdeletions? The simplest one is:

```
SNARL     A        LN  RS
NORTH         H    NOR    T
CLINT     C    ILN        T
LATHE     A  EH  L        T
LOCHS       C  H  L  O  S
CHAIR     AC  HI     R
CANOE     ACE     NO
OSTIA     A     I   O  ST
OILER       E  IL  OR
SHINE       EHI  N    S
CREST     CE          RST
```

Each word has two letters in common with each other word, and each pair of letters appears in two different words.

A complementary word group to the one above, one which uses

the same group size but a different word length (the word lengths of two complementary groups sum to the group size), is given below.

A complementary word group to *ado, ore, bar, boy, yea, bed,* and *dry,* presented earlier, is *nail, sale, sine, lend, idea, sand,* and *slid.* A word group complementary to the thirteen four-letter words, consisting of thirteen nine-letter words in which each word has six letters in common with every other and each letter-pair appears together in six words, is almost certainly impossible to construct.

P O N D E R	D E	N O P R			
A U D I O N	A D	I N O			U
U R S I N E		E I N		R S	U
O U S T E D	D E	O		S T U	
P I S T O N		I N O P		S T	
P E A N U T	A	E N	P		T U
P A R O U S	A			O P R S	U
S T R A N D	A D	N		R S T	
P U T R I D	D	I		P R	T U
A S P I D E	A D E I		P	S	
A R E I T O	A	E I		O	R	T

In the two complementary word groups diagrammed above, one uses the letters *ACEHILNORST* and the other, *ADEINOPRSTU.* Can one construct a pair of complementary word groups that use the same underlying set of letters? This is demonstrated in Figure 63a.

Figure 63a Two Complementary Word Groups Using the Same Letters

A C E I l n O r s T u	C O A T I E	snurl
A c E i l n O R S t U	A R O U S E	clint
A c e I L n o R s T U	R I T U A L	cones
a c E i L N O R s T u	L E N T O R	caius
A C E i L N o r s t U	C U N E A L	roist
a C E I L n o R S t u	S L I C E R	touna
A c e I L N O r S t u	A L I S O N	cruet
a C e I l N O R s t U	U R O N I C	slate
a C e i L n O r S T U	L O C U S T	reina
a c E I l N o r S T U	T E N U I S	coral
A C e i l N o R S T u	C R A N T S	louie

All words except *Touna* are found in the Second Edition of the unabridged Merriam-Webster; *Touna* is in the *Times Index-Gazetteer.*

If either the partial overlap property or the letter-pair property is waived, retaining the other, many more word groups can be devised. In Figure 63b the letter-pair property is retained; in Figure 63c, the partial overlap.

Figure 63b Word Groups in Which Each Letter-Pair Appears in Exactly M Words (WW, May 1977)

stockpile AEINPT, each pair in 6 different words: peai, aine, itea, atip, anti, pain, pate, neat, pane, pite, tine, pine, pant, pent, pint

stockpile AEINRST, each pair in 10 different words: reina, irate, anise, tinea, tasie, raise, tarns, stern, trins, astir, aster, rites, stein, stain, antes, rinse, saner, rains, niter, antre, train

stockpile AEGINRST, each pair in 15 different words: string, streng, grants, reigns, tigers, ingest, tinger, insert, astern, argent, grates, agents, angers, strain, gratis, giants, grains, rating, satire, tisane, staige (in *Web 1*), arisen, agrise, easing, retain, triage, eating, regain

stockpile AGEHMOTUY, each pair in only one word: emu, thy, ago, tau, gym, hoe, you, ham, get, hug, tom, yea

stockpile ADEILNOT, each pair in 3 different words: idea, iota, dote, nolt, lend, nail, aloe, tald, tile, lido, dint, Ione, dona, neat

stockpile AEINOPRST, each pair in 3 different words: torn, ions, sent, pose, neat, spar, aire, Ateo, porn, anis, rest, opie, pant, soar, rein, spit, trip, iota

stockpile ADEINORSTU, each pair in 2 different words: rent, dots, darn, duns, stir, aitu, Aino, dieu, Osea, roue, date, sine, roid, sura, unto

stockpile ADEINORST, each pair in 5 different words: stond, sotie, intro, stair, radio, trade, Diane, rends, aeons, arose, Donat, tides, irone, tarns, adios, doter, tinea, rinds

stockpile ADEILNORST, each pair in 4 different words: irate, dints, snort, danli, tonal, stead, anode, trild, rains, idose, aliso, lords, toile, slent, irone, laser, Troad, lernd

stockpile ADEINORST, each pair in 5 different words: ostein, adorns, tirade, storid, astern, Oneida, rinsed, ration, estado, rodent, ariose, dinast

stockpile ADEINOPRST, each pair in 5 different words: aspine, trepid, strand, sprint, teopan, Portia, ordain, ditone, adopts, Sadite, ariose, spored, tenors, pander, points

The first four word groups in Figure 63c have the additional property that each letter appears in exactly two words. This is a stronger version of the partial-overlap property. The fourth word group, involving twenty-one different letters allocated twice apiece to seven six-letter words, was constructed by Mary J. Hazard.

Figure 63c   Word Groups in Which Each Word Has Exactly N Letters in Common with Each Other Word (WW, May 1972, May 1977)

---

stockpile ACENOT, one-letter overlap: can, cot, ate, one (each letter in 2 words)

stockpile ACEILMNORS, one-letter overlap: scan, sore, coil, marl, mine (each letter in 2 words)

stockpile ACEHILMNOPRSTUW, one-letter overlap: wrist, whole, charm, count, plain, spume (each letter in 2 words)

stockpile ABCDEFGHIKLMNOPRSTUWY, one-letter overlap: whumps, wicked, blight, flunky, dognap, embryo, crafts (each letter in 2 words)

stockpile ABDEILMNORST, one-letter overlap: slam, more, mind, neat, told, stir, bard, snob, bile (each letter in 3 words)

stockpile ADEGILOPRS, two-letter overlap: ogled, grape, poise, grids, plaid, solar (each letter in 3 words)

stockpile ACDEILNOPRSTUY, two-letter overlap: litany, clypes, adopts, coined, purins, dourly (each letter in 3 words)

stockpile AEGHILNOPRST, two-letter overlap: ignore, phrase, plight, talons (each letter in 2 words)

stockpile ADEGILNRT, three-letter overlap: rating, dental, glider (each letter in 2 words)

stockpile ADEGIMNRST, three-letter overlap: grinds, mating, grates, remand, misted (each letter in 3 words)

stockpile AEINORST, four-letter overlap: atones, ratios, retina, senior (each letter in 3 words)

stockpile AEGILNORST, six-letter overlap: sterling, oriental, tangelos, seraglio, organist (each letter in 4 words)

stockpile AEFILMNOPRST, four-letter overlap: ensiform, platform, panelist (each letter in 2 words)

stockpile ACEDGILNORST, six-letter overlap: goldcrest, nostalgic, declaring, ordinates (each letter in 2 words)

stockpile ACEDGHILNOPRSTU, five-letter overlap: canephorus, cingulated, droplights (each letter in 2 words)

These four groups are, in fact, closely related to word groups used as a mnemonic aid in performing certain card tricks. The mathemagician deals ten pairs of playing cards facedown on the table and invites the subject to look at the face values of one pair while the mathemagician's back is turned. The mathemagician then deals the cards out in a four-by-five array, faceup, and the subject is asked to identify the row or rows in which his two face values appear. The mathemagician then identifies the cards.

The successful execution of this trick depends upon the fact that there are exactly ten different ways a pair of cards can be distributed among four rows: both cards in row 1, cards in rows 1 and 2, both cards in row 2, and so on to both cards in row 4. The mathemagician uses the mnemonic *Bible atlas goose thigh*. The first pair of cards occupies the positions of the *B*s in *Bible*, the second pair of cards occupies the positions of the *L*s in *Bible* and *atlas*, the third pair of cards occupies the positions of the *A*s in *atlas*, and so on to the *H*s in *thigh*.

The mnemonic is closely related to the first word group in Figure 63c; the three-letter words have been enlarged to five-letter ones by adding a pair of letters to them, different for each word.

```
B I B L E    E   I L      B B
A T L A S        L S T A A
G O O S E    E G     S   O O
T H I G H      G I     T H H
```

This trick can be expanded to fifteen pairs of cards using the mnemonic *lively rhythm muffin supper savant*, and to twenty-one pairs using the mnemonic *meacock rodding guffaws twizzle rhythms knubbly*. Christopher McManus has found many more by computer. The commonest mnemonics, in which all words are in the *Official Scrabble Players Dictionary* and the *Random House Concise Dictionary*, include

> bombard gruffly hunched jotting pimples skyjack
> bowknot crackup distaff hyphens mumbled wriggly
> checkup gruffly symptom tankard wishing wobbled

There are other ways to construct the mnemonic, using more words but not assigning card pairs as efficiently to the various rows. One mnemonic uses the word set *tire balk pond gums duke limp tang robs*, which can be arranged as a transposition square, defined in Section 62. Similarly, the word set *wind lock grab hump jest junk herd caps gilt womb* can be arranged as an incomplete transposition five-square.

```
E I T R          N D . I W
K L A B          K . C L O
D P N O          . R A G B
U M G S          U H P . M
                 J E S T .
```

For a mnemonic using a full card deck (twenty-six pairs), construct a double pangram such as the following by Christopher McManus from the Second Edition of the *Official Scrabble Players Dictionary: qoph jazz hymn jinx vext word buff pled byrl kick cwms qats vugg.*

Ted Clarke devised yet another mnemonic, one which requires the subject to identify only the row or column the pair of cards is located in. For nine pairs of cards, the mnemonic to use is *romper logged limpid;* for eight, *cock pomp lama leek.* In the mnemonic *loony stunt scuff icily,* the two Ls do not appear in a single row or column as the other nine letters do. If the subject protests that his card pair does not appear in a single row or column, it is still identifiable.

64 CRASHING AND NONCRASHING WORD GROUPS

If two words of the same length contain the same letter in the same position, as *dEvil* and *fEtch,* they are said to *crash,* a word originally suggested by David Silverman to describe a game based on this concept. The longest pair of noncrashing words with the same letter-pattern in the Pocket Merriam-Webster is *conceptualism exceptionably,* and in the unabridged Merriam-Webster, *gynaecomorphous demulsification.*

How large a list of mutually noncrashing words can be collected? This depends upon the word-length and the dictionary allowed. For the Pocket Merriam-Webster, Figure 64a exhibits lists of seventeen noncrashing three-letter, four-letter, and five-letter words; for six-letter words, only fifteen noncrashers appear possible.

Figure 64a   Noncrashing Word Lists in the Pocket Merriam-Webster
(WW, May 1972, Aug. 1972)

a d d	a mm o	a n g s t	a s t h m a
b r a	c z a r	b l u f f	b l a z o n
c a r	e t c h	c o y p u	c y s t i c
d e w	f i z z	d r i n k	e m b r y o
e b b	h u s k	e t h y l	f r e e z e
f l y	i k o n	f j o r d	g u f f a w
g n u	k n e w	g i z m o	h i c c u p
h i t	l y n x	h e l v e	k n o b b y
i m p	n e w t	i c t u s	l e n g t h
j o g	o g l e	l y n c h	m a d d e r
n t h	p l u m	o x b o w	o b l o n g
o w l	r a j a	p s a l m	s c r u f f
p y x	s p r y	r u m b a	t o w a r d
r u n	t w i g	s p r i g	u p h i l l
s k i	U r d u	t h e g n	w h i l s t
u s e	w h y s	u d d e r	
w h o	y o g i	w a c k y	

In Problem 86: Irrelevance in *Beyond Language,* Dmitri Borgmann enlarged these records slightly (to seventeen, seventeen, eighteen, sixteen) by using unabridged Merriam-Webster words.

Noncrashing word lists can be lengthened if one is prepared to admit dictionary boldface entries that are ordinarily spelled in capitals and pronounced letter by letter, as *TNT, TV,* or *TB.* The September/October 1981 issue of *Games* magazine allowed these types of words in a contest designed to reveal the maximum number of noncrashing four-letter words in the Third Edition of the unabridged Merriam-Webster; the winner found the twenty-one words listed in the first column of Figure 64b. Without relying on such entries, Stephen Root found twenty noncrashing five-letter words in the Third Edition; these are listed in the second column of Figure 64b. The *Oxford English Dictionary,* full of obsolete spellings of words, provided Jeff Grant with an amazing twenty-three noncrashing four-letter words and twenty noncrashing five-letter words; these are listed in the third and fourth columns of Figure 64b. If the plausible letter-combination *ucko* appeared in the *Oxford English Dictionary,* it could replace *ecko,* and *esox* could then be added to the third list for a total of twenty-four noncrashing words.

Figure 64b   Noncrashing Word Lists in the Third Edition of the
Unabridged Merriam-Webster and in the *Oxford English
Dictionary* (WW, May 1982)

a b b e	a n g s t	a b b a	a f f i x
b a f f	b r i g g	b r wk (brook)	bwr ch (burgh)
c l e g	c l amp	c z a r	c h a um
d j i n	dwe l l	d j i n	d i l d o
e d d y	embo x	e c k o	e s e r y
f r um	f j o r d	f i s c	f j e l d
g n aw	g y p p o	g l y g	g l y n n
h u z z	h u z z a	h v n t	h e x y l
i s n't	I g d y r	I d d y Umpty	i g h t s
j ow l	j i f f s	j u j u	kn i j f (knife)
Khmu	k t h i b	k n e v (know)	l a k k a
Lv o v	l o c h e	l ymb	mu s s e (muss)
my t h	McKa y	MPHM (mph)	n d u g u
Oms k	o xme n	n e v i (nevus)	o x b ow
PFCs	p s y c h	o f t e (oft)	p o p p i (poppy)
r e p p	r e n d u	p o p p (pop)	r y g h t (right)
s k y r	s k u n k	r a z z	s k o b b (scob)
Tc h i	t h r om	s k u l	t r wmp (trump)
u p g o	u p s k i	t h rw	u t t e r
v i l d	wa l t z	vmf f (umph)	v pma k (upmake)
x t r a		wg g s (ug)	
		xw l d	
		y t c h	

The four three-letter words *pen pot set sen* form a symmetric crash group. Each word crashes exactly once with another word: *Pen* with *Pot*, *pEn* with *sEt*, *peN* with *siN*, *poT* with *seT*, *pOt* with *sOn*, *Set* with *Son*. Furthermore, each letter in every word participates in a crash; there are no extraneous letters in the group. One can similarly find a symmetric crash group of six five-letter words: *hated horny wires would fitly fauns*, or a minor variant with *M* substituted for *W*. However, it has thus far proved impossible to find a symmetric crash group of eight seven-letter words: *DUALIST FLOTANT vERSINE PUNNAGE NAOLOGY PEATERY ceNSORS FARNESS* is a near-miss. If *v*, *c*, and *e* could be replaced by *N*, *D*, and *L*, then this would form a crash group. It should be possible for a computer to find an unblemished example.

65 LETTERS ON SOLIDS

Various word groups can be associated with the five Platonic solids: the tetrahedron, the cube, the octahedron, the dodecahedron, and the icosahedron. For example, one can label the vertices of a Platonic solid with different letters of the alphabet so that words can be formed out of the letters at the vertices bounding each face. When the faces are triangular (tetrahedron, octahedron, and icosahedron) it is always possible to read the word by proceeding sequentially around the vertices; however, when the faces are square (cube) or pentagonal (dodecahedron) it may be necessary to rearrange the letters before words are formed.

Alternatively, one can label the faces of the Platonic solids with letters, and read off words from the faces sharing a common vertex. In this case, the dodecahedron and icosahedron exchange roles, as do the cube and octahedron; the tetrahedron labeling is the same no matter whether faces or vertices are used.

It is difficult to show how this is done, unless one unfolds the Platonic solids so that they lie flat on the page. This is done in Figure 65a (the pentagons are slightly distorted). The corresponding words are:

> TETRAHEDRON eat sat sea set
> CUBE oval dire dove rave lira idol
> OCTAHEDRON nor pro pot not ran par pot pan
> DODECAHEDRON chowk bumps chimp rhomb spild rugby genty grown waken study alick delta
> ICOSAHEDRON ago ado aid air rag hot dog Ted die tie fir fur rug hog hug nth hun fun fen net

Figure 65a Unfolded Platonic Solids (WW, Feb. 1980)

```
         R  (icosahedron)        (octahedron) A - R       (cube) A - V
        / \                                  / \ / \             |   |
  I - A - G - U   G                    T - P - O             L - O
    \ / \ / \ /   / \                       / \ /                |   |
    D - O - H - U - R - A              T - N - O             L - I - D - O
    / \ / \ / \ / \ / \ /                \ / \ /               |   |   |   |
    E - T   T - N - F - I                A - R             A - R - E - V
          / \ / \ / \                                          |   |
          T - E   E - D                                        A - V
```

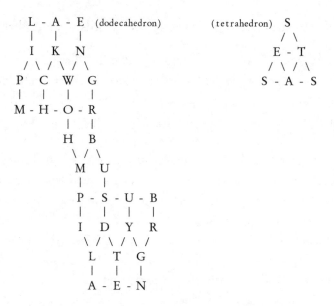

```
   L - A - E  (dodecahedron)        (tetrahedron)  S
   |   |   |                                      / \
   I   K   N                                     E - T
  / \ / \ / \                                   / \ / \
  P   C   W   G                                 S - A - S
  |   |   |   |
  M - H - O - R
          |   |
          H   B
           \ / \
            M   U
            |   |
            P - S - U - B
            |   |   |   |
            I   D   Y   R
             \ / \ / \ /
              L   T   G
              |   |   |
              A - E - N
```

The dodecahedron is by far the hardest one to label, as one must use twenty different letters of the alphabet, each three times, in twelve five-letter words. All words are found in the unabridged Merriam-Webster.

66 LETTERS ON TILES

It is well known that hexagons can be used to tile a flat surface. If letters are inscribed on the hexagons, a three-letter word can be formed by a set of three hexagons meeting at a common vertex.

Three symmetric patterns can be created out of a set of hexagonal tiles: an equilateral triangle, a larger hexagon, and a Star of David. Each pattern comes in an assortment of sizes; the patterns below are the largest ones known if no repeated letters are allowed and the words are confined to the Pocket Merriam-Webster.

```
            X
           / \
          A - L
         / \ / \
        M - D - E
       / \ / \ / \
      S - U - B - W
     / \ / \ / \ / \
    Y - P - G - O - N
   / \ / \ / \ / \ / \
  C - R - I - F - T - H
```

lax	mud	sup	won	fig
mad	bud	pug	cry	fog
lad	bed	bug	pry	oft
led	web	bog	rip	not
sum	spy	bow	pig	nth

A hexagon of nineteen letters and twenty-four words is somewhat easier to construct.

```
        W - M - Y
       / \ / \ / \
      S - E - G - P
     / \ / \ / \ / \
    O - T - B - I - N
     \ / \ / \ / \ /
      H - A - R - F
       \ / \ / \ /
        D - C - U
```

sew	gyp	beg	hot	rib	cad
mew	sot	big	hat	fir	car
gem	set	pig	bat	fin	cur
gym	bet	pin	bar	had	fur

A Star of David with thirteen letters and twelve words is extremely easy.

```
          D
         / \
    C - L - I - N
     \ / \ / \ /
      A   P   T
     / \ / \ / \
    Y - R - E - B
         \ /
          U
```

lid	pit	per
lac	tin	pet
lap	ray	bet
lip	rap	rue

These letters spell *unpredictably*

It is impossible to place hexagonal tiles with twenty-six different letters to form three-letter words, as there is no Pocket Merriam-Webster word of three letters containing Q. However, twenty-five can be accommodated.

```
            M
           / \
      H - G - Y - K
       / \ / \ / \
  J - B - U - P - S
   \ / \ / \ / \ / \
    A - D - N - I - X
   / \ / \ / \ / \ /
  R - C - O - T - F
     \ / \ / \ / \
      W - L - E - Z
         \ /
          V
```

gym	sky	pin	nod	low
hub	jab	sip	not	lot
hug	bad	six	tin	let
pug	bud	car	fit	eft
gyp	dun	cad	fix	fez
spy	pun	cod	cow	lev

Suppose that one has an infinite array of hexagonal tiles. The following three-letter, nine-letter, and twelve-letter patterns can be infinitely extended:

```
E - R - A - E - R - A ...              are
 \ / \ / \ / \ / \ / \
A - E - R - A - E - R ...
 \ / \ / \ / \ / \ / \
  R - A - E - R - A - E ...


G - U - R - G - U - R ...       ran   bad   din   bud   gut
 \ / \ / \ / \ / \ / \          rag   and   dig   rub   dug
T - N - A - T - N - A ...        tag   bit   rib   run
 \ / \ / \ / \ / \ / \          bat   tin   rig   tun
  I - D - B - I - D - B ...
   \ / \ / \ / \ / \ / \
    G - U - R - G - U - R ...


F - I - L - B - E - R - F ...    pal   den   fan   red
 \ / \ / \ / \ / \ / \ / \       lab   per   fin   rod
G - P - A - N - D - O - G ...     fig   lob   pig   bog
 \ / \ / \ / \ / \ / \ / \  .    ban   rap   din   for
  E - R - F - I - L - B - E ...   neb   far   lid   fog
   \ / \ / \ / \ / \ / \ / \     lip   beg   old   peg
    D - O - G - P - A - N - G ...
```

The letters of the second and third arrays do not form words; however, one can construct one on the word *unprofitable* by using the Pocket Merriam-Webster words *pin bin rib rub fur pul lip oil oar far fan flu elf leo toe oat pat pan few neb bet tub put* and the unabridged *rio*.

Similarly, triangles can be used to tile a flat surface. Six adjacent triangular tiles form a hexagon with rays meeting at a central point; thus, letters inserted on these tiles can be combined to form six-letter words arranged around this common vertex. In general, it is necessary to rearrange the letters to spell words.

Triangular tiles can be assembled into hexagonal patterns using 6, 24, 54, 96 ... individual triangles. The first is trivial; any six-letter word can be inscribed on it. The second is far more challenging; it can be filled with 24 different letters of the alphabet (*Q* and *X* omitted) so that seven Pocket Merriam-Webster words are formed:

```
    C   F          tunics              R          trales
   / \ / \         refund             / \         rastle
  T   N   D        revamp            A   T         resalt
  I   U   E        walrus            L   S
 / \ / \ / \       logjam           / \ / \
K   S   R   P      blowzy          T   E   A
H   W   A   V      whisky          S   R   L
 \ / \ / \ /                        \ / \ /
  Y   L   M                          A   T
  Z   O   J
   \ / \ /
    B   D
```

If one has an infinite array of triangular tiles, six different letters can be inscribed on them to form three hexagonal cycles, as shown at the right above. All three words are found in the unabridged Merriam-Webster.

The next larger triangular pavement of infinite extent uses twenty-four different letters to form twelve hexagonal patterns. It is impossible to find Merriam-Webster words satisfying the geometrical requirements; at least six words must have only one vowel, and nine must contain the rare letters Z, X, or J (having eliminated V and Q at the outset). Falling back, one can instead design a pattern using twelve different letters (each one used twice) with the added restriction that each of the twelve words be different and contain no repeated letters. The infinite pattern is shown in Figure 66a.

Figure 66a An Infinite Triangular Array Using Twelve Different Letters, Each Used in Six Different Words

```
    N   S   T          Diurna    noised
   / \ / \ / \         Sunday    tylose
  I   A   U   Y        snouty    loiter
  R   D   N   S        tauryl    railed
 / \ / \ / \ / \       dourly    tisane
A   U   Y   O   E      yonder    situal
T   L   R   D   N
 \ / \ / \ / \ /
  Y   O   E   I
  S   T   L   R
   \ / \ / \ /
    E   I   A
    N   S   T
     \ / \ /
      A   U
```

Squares represent the third way to tile a flat surface. Ed Pegg constructed a five-by-five square array using twenty-five different letters which contains sixteen four-letter words from the unabridged Merriam-Webster.

```
X W R N J      waxy    braw    burn    junk
Y A B U K      amyl    blah    chub    puck
M L H C P      slim    hilt    etch    cope
S I T E D      zigs    gift    deft    dove
Z G F D V
```

67 MAXIMALLY DIFFERENTIATED WORD SETS

Consider a set of words, each of the same length, and each having no repeated letters. How large a list of such words can be assembled from this set so that no two words in the list have more than k letters in common?

If k is set equal to zero, such a list is a near-pangram, introduced in Section 27, where lists of eight three-letter words, six four-letter words, five five-letter words, four six-letter words, and three seven-letter words were presented. These are the largest lists possible, since the alphabet has only twenty-six letters.

If k is set equal to one, so that each pair of words on the list has none or one letter in common, the list becomes more difficult to construct. In his book *Amusements in Mathematics* (1917), Henry E. Dudeney considered a reduced form of this problem, for three-letter words and an alphabet going from *A* through *O*. For the full alphabet, the largest possible such list of three-letter words is sixty if one insists that all words contain at least one vowel and one consonant. Each of the $6 \times 20 = 120$ possible vowel-consonant pairs can appear only once in a word in the list, and each three-letter word uses up two vowel-consonant pairs. If a sixty-first word is added, it must contain a vowel-consonant pair appearing in the first sixty words, and hence have two letters in common with that word.

In the Pocket Merriam-Webster, a list containing fifty-three vowel-consonant words has been found; to this the only all-consonant word in the Pocket Merriam-Webster, *nth,* can be added, making a total of fifty-four.

> gym pyx sky why try fly jay ivy buy coy dye jut sum dun fur
> lug cup hue auk ohm box jog vow lop oft sod nor vex fez Jew
> elk beg sen per met ice air zip fix jib kid gin his mil wit adz
> wax cam van lab fag hap sat nth

This list has a property much prized in information theory: even if one letter is changed and the letters rearranged, one can still retrieve the original word.

The maximum possible number of four-letter words with at most one letter in common between any pair of them is forty, allocated among words having one vowel and three consonants or one consonant and three vowels. A list of thirty such words has been found in the Pocket Merriam-Webster:

> jamb czar vast gawk flap hand quai whiz jinx pick bird gift
> slim josh foxy bloc monk prow chef jerk veld went pegs surf
> hump duct July bung myth sync

68 WORD PACKS

For seventy years crossword puzzles have been America's most popular word recreation; in recent years they have been joined by word-search puzzles. How dense a network can be constructed for either of these structures, as measured by the ratio of the total number of letters in the words used to the area of the grid in which the words appear? To fix ideas, assume that the grid must be rectangular, although most crossword puzzles and word-search puzzles restrict themselves to the square.

This ratio obviously increases with the size of the allowed vocabulary. Furthermore, it appears to increase with the size of the grid until edge effects are minimal; the largest words in the grid are substantially smaller than the grid dimensions. To investigate the ratio, it is useful to recast the problem. Assume that one has a given set of words; what is the area of the smallest rectangle into which these can be squeezed? Lists that come to mind are the chemical elements, the names of the states, or the different surnames of the presidents.

The thirty-seven different presidential surnames can be packed into a $22 \times 18 = 396$ rectangle with all names connected. If isolated names are allowed (a crossword no-no), then a $17 \times 23 = 391$ rectangle is possible. Both are by Leonard Gordon; the former is shown in Figure 68a.

Figure 68a A Well-Packed Presidential Crossword (*WW*, Feb. 1994)

```
HARDING     FILLMORE        R
A       I   T   O       O           O
GRANT X Y   R   J   N               O
R       COOLIDGE    R           A   S
LINCOLN E       F   O   PIERCE
S       E   R       F   E           T   V
POLK  VAN  BUREN         BUSH    E
N       E           R           U   L
G   WILSON  EISENHOWER          T
A J     A       B   O
REAGAN  TRUMAN          ADAMS   C
F C D       C       K       C   L
I K         HOOVER  C   K       I
E S H       A       N   MADISON
L O WASHINGTON          R   N   T
D N Y       A   E       T   L   O
        E   N   F   D   E   E   N
    JOHNSON         TAYLOR  Y
```

For a word-search grid, the apparently best strategy is to form overlap chains like *trumaNotgnihsaWilsoNixoNosnhoj,* and connect these with a few short horizontal (or diagonal) surnames. Leonard Gordon has been able to pack a $5 \times 42 = 210$ rectangle, shown in Figure 68b.

However, this is so far from the conception of a "normal" word-search puzzle that it is worth asking how much is lost by insisting on a square grid with at least three surnames in each of the eight possible directions. Leonard Gordon has demonstrated that it can be done in a square with side fifteen; this is shown in Figure 68c.

Figure 68b   A Well-Packed Presidential Word-Search Rectangle
(*WW*, Aug. 1994)

```
t k l j h      l a  h n      a e N s a
r e i e a      s y r n o     C v e i f
u n n f r      o e e s M     l e r E t
m n c f R      n S v o a     e l u r h
a e o E i      d m o N d     v T b o a
N d L r s      l a o a i     e a n m r
o Y n s o      e d H g s     l y a l d
T e c o n      i A s a o     a l v l i
g l o N P      f r u e N     N O x I N
n n o O i      r t B R o     D R o F g
i i L s e      a h u e t
h K i k r      G u c w n
s c d c c      r R h o i
a m g a E      e o A h l
W  e J o       t o n N c
i h  o r     r s a e T
```

Figure 68c   A Well-Packed Presidential Word-Search Square (*WW*,
Nov. 1994)

```
P e b r g n J o H N S o n e
i o g u e A i e  a o m i   y
e  l d C v r x f  r S a e
r r  K i h o f o f e d L d f
c o s e c l a o i N e n i I a
e O n n a h o n H e i r l n W
N s l n r a  O a k l l s a g
o e o e t y w n C N m D s o
t v c d e E o M e o r h b n n
n e n y R s a r R o i  u a e
i l i e i d u E f n   s m o
l t L r i b a  g a r t H U R
c y r s n g  T n a r g  r n
t a o a a r O l y a T a f T o
h n v n d N a l e v e l c  m
```

Capitalized letters share two (or, in three cases, three) presidential surnames.

One can create an even denser packing in which the challenge of determining the embedded surnames is considerably greater than it is in a word search: the king's move word pack. In Section 25, words were graphed using king's move in which each letter could appear only once; here, letters can be repeated as often as necessary, and the goal is to minimize the total number of letters used. Ninety-three is the best thus far achieved, but a computer could probably lower this. As a rule of thumb, each word pack halves the area of the previous one.

If one is restricted to words of a given length, how densely can one crossword-pack exactly n words? Leonard Gordon has developed two different packing strategies applied to four-letter and five-letter words. These pack words into long strips that are at most one letter wider than the word-length. More conventional square packings can be designed to do as well: 26 four-letter words in a 9-by-9 square, 56 four-letter words in a 14-by-14 square, 34 five-letter words in an 11-by-11 square, 82 five-letter words in a 17-by-17 square, 84 six-letter words in a 17-by-17 square, and 116 seven-letter words in a 23-by-23 square. Gordon provided actual crosswords for all but the seven-letter square. The corresponding total letters/area packing ratios are, respectively, 1.28, 1.14, 1.40, 1.42, 1.74, and 1.53. The latter ratios compare favorably with Sunday crossword puzzles, which are free to allow words of any length; Sunday puzzle ratios typically range from 1.6 to 1.7.

SEVEN
NUMBER WORDS

THIS CHAPTER CONSIDERS a special class of words: the cardinals *one, two, three,...*It is surprising how much can be done with these in recreational linguistics, not only by applying ideas presented in more general form in the preceding chapters, but also by introducing wordplay uniquely adapted to the properties of the number system.

Before looking at number wordplay, it is interesting to note the relative frequencies of occurrence of the cardinals *one, two, three,...* and the ordinals *first, second, third, ...* as revealed by Kucera and Francis's *Computational Analysis of Present-Day American English* (Brown University, 1967), a corpus of a million words drawn from five hundred segments of text printed in the United States in 1961. As shown in Figure 70a, the frequencies decrease in a somewhat irregular fashion; there is a certain amount of "heaping" at numbers divisible by five, reflecting the tendency to round off, and there is a strong ordinal bulge from *fifteenth* through *twentieth,* no doubt reflecting historical references to various centuries.

Figure 70a   Frequencies of Cardinals and Ordinals in a Million
Words of Text

	Cardinal		Ordinal	
	Observed	Fitted	Observed	Fitted
1	3292	3000	1360	1500
2	1412	1160	373	375
3	610	588	190	167
4	359	374	74	94
5	286	269	38	60
6	220	212	26	42
7	113	162	31	30
8	104	133	23	24
9	81	111	20	19
10	165	95	7	15
11	40		4	
12	48	72	5	10
13	11		2	
14	31	57	3	8
15	56		9	
16	20	47	12	6
17	24		11	
18	17	39	22	5
19	18		42	
20	80	34	20	4
21	8		3	
22	8		3	
23	7		0	
24	14		1	
25	25	24	0	2

If the former is smoothed out over adjacent integers, and the latter
ignored, one can fit both series reasonably well by the mathematical
formulas

$$\text{Cardinal Frequencies} = 3000/(n)^{3/2}$$
$$\text{Ordinal Frequences} = 1500/(n)^2$$

71   SELF-ENUMERATING SENTENCES

Number words play a central role in self-enumerating sentences, ones that correctly state the quantities of their com-

ponent parts. The simplest form of a self-enumerating sentence is:

> This sentence contains five words.

It is not much harder to characterize a sentence by its total number of letters.

> This sentence contains thirty-six letters.
> This sentence contains thirty-eight letters.

Robert Kurosaka combined the two ideas.

> In this sentence there are sixteen words, eighty-one letters, one hyphen, four commas, and one period.

Howard Bergerson enumerated the number of words of various types in the following:

> In this sentence, the word AND occurs twice, the word EIGHT occurs twice, the word FOUR occurs twice, the word FOURTEEN occurs four times, the word IN occurs twice, the word OCCURS occurs fourteen times, the word SENTENCE occurs twice, the word SEVEN occurs twice, the word THE occurs fourteen times, the word THIS occurs twice, the word TIMES occurs seven times, the word TWICE occurs eight times, and the word WORD occurs fourteen times.

Lee Sallows is the author of self-enumerating sentences far more difficult to construct, ones in which the individual letters are enumerated. He found it necessary to build a special-purpose computer to search for such sentences; details are given in his booklet "In Quest of a Pangram" (privately published in 1984) and in the October 1984 "Computer Recreations" column in *Scientific American* magazine. Nowadays the same job can be performed by a personal computer. A typical sentence reads

> This sentence contains three a's, three c's, two d's, twenty-six e's, five f's, three g's, eight h's, thirteen i's, two l's, sixteen n's, nine o's, six r's, twenty-seven s's, twenty-two t's, two u's, five v's, eight w's, four x's, five y's, and only one z.

Since the cardinal numbers from one through fifty use only sixteen different letters of the alphabet, it may be possible, by careful phrasing of the sentence, to reduce the number of different letters to only eighteen (*A* and *D* are needed for the word *and*).

Somewhat more startling is the existence of pairs of sentences that are identical except for the number of letters enumerated. An example:

> This autogram contains five a's, one b, two c's, two d's, thirty-one e's, five f's, five g's, eight h's, twelve i's, one j, one k, two l's, two m's, eighteen n's, sixteen o's, one p, one q, six r's, twenty-seven s's, twenty-one t's, three u's, seven v's, eight w's, three x's, four y's, and one z.

> This autogram contains five a's, one b, two c's, two d's, twenty-six e's, six f's, two g's, four h's, thirteen i's, one j, one k, one l, two m's, twenty-one n's, sixteen o's, one p, one q, five r's, twenty-seven s's, twenty t's, three u's, six v's, nine w's, five x's, five y's, and one z.

The second sentence has five fewer *e*'s, one more *f*, three fewer *g*'s, four fewer *h*'s, one more *i*, one less *l*, three more *n*'s, one less *r*, one less *t*, one less *v*, one more *w*, two more *x*'s and one more *y* than the first sentence does. These differences are, of course, related to the letter-differences in the number words in the second and third columns below.

E	thirty-oNe	tweNty-six
F	fiVe	six
G	fiVe	two
H	eight	four
I	twelVe	thirteeN
L	two ——s	oNe
N	eighteeN	tweNty-oNe
R	six	fiVe
T	tweNty-oNe	tweNty
V	seVeN	six
W	eight	NiNe
X	three	fiVe
Y	four	fiVe

For example, the *v*'s in the left column (4) exceed the *v*'s in the right column (3) by one, and the *n*'s in the right column (8) exceed the *n*'s in the left column (5) by three. This balancing of different number-names is reminiscent of the well-known observation that TWO + ELEVEN = ONE + TWELVE both numerically and literally. (This apppears in the April 1948 issue of *The Enigma,* the monthly publication of the National Puzzlers' League, but probably was discovered earlier by others.)

Later, Sallows succeeded in including at the start of the sentence a statement about the total number of letters present:

> This sentence contains one hundred and ninety-seven letters: four a's, one b, three c's, five d's, thirty-four e's, seven f's, one g, six h's, twelve i's, three l's, twenty-six n's, ten o's, ten r's, twenty-nine s's, nineteen t's, six u's, seven v's, four w's, four x's, five y's, and one z.

Lee Sallows proposed writing the following "book" in which each page after the first (a priming text) enumerates its predecessor:

> Page 1: x
> Page 2: one x
> Page 3: one e, one n, one o, one x
> Page 4: five e's, five n's, five o's, one x
> Page 5: five e's, three f's, three i's, two n's, two o's, three s's, three v's, one x...

How does this plot end? The list on any page will contain at most sixteen entries (the ones found in number-names *one* through *twenty*), none of them large. The possible variations are finite, so that sooner or later the numbers (i.e., five, five, five, one on Page 3) on Page m will appear on Page n, perhaps in a different order. Page n and Page m are anagrams of each other; their letter-frequencies agree. This means that page $n+1$ is identical to page $m+1$; from now on, the book cycles with period $n-m$.

A computer program reveals that the above book eventually cycles with a period of 155. If one uses other priming text than x, computer simulation reveals four cycles, the others with periods 14, 1, and 1. All priming texts lead inexorably into one of these whirlpools, or strange attractors as mathematicians call them.

Logologists, unlike mathematicians, are most interested in the cycles of length 1. These correspond to books in which every page after some starting sequence of pages reads like one of the following:

> fifteen e's, seven f's, four g's, six h's, eight i's, four n's, five o's, six r's, eighteen s's, eight t's, four u's, three v's, two w's, three x's.

> sixteen e's, five f's, three g's, six h's, nine i's, five n's, four o's, six r's, eighteen s's, eight t's, three u's, three v's, two w's, four x's.

These are the only two known English-language examples of what Sallows calls *reflexicons*—word lists that describe their own letter counts. In a sense, they are more elegant than the self-descriptive sentences introduced earlier; extraneous introductory matter has been eliminated. One can strip away further extraneity by leaving out the 's endings, producing such reflexicons as

> five f, five i, five v, five e
> twelve e, six f, three h, seven i, two l, two n, five o, five r, five s, six t, three u, six v, four w, four x

For even more compression, arrange the phrases such as *five f* or *twelve e* in a crossword grid, so that certain letters are shared. In such a crossword, n phrases intersect n-1 times, unless there is a closed loop, in which case they intersect n times. The closed-loop case offers the possibility of searching for a crossword in which each intersection contains one of the n different letters represented in the phrases. Victor Eijkhout found a marvelous crossword in which not only is each letter represented at an intersection, but the crossword consists of a single twelve-linked bracelet. This is depicted in Figure 71a.

Figure 71a A Self-Descriptive Crossword with a Single Loop and Each Letter at a Crossing (WW, Aug. 1992)

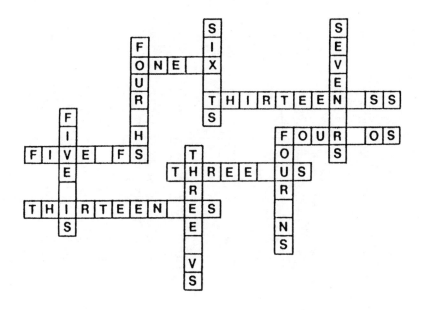

Note that the phrases as assembled in a crossword are self-descriptive, but they do not remain so if disassembled and presented merely as a list.

One can abandon the requirement that each letter be represented at an intersection, and instead ask what is the minimum-area rectangle in which a self-descriptive crossword can be embedded. Lee Sallows has discovered one in a 14×16 rectangle, shown in Figure 71b. It is not known whether or not this is the minimum; thousands of different crosswords can be formed from the same set of phrases.

Figure 71b   A Self-Descriptive Crossword in a Minimum Area (*WW*, Aug. 1992)

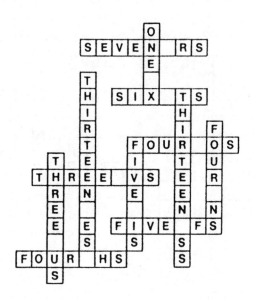

72   CARDINAL CONVERGENCE

The number *four* in English is the only truthful number, for its value equals its number of letters. It can be proved that all cardinal numbers in English converge to *four* in the sense illustrated by the following example: *one hundred twenty-three* has 21 letters, *twenty-one* has 9 letters, *nine* has 4 letters, *four* has 4 letters.

Other languages have more complex convergence structures, as illustrated by Sidney Kravit's "The Lucky Languages" in the 1974 *Journal of Recreational Mathematics*:

> Spanish: cardinals converge to the 4-6 cycle (*cuatro-seis*) or to 5 (*cinco*)
> French: cardinals converge to the 3-5-4-6 cycle (*trois-cinq-quatre-six*)
> German: cardinals converge to 4 (*vier*)
> Italian: cardinals converge to 3 (*tre*)
> Latin: cardinals converge to the 3-4-7-6 cycle (*tres-quatuor-septem-sex*)

In Greek, the cardinals converge to 5 or the 4-8 cycle in the masculine case, and to 5 or the 4-7 cycle in the feminine case. Russian is the most complex of all, converging to 3, 11, or the 4-7 cycle.

In Problem 128: The Pentagon in *Beyond Language* (Scribner's, 1967), Dmitri Borgmann considered a different sort of convergence: each number is represented by the sum of its letter values instead of the number of its letters. There is no cardinal with name the same as its letter value sum, but all numbers converge to the cycle -216-228-288-255-240- (*two hundred sixteen* has a value of 228, *two hundred twenty-eight* has a value of 288, etc.). All cardinals converge to this cycle in eighteen or fewer steps, even those in the vigintillions. Actually, it requires only two steps for a number in the vigintillions to reduce to a number in the hundreds. As noted in Section 74, no number-name has more than 758 letters, corresponding to a score of nine thousand or so; in turn, any number less than ten thousand will have a score of less than five hundred. Once a score reaches the 150–300 range, however, it is possible to wander awhile before the final cycle is reached. For instance, 4 reaches 240 through the sixteen intermediate steps 60-97-152-232-290-219-218-205-174-278-291-253-254-258-247-281. Among the numbers from 1 through 999, 240 is the cycle entry point of the overwhelming majority, or 937; 216 is the entry point for 28 numbers, 288 for 15, 255 for 14, and 228 for none at all. (The smallest number converging to 228, other than 216, is 4,050.)

If the alphabet were rearranged, the cycle -216-228-288-255-240- would be replaced by one or more cycles of various lengths. Finding alphabetic rearrangements corresponding to particular types of convergence patterns is a challenging task. Section 76 exhibits an alphabetic rearrangement leading to thirty-eight cycles of length one (numbers that merely repeat themselves). On the other hand, how long a cycle can be constructed, or how long a series of numbers can be devised before a cycle is reached? Most cycles have vigintillions of different numbers that feed into them, but certain alphabetic rearrangements create degenerate cycles (ones having only a few entrants). For example, any alphabet starting *ISX*...contains the number 6, which endlessly cycles itself, and there exist no other numbers that converge to 6. More elaborately, the rearrangement *ENVIWT.O..LS*...results in 10 converging to 9, and 1, 11, 7, and 2 converging to 19. How many such degenerate cycles are possible? How large can a degenerate cycle be? The rearrangement *TYOFGS.VI.......H.WRNX...E* creates the cycle -30-50-20-70-90-80-60-40-, into which only 1, 3, 41, 51, and 61 feed.

73 ALPHABETIZING THE CARDINALS

Suppose that the numbers between *one* and *one thousand vigintillion* (minus one) are arranged in alphabetical instead of numerical order; the first three entries of such a list are *eight, eight billion,* and *eight billion eight.* Is there any number name in this list that matches its position in the numerical list?

The number names *thousand, million, billion,* etc., are defined in multiples of one thousand; therefore, it is first worth looking at the reduced matching problem for the first 999 integers. A group of Massachusetts Institute of Technology mathematicians issued a small booklet "Alphabetic Number Tables: 0-1000" in 1972; an examination of this quickly reveals that there are no matches, the nearest misses being *six hundred eighty-two* in position 676, *six hundred eighty-three* in position 675, and *eight* in position 1.

The basic structure of the full alphabetical list of numbers is quite similar to the list of the first 999. All but 0.1 percent of number-names start with the phrase (cardinal number between 1 and 999) *vigintillion;* the remainder are scattered through the list in the interstices between various blocks of one-vigintillion size. This intercalation will affect the numbering of the list, but not very much; at most, the ordered numbers will change by one in the third place. But, as shown above for the list of the first 999, the nearest potential match misses by six units in the third place. In other words, there are no matches between the alphabetical and numerical lists.

Actually, the matching problem can be formulated for number lists of any length, not just those ending with *one thousand* (minus one) or *one thousand vigintillion* (minus one). The first nine lists are given in Figure 73a, with the matches capitalized. Five out of the nine lists exhibit matches, as do fifty-five out of the first ninety-nine.

Figure 73a Matches Between Alphabetical and Numerical Lists of
Cardinals (*WW*, Feb. 1981)

ONE	ONE	ONE	four	five	five	five	eight	eight
	TWO	three	one	four	four	four	five	five
		two	THREE	one	one	one	four	four
			four	three	six	seven	one	nine
				two	three	six	seven	one
					two	three	SIX	seven
						two	three	six
							two	three
								two

Figure 73b gives the list size required for a match to occur for each cardinal from *one* through *twenty*. *Eight* is the only cardinal for which there is no matching list of any size; *eight billion* is another.

Figure 73b List Sizes for the First Twenty Numerical-Alphabetical
Matches (*WW*, Feb. 1981)

1	1–3	6	8	11	87	16	41
2	2	7	11–13	12	13	17	44
3	4	8	never	13	16	18	815
4	11–14	9	40	14	46	19	49
5	18–49	10	14	15	800	20	30

The fraction of lists with one or more matches, 0.56, agrees rather well with a result from mathematics. If one randomly shuffles the integers from 1 through n, the probability that there will be one or more matches between the original list and the shuffled one approaches for large values of n the expression $1 - (1/e) = 0.63$, where e, the base for natural logarithms, is a mathematical constant equal to approximately 2.72. Since the alphabetical list is not randomly shuffled but highly structured, it is somewhat surprising that these two probabilities agree as closely as they do.

As Figure 73a indicates, it is possible to generate more than one match for certain list sizes. The list of the first thirteen cardinals has matches at 4, 7, and 12; the list of the first thirty-one cardinals has matches at 5, 24, and 27. Jeremy Morse found several lists of one thousand or less with four or five matches:

202-list: 101,200,201,202   463-list: 144,147,316,336
211-list: 101,200,204,207   465-list: 145,170,334,337
212-list: 101,200,204,207   213-list: 101,200,204,207,212
214-list: 101,200,204,210   231-list: 101,200,205,224,227

Lists of vigintillion size can generate as many as eight matches.

If *eight* is the first cardinal number in the alphabetical list, what is the last? Edward Wolpow believes that it is *two vigintillion two undecillion two trillion two thousand two hundred two.* In a similar vein, the first prime number is *eight billion eighteen million eighteen thousand eight hundred fifty-one* (8,018,018,851) and the last, reported in the April 1981 Mathematical Games column of *Scientific American*, is *two vigintillion two undecillion two trillion two thousand two hundred ninety-three.* The first square is *eight billion eighteen million eight hundred forty-four thousand three hundred four* (8,018,844,304, the square of 89,548), and the last, calculated by Alan Frank, is *two vigintillion, two undecillion, two hundred two decillion, two hundred eleven nonillion, six hundred ninety-eight octillion, two hundred ninety-seven septillion, seventy-nine sextillion, twenty-seven quintillion, two hundred thirty-two quadrillion, six hundred sixty-three trillion, two hundred forty-nine billion, sixty million, one hundred sixty-seven thousand nine.*

If number names are reverse alphabetized (last letter alphabetized first, then the second-to-last letter, etc.), the first name on the list is *three hundred* and the last, *six hundred sixty vigintillion, sixty septillion, sixty sextillion sixty.*

74   NUMBER ODDITIES

The longest number-name, according to Edward Wolpow, has 758 letters; there are about one sextillion such numbers, the alphabetically first one consisting of 878 repeated 22 times, and the alphabetically last consisting of 373 repeated 22 times.

The smallest number using twenty-three different letters of the alphabet (*J, R,* and *Z* are never seen) is *one octillion, one septillion, one quadrillion, one billion, one million, two thousand five hundred sixty-eight.* The shortest number-name with this property has 56 letters: *five septendecillion, six quadrillion, eighty billion, two million.*

If the number-names are written out in numerical order (*one, two, three,...*) and a cumulative total is kept of the number of times each letter of the alphabet appears, the only letters that lead all others are *O* (at the end of *one, two*) and *E* (beginning with *one, two, three* and continuing on to *one thousand vigintillion*). The second most common letter is *I*. Through *one thousand*, *E* has appeared 3,131 times and *I*, 1,310; through *one billion*, *E* has appeared 9.39 million times and *I*, 5.93 million times. The gap is nearly closed at *one sextillion*, when the cumulative number of *I*'s is 0.937 the cumulative number of *E*'s.

If the number-names are written in their proper places in the Second Edition of the unabridged Merriam-Webster, three (822, 1702, 2748) match their page numbers; for the third edition, two do (1576, 2475).

Each number-name consists of a sequence of words separated by spaces and hyphens. The most words that can be put in alphabetical order is eleven: *eight hundred nine novendecillion one quintillion seventy-six thousand twenty-two*. The most that can be put in reverse alphabetical order is thirteen: *twenty-three sexdecillion seventy-seven quattuordecillion one nonillion ninety-nine million eighty-eight*. Neither example is unique.

The number-names from *one* through *ten* can be embedded in words or augmented by internal pentagrams to form words, as illustrated in Figure 74a.

Figure 74a   Number Words in Other Words

d ONE	O v e r t o NE
o u TWO n	TWe l v e mO
THREE p	THRE n o d i z E
c a r FOUR	FOU n d a t o R
FIVE s	F o r m a t I VE
S I X e t e e n e	S e n a t r I X
m i SEVEN t	S Em i p r o VEN
h E I GHT	E a r t h l I GHT
c a NINE	N e c t a r INE
TEN t	TE a s p o o N

SIXeteene is an obsolete form of *sexton*, found in the *Oxford English Dictionary*, and *FIVEs* is a horse disease mentioned in *The Taming of the Shrew*. The words *TENONEd, miNINETWOrk* (in *Webster's*

Vest-Pocket Dictionary), *TENTWOrt* (in the *Oxford English Dictionary*), and *roTENONE* contain two consecutive number-names.

The letters of *one* through *nine* (except for *two*) can be distributed in order within cardinal numbers not containing the digit in question. The smallest known examples are *fOrty-NinE, Two HundREd onE, Five thOUsand thRee, Four hundred thIrty-seVEn, Seventy-fIve seXtillion, Six hundrEd eleVEN, onE vIGintillion tHirTy, oNe hundred thIrty-oNE*. A more challenging problem: Embed the letters of *one* through *ten*, each in order, within a single cardinal. If letters can be reused, the shortest appears to be the thirty-eight-letter EIGHTy-*FIVE* *T*HOUsa*N*d *SI*X hu*N*d*R*Ed *EVE*Nty-TWO (reused letters in italics). If the thirty-nine different letters cannot be reused, the shortest is probably the fifty-seven-letter *EIGHT*y-*FIVE SE*p*TEN*dec*I*lli*ON TWE*l*VE T*HO*u*sa*N*d *SIX* hu*N*d*R*Ed *FOURtEE*N. Note that *ten* consists of *te* in *septendecillion* and *n* in *fourteen; nine*, of *n* and *i* in *septendecillion*, *n* in *hundred*, and *e* in *fourteen*.

Some number-names can be transposed to other words in the Pocket Merriam-Webster; others require the addition of one or more letters before such transpositions are possible. The shortest examples known for *one* through *twenty* are given in Figure 74b.

Figure 74b   Transpositions and Transadditions of the First Twenty Number-Names

eon = one		leavened = eleven + AD
tow = two		wavelet = twelve + A
ether = three		tethering = thirteen + G
flour = four + L		counterfeit = fourteen + CFT
verify = five + RY		stiffener = fifteen + RS
axis = six + A		existent = sixteen + T
evens = seven		retentiveness = seventeen + IRTS
height = eight + H		heightened = eighteen + DH
inner = nine + R		internecine = nineteen + CIR
net = ten		noteworthy = twenty + HOOR

Apparently, *twenty-one* cannot be transadded even if the unabridged Merriam-Webster is allowed. Figure 74c gives various larger number-names that can be transadded to unabridged Merriam-Webster words. The word *interchangeability* contains eleven different number-names in scrambled form: 3, 8, 9, 10, 13, 30, 39, 80, 89, 90, 98.

Figure 74c Transadditions of Larger Number Names

30 thirsty	60 sexuality
31 retinopathy	61 extensionally
33 thyroparathyroidectomize	63 heterosexuality
36 thyrotoxicosis	69 exsanguinity
37 hypersensitivity	70 sensitively
39 interchangeability	80 weighty
40 frosty	81 homogeneity
41 confectionery	89 interchangeability
43 polytetrafluoroethylene	90 intently
49 confectionery	91 conveniently
50 stiffly	96 extensionality
51 affectionately	98 interchangeability
59 inefficiently	99 inconveniently

There is a small group of words that are the transpositions of two or more number-names: *one four* fortune, *eight ten* teething, *eleven sixty* extensively, *one six ten* extension.

Figure 74d depicts an insertion-deletion network (Section 41) containing eight cardinals, the most possible using Pocket Merriam-Webster words.

Figure 74d Cardinals in the Pocket Merriam-Webster Insertion-Deletion Network (*WW*, Aug. 1987)

```
          here—ere—sere—see—seen—SEVEN
           |
          her                    ion—in—fin—fine—fie—FIVE
           |                      |
THREE—thee—the—he—hoe—hone—ONE—on—ton—to—TWO
           |                      |
          then                   tone—toe—tore—fore—for—FOUR
           |                                          |
          TEN                                   FORTY—fort
```

75 ALPHAMAGIC SQUARES

A square of numbers (usually positive integers) is magic if the sum of the numbers in every row, column, and diagonal is the same. These have been studied by mathematicians for centuries; however, the logological analogue is much less well-known. Lee Sallows introduced it in the Fall 1986 and Winter 1987 issues of *Abacus,* a computer journal published by Springer-Verlag for only five years (1983–88); later he excerpted nontechnical material from these articles.

An alphamagic square is a magic square in which the sums of the letters of the number-words also form a magic square. Thus:

5	22	18	five	twenty-two	eighteen	4	9	8
28	15	2	twenty-eight	fifteen	two	11	7	3
12	8	25	twelve	eight	twenty-five	6	5	10

Note that the letter-counts are all different; each one from three to eleven is represented. In general, repetition of numbers in the derived square is permitted.

Alphamagic squares can be grouped in families. One can add one hundred to each number in an alphamagic square and it will remain alphamagic. Less trivially, a magic square containing numbers all ending in 1, 4, or 7 can be converted to one containing all numbers ending in 2, 5, or 8 because the number of letters in *one* and *two, four* and *five,* and *seven* and *eight* is the same. To illustrate:

44	61	57	9	8	10		45	62	58	9	8	10
67	54	41	10	9	8		68	55	42	10	9	8
51	47	64	8	10	9		52	48	65	8	10	9

Certain four-by-four alphamagic squares are ridiculously easy to construct. All are based on a mathematical construct called a Graeco-Latin square. Without burdening the nonmathematical reader with details, it is enough to note that all alphamagic squares of this type resemble the sample below:

26	37	48	59	9	11	10	9
49	58	27	36	9	10	11	9
57	46	39	28	10	8	10	11
38	29	56	47	11	10	8	10

In this alphamagic square, each row and each column contain one apiece of the tens-digits 2, 3, 4, or 5, and each row and each column contain one apiece of the units-digits 6, 7, 8, or 9. Any permutation of these digits preserves the alphamagical property.

It is far more difficult to construct a four-by-four alphamagic square avoiding this permutational structure. The only two alpha-magic squares Lee Sallows could find are given below, along with a single five-by-five alphamagic square with a center consisting of a three-by-three alphamagic square:

31	23	8	15
17	5	21	34
26	38	13	0
3	11	35	28

18	12	23	5
3	25	19	11
16	13	1	28
21	8	15	14

59	89	17	44	61
67	4	101	57	41
15	107	54	1	93
82	51	7	104	26
47	19	91	64	49

76   SELF-DESCRIPTIVE NUMBER-NAMES

If one sets $A=1$, $B=2$, ..., the number name *one* scores $15+14+5 = 34$, the number-name *two* scores $20+23+15 = 58$, and so on. Edward Wolpow (*WW*, Aug. 1981) noted that no number-name is self-descriptive (is equal to its score), but he found two near-misses: *two hundred nineteen* scored 218 and *two hundred fifty-three* scored 254. Dave Morice suggested that this lack of simultaneity could be recti-fied by rearranging the alphabet. For example, if it began *ISX* (or any permutation of those letters), then *six* would score 6. Not all of the early number names can be so well accommodated; in fact, it is impossible for 1 through 5, 7, 8, 11 through 18, 21 through 28, 31, and 32.

How many number-names can be simultaneously made self-descriptive by a suitable alphabet rearrangement? Leonard Gordon suggested the following strategy:

(1) construct n self-descriptive number-names from the set *twenty, thir-ty, ..., ninety*
(2) construct m self-descriptive number-names from the set *two hun-dred one, two hundred two, ..., two hundred nine*
(3) combine these to construct an additional mn names
(4) check to see if *two hundred eleven* or *two hundred twelve* can be included by suitable placement of L in the alphabet

Experimentation suggested that m and n could both be set equal to five. Selecting *fifty* through *ninety* and *one, two, three, four,* and *nine,* one can use various algebraic arguments to reposition the let-ters. The rearrangement *.ESIV.F.WR.Y.UD..H.TXOLG.N* (the remaining nine letters can be inserted in any order in the spaces) created thirty-seven self-descriptive number-names: 50, 60, 70, 80, 90, 201, 251, 261, 271, 281, 291, 202, 252, 262, 272, 282, 292, 203, 253, 263, 273, 283, 293, 204, 254, 264, 274, 284, 294, 209, 259, 269, 279, 289, 299, 211, and 212. Further progress could not be made without the aid of a computer. Leonard Gordon searched for selections incorporating the above thirty-seven number-names plus *two hundred fifteen* or *two hundred eighteen,* and succeeded in adding the former to the list for a total of thirty-eight self-descriptive number names using the alphabet *REFSW.VG..IXYD.....T.NULOH.*

Lee Sallows generalized the problem, suggesting the assignment of numbers to letters at will with only one restriction: the same number could not be assigned to two different letters. Using algebraic arguments, he was able to assign numbers to letters that made *one* through *twelve* self-descriptive, but proved that *thirteen* was impossible to add by the following simple argument: canceling similar letters in the equation *thirteen = three + ten* yields $I = E$ which is not allowed. The assignment, not unique, that he found is:

E	F	G	H	I	L	N	O	R	S	T	U	V	W	X
3	9	6	1	-4	0	5	-7	-6	-1	2	8	-3	7	11

To this, one can add the number-name *zero* by assigning Z the value 10. Figure 76a demonstrates how *thirteen* can be added using a little chicanery. The self-descriptive number-name problem was discussed by Ian Stewart in his column "Mathematical Recreations" in the March 1994 *Scientific American* magazine.

Figure 76a   The Einschwein Swindle (WW, Aug. 1991)

Paying a recent call on my old friend Professor Einschwein, the world-famous Transylvanian logologist, I was privileged to learn about his latest numerological invention. Drawing forth a curious pack of cards, he showed me that each card bore a single letter of the alphabet on one side and a single integer, sometimes positive, sometimes negative, on the other.

"You see that every distinct letter is paired with its own distinct number on the reverse side, and that some cards are duplicated." I verified this, noting a total of 20 cards: E with 0, F with 14, G with -2, H with 9, I with -3, L with 11, N with 6, O with -5, R with -10, S with 7, T with 4, U with 5, V with -6, W with 3, X with 2 and Z with 15. The E card was duplicated two times, the N and T cards once each.

"Now, observe carefully," he said. Spreading out the cards on the table, letter sides up, the Professor carefully selected four, sliding them with his index finger into a single line so as to spell the word ZERO. Next, turning the cards over one by one, he invited me to add up the numbers so revealed. Their sum was zero. "That's cute," I responded, "but don't I recall seeing something along these lines in a recent *Word Ways*?" "Have patience," he purred, "we are not finished. Check me at every step!"

Einschwein continued in the same vein, ZERO followed by ONE, TWO, THREE, etc., until he had reached TWELVE. I watched him like a hawk throughout. There was no question of any new cards being palmed. Each time the cards needed were slid into line as before and then turned over. The sum of the numbers always tallied with the number word spelled. "It's a nice trick, Professor," I said. "But that's it; you can't get beyond TWELVE. THIRTEEN is unlucky, as proved in that article I saw in the February 1990 issue, 'The New Merology'."

Slowly and deliberately he lined up the letters to spell THIRTEEN. With a sinking feeling I watched him turn the cards over one at a time. Incredibly, their sum was indeed 13!

"But this is against logic!" I cried. "Not only do I remember the earlier impossibility proof that cancelling common terms in the equation $T+H+I+R+T+E+E+N = T+H+R+E+E + T+E+N$ shows that $I = E$, and thus I and E could never have different values. I also remember that we can go even further. From $N+I+N+E = 9$, we know that $I = 9-2N-E$. But since $I = E$, then $E = 9-2N-E$, from which $2E = 9-2N$. Yet, since 2E is even, while 9-2N must be odd, we have a contradiction. Thus, if THREE, NINE, and TEN are self-descriptive, no assignment of letters, distinct or otherwise, could ever make THIRTEEN perfect as well!"

"For vy are you shouting at me already?" cried Einschwein plaintively, his Transylvanian accent momentarily in the ascendant. "You vant ve should repeat ze demonstration for you all over again?"

The solution depends on the fact that N rotated 180 degrees is still N, converting the 6 on the back of the card to a 9. Einschwein merely made sure that the card labeled N used in THIRTEEN was rotated before spelling out the number-name.

In French, the number-names 1 through 13 can be made self-descriptive; in Spanish, 1 through 11; and in German, 1 through 49, if umlauted *U* is treated the same as nonumlauted *U*.

The numbers assigned to letters do not match, even after converting negative numbers to positive ones, the set of number-names they describe. In the diagram below, Lee Sallows rectifies this defect. There are sixteen numbers in the checkerboard, the shaded ones to be understood as negative. If one spells out the number-name of any of these sixteen numbers, adding or subtracting the corresponding numbers as indicated, the sum is equal to the number so spelled out. For example, *six* corresponds to the numbers 16, 17, and -27, which add up to 6.

E 4	I 17	N 2	S 16
L 24	F 9	T 20	R 6
W 25	U 12	G 22	O 7
V 1	X 27	Y 11	H 3

How many number-names can be simultaneously made self-descriptive under the general conditions specified above? To simplify the problem, consider only the names between *zero* and *ninety-nine*. Using a strategy similar to the one above, one can combine *one, two, three, four, five, seven,* and *eight* with *twenty, thirty, forty, fifty, sixty, seventy, eighty,* and *ninety* and solve fifteen linear equations in fifteen unknowns to obtain seventy-one self-descriptive number-names. To this one can assign a value for *L* which will add *eleven* and *twelve* to the set, and *Z* to include *zero*. The seventy-four self-descriptive numbers are 0, 11, 12, 20–25, 27, 28, 30–35, 37, 38, 40–45, 47, 48, 50–55, 57, 58, 60–65, 67, 68, 70–75, 77, 78, 80–85, 87, 88, 90–95, 97, and 98. The corresponding assignment of numbers to letters is:

E	F	G	H	I	L	N	O	R
107	-191/2	-33/2	-503/2	178	7/2	-129	23	99/2

S	T	U	V	W	X	Y	Z
213/2	-9	27	-369/2	-12	-575/2	72	-359/2

One can use *six* or *nine* instead of *seven* to obtain a different assignment.

If one wishes to restrict the solution to integer values only, one must leave out the number-name *fifty*, resulting in the loss of eight self-descriptive number-names for a total of sixty-six.

E	F	G	H	I	L	N	O	R	S	T	U	V	W	X	Y	Z
20	-18	-7	0	4	-6	-42	23	-28	10	-9	27	-1	-12	-17	72	-15

Removing the restriction that number-names lie between *zero* and *ninety-nine*, one can assign suitable values to D (for *hundred*), A (for *thousand*), M (for *million*), B (for *billion*), Q (for *quadrillion*), P (for *septillion*) and C (for *octillion*) to multiply the 73 nonzero number-names by a factor of 128, for a total of 9,344 self-descriptive ones.

On the other hand, by using fractions other than the multiples of one-half, the following self-description is achieved:

ONE = 1/3 + 1/2 + 1/6
TWO = 2/3 + 1 + 1/3
THREE = 2/3 + 7/6 + 5/6 + 1/6 + 1/6
FOUR = 4/3 + 1/3 + 3/2 + 5/6
FIVE = 4/3 + 11/6 + 5/3 + 1/6
SIX = 2 + 11/6 + 13/6

E	F	H	I	N	O	R	S	T	U	V	W	X
1/6	4/3	7/6	11/6	1/3	1/2	5/6	2	2/3	3/2	5/3	1	13/6

Note that all the numbers from 1 through 13 with divisors of 6 have been used.

77   BASE 27

The number-system uses ten symbols, 0 through 9, in a place-value notation. Many people are aware that other bases can be used; binary, a number-system based on only the symbols 0 and 1, is extensively employed in logic and computer science. Why not create a number-system based on twenty-six values, the letters from *A* to *Z*? Such a system was proposed by Philip Cohen, but it suffers from a grievous defect. If, for example, one assigns the zero digit in the base-26 system to the letter *A*, then words such as *wake* and *awake* have the same numerical value. One wants a system in which each word corresponds to a unique number. Lee Sallows was the first to perceive a remedy—create a base-27 system in which the zero-digit is assigned to a space. Not only did this restore the desired uniqueness property, but it also provided for the assignment of numbers to dictionary phrases or, for that matter, whole sentences or paragraphs of text (not containing numbers or other symbols).

If, then, one sets $A=1$, $B=2,\ldots$, $Z=26$, the reduction of base 27 numbers (words) to base 10 numbers for the purpose of arithmetical manipulation is straightforward but tedious without a computer. Take, for example, $cat = 3 \times 27 \times 27 + 1 \times 27 + 20 = 2187 + 27 + 20 = 2234$. The conversion of a base 10 number to its corresponding word is achieved by successive divisions by 27. For example, $74417/27 = 2756$ with remainder of 5 (*E*), $2756/27 = 102$ with remainder of 2 (*B*), $102/27 = 3$ with remainder 21 (*U*), and the final 3 is labeled *C*. In other words, 74417 corresponds to *cube*.

Sallows exploits this identification of words to numbers by converting words to their base 10 numbers, performing various arithmetical operations on the latter, and reconverting the result to a string of letters (which sometimes forms a word). For example, there are many pairs of four-letter words that add to another word of four letters, such as *anti* + *bulk* = *diet*, *cube* + *polo* = *tint*, or *inch* + *mail* = *volt*, but only a few long ones such as *gauche* + *hairdo* = *occult* or *antics* + *reveal* = *stones*. Multiplication is also possible: *at* × *king* = *stove*, *zip* × *cram* = *corpses* (a body-bag exercise?). More elaborate exercises are possible: *boy* × *egg* + *dee* × *saw* = *boy* × *ill* + *dee* × *ply* = *closet*, and the Pythagorean theorem is simply illustrated by *an* × *an* + *I* × *I* = *am* × *am*.

At a more sophisticated level, one can look for the linguistic version of congruences, which exhibit the remainder after one number is divided by another: 10 (mod 4) = 2, 9 (mod 3) = 0. In words, one obtains *circle* mod *love* = *flag*, or *hangs* mod *green* = *jibe*. It is even possible to find moduli that are correct both lexically and numerically: (*forty-two* + *forty-nine*) mod *six* = *one*, and (42 + 49) mod 6 = 1.

Irrational numbers, written in base 27 notation, consist of long, seemingly random sequences of letters and spaces. Sallows speculated that the first coherent sentence in the expansion of *pi* or *e* might be *-GOD-EXISTS-* or *-THIS-NUMBER-IS-IRRA-TIONAL-*. Presumably both of these messages, plus any other, will appear if one examines a sufficiently great number of digits in the expansion!

EIGHT
AFTERWORD

THIS BOOK FOCUSES on words as collections of letters, looking at the various ways in which they can be patterned or transformed, and tracing out the relationship among different types of letterplay. It is more akin to mathematics than it is to linguistics, which is more concerned with words as carriers of meaning. Certain topics—words viewed as a whole—do not fit well into this taxonomy; these are examined in this chapter. We begin with two quite different geometric characterizations of words, and conclude with a discussion of word length.

§1 THE ALPHABET CUBE

Two-letter words can be plotted as intersections on a square lattice having rows and columns labeled with the letters of the alphabet:

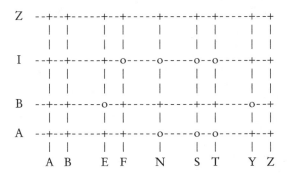

Three-letter words can be similarly plotted on a cubic lattice, and longer words can be plotted on various hypercubic lattices that are mathematically describable even though difficult to visualize. In what follows, we restrict ourselves to a discussion of three-letter words for ease of comprehension. David Morice has visualized the cubic lattice as twenty-six planes, each containing a 26-by-26 grid of tiny lights that can be activated either individually or in groups by commands entered on a central panel.

Various letterplay topics can be illustrated by the operation of this machine. For example, pressing the button labeled Palindrome, all the lights in a plane cutting diagonally through the Alphabet Cube are illuminated. If one also presses the Word button, then only those lights that actually form words (*dad, bib, pop, tot,* etc.) come on.

If one wishes to study letter shifts (words such as *OWL-pxm-qyn-rzo-SAP*), one presses the button labeled Letter-Shift and specifies which three letters are to be letter-shifted. Up to three rows of lights, all parallel to the general diagonal from *AAA* to *ZZZ*, twinkle on.

The transpositions of a given letter set (such as *ZAM, ZMA, AZM, AMZ, MAZ,* and *MZA* below) are found at the vertices of a hexagon on a plane of lights perpendicular to the general diagonal. Alternatively, they may be found at the vertices of an equilateral triangle.

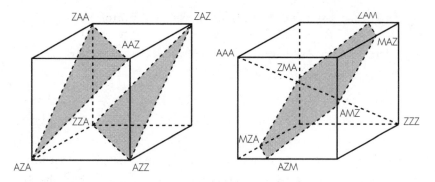

All words that crash with a given word (have the same letter in the same position, as *cAt* and *pAn*) are represented by three mutually perpendicular lines of lights that intersect the word being crashed.

Many other letterplay concepts can be translated into geometric form; this gives a flavor of the possibilities. Some cannot be fully appreciated by the reader without referring to other sections of this book. For instance, the Alphabet Cube will display a rectilinear three-dimensional maze if a Word Ladder (*pat-pan-pen-men-mew-few*) is called for (see Section 42).

82 WORD WORMS

The disadvantage of the Alphabet Cube is that words of different lengths inhabit different mathematical universes. It is desirable to have a single geometric representation for words of all lengths; this is provided by the mathematical concept of the vector. In two dimensions, a vector is a line of a specified length pointing in a specified direction. A word can be constructed out of a sequence of such lines, somewhat resembling a segmented snake.

How should letters be assigned to vectors? On 7 July 1992 Keith Jones suggested on the IBMTEXT computer bulletin board that the twenty-six letters of the alphabet could be identified with the twenty-six "outside" cubelets stacked in a three-by-three-by-three cubic lattice. Three days later, Grant Willson endorsed the concept and added the key ingredient: the cubic lattice could be used as a template to lay down the successive letters in three-dimensional space. Although there are an astronomical number of ways to assign letters to cubelets, the following pattern is perhaps the most natural:

Top Layer	Middle Layer	Bottom Layer
A B C	J K L	R S T
D E F	M . N	U V W
G H I	O P Q	X Y Z

Using this array as a template, one can trace out words in three-dimensional space. To form the word *AND,* for example, first draw a line from the dot in the central cube to the center of the cube in the upper left corner, containing *A.* Next, move the lattice, without twisting or turning it, so that the central cube is located where the *A*-cube was, and draw a line from the (relocated) dot to the center of the cube containing *N.* Move the lattice again so that the central cube is located where the *N*-cube was, and draw a line from the dot to the center of the cube containing *D.* These three lines form a word worm, as shown in the picture below, which also diagrams the word worm corresponding to *MEN.* If the sides of the cubelets are of unit length, the word worm corresponding to *AND* consists of a line of the square root of 3 in length, followed at an angle of 60 degrees by a line of unit length, followed at an angle of 45 degrees by a line of the square root of 2 in length. (For convenience, all lines are identified by their squared lengths.)

There are an amazing number of varieties of word worms; in fact, any word worm of four or more letters has a shape that is almost certainly unique. An open question: What is the longest pair of words that form the same worm? There are three different one-letter word worms: straight lines of length 3 (*A,C,G,I,R,T,X,Z*), length 2 (*B,D,F,H,J,L,O,Q,S,U,W,Y*) or length 1 (*E,K,M,N,P,V*). Most two-letter ones are bent lines (*AA* is the only exception); a few (*BY, LO, SH*) fold back upon themselves. In fact, there are twenty-eight varieties, which can be characterized by a code *a(b)c*, where *a* is the squared length of the first segment, *b* is the angle between the segments, and *c* is the squared length of the second segment. For example, *IT* and *AT* are 3(60)3, *GO* and *IF* are 3(150)2, *IS* and *TO* are 3(30)2, *DO* and *US* are 2(120)2, *OF* and *SO* are 2(60)2, *BE* and *HE* are 2(135)1, and *ON* and *WE* are 2(45)1. All but four are representable by *Official Scrabble Players Dictionary* words; the missing ones are 3(0)3, 2(180)2, 1(180)1, and 1(0)1, all straight lines or fold-backs.

For three-letter words, 728 varieties exist; a type-collection has yet to be assembled. It is worth focusing on varieties having special properties. Probably the one of greatest interest is the Ouroboros worm, one that bites its own tail (forms a closed loop). The name *Ouroboros* honors the 1922 science-fiction story by E. R. Eddison, "The Worm Ouroboros," in which the Worm of Time grasps its tail in its mouth (in Greek, *oura* is tail and *bora* food). It is a straightforward computer problem to search for these beasts.

The only three-letter Ouroboros worms are the 30-60-90 right triangle with sides (1,2,3), the isosceles triangle with sides (1,1,2), and the equilateral triangle with sides (2,2,2). (Recall that all lengths are given in squared units.) *Official Scrabble Players Dictionary* examples of these are *ANY (NAY), CUP, LEX, MIS (SIM, ISM), PAW (WAP),* and *TOE* for the right triangle: *KEY, MEW,* and *PES* for the isosceles; and *BOW* for the equilateral.

Foldback worms form another special case of interest: *EVE, VEE, LOO,* and *SHH* are straight, and *AZO, BYE, BYS, FUB, BUD, FUG, FUN, LOB, LOG, LOP, LOT, LOW, LOX, OLD, OLE, VEG, VET, VEX, ZAP,* and *ZAX* are bent at various angles.

When one looks at four-letter words, Ouroboros worms become more interesting, as some are planar and some are not. No square worm has been found, although it is theoretically possible (*JOQL, MENV,* etc.). *ROIL* is a rectangle with sides (2,3,2,3); *FOUL* is a rhomboid with internal angles of 60 and 120 degrees and sides (1,3,1,3); *COOT* is an isosceles triangle with sides of length 3 and a base of length 4. Nonplanar Ouroboros worms come in several varieties. The most elegant, perhaps, is *TAXI,* which traces out two-thirds of the edges of a tetrahedron (a triangular pyramid): four lines of length 3, each angled at 60 degrees with respect to its neighbors. There are a number of isosceles relatives of TAXI that consist of two equal-length lines on either side of a fold: *PULE* (fold of 90 degrees, lines of length 1 and 2); *WOKE, HUNK, NOSE, ONES, SONE* (fold of 45 degrees, lines of length 1 and 2); *DUIT* (fold of 30 degrees, lines of length 2 and 3). And there are several words in which the lengths on either side of the fold do not match: *ZEDS, ZEBU, SCOP, COPS, PLAY, PALY, LUNG, UNCO.*

A variation on the folding theme is provided by *ELMY, EONS,* and *NOES.* These Ouroboros worms consist of two right triangles with sides (1,2,3) folded along their hypotenuses at a 45-degree angle.

Nondegenerate Ouroboros worms are relatively rare, ranging from about 1.5 percent of three-letter words to 0.1 percent of sixteen-letter ones. (Degenerate worms are those that have foldback sections, such as *SH* in *SHIMS;* examples of degenerate Ouroboros worms include *BEVY, LOVE, SHOVEL, SHRIVE, REVIVE,* and *WIZARD,* all of which look like a set of spikes.) The only three sixteen-letter Ouroboros worms with no foldbacks are *CONSANGUINEOUSLY, DISINGENUOUSNESS,* and *MISPRONOUNCEMENT.* These are slightly flawed by having internal intersections (as in *MISPLAY,* which contains two joined loops *MIS* and *PLAY* in a figure-eight pattern). The longest known Ouroboros worms that have a fully open loop are *TRYPANORHYNCHAN* and *SEMICONSPICUOUS.*

Intermediate intersections become rather common in long words; for words of twenty letters or more, about 70 percent have this property. The longest known word without self-intersections is the twenty-seven-letter *ETHYLENEDIAMINETETRAACETATE.*

All of the Ouroboros worms exhibited thus far are equivalent to a (distorted) ring. Is it possible to find an Ouroboros worm without intermediate intersections that is topologically equivalent to a knot?

A little trial and error convinces one that the minimum number of vectors (letters) needed to tie a worm into a knot is nine; the "word" *TYDBNYRDI* does the job. It is very hard to visualize the knottedness of a word without a model (such as a Tinkertoy set), and difficult to write a computer program that can search for this property in a word list. It seems extremely unlikely that any dictionary words exist for which the Ouroboros worm is a knot; however, a knotted phrase might be findable.

83   LONG WORDS

It is impossible to give an answer to the question "What is the longest solidly written word in the English language?" that will satisfy everyone. The longest words that one is at all likely to encounter in general text are the twenty-two-letter *deinstitutionalization* and *counterrevolutionaries.*

How common are really long words? In the million-word corpus of Kucera and Francis's *Computational Analysis of Present-Day American English* (Brown University Press, 1967), the longest solidly written word, *alkylbenzenesulfonates,* also has twenty-two letters. Data on words of eighteen letters or more in Kucera and Francis suggest that each added letter halves the frequency of occurrence; for every one hundred eighteen-letter words there are about fifty nineteen-letter ones, twenty-five twenty-letter ones, and so on. If one twenty-two-letter word occurs in a million words of text, this would predict one thirty-two-letter word in a billion words and a forty-two-letter word in a trillion. However, the halving rule is suspect when applied to highly technical articles in chemical or medical journals, where agglutinative words are the rule.

The longest word found in standard English-language dictionaries is *pneumonoultramicroscopicsilicovolcanokoniosis* (alternatively, *-coniosis*), first appearing in the Addenda section of the Second Edition of the unabridged Merriam-Webster, and subsequently in the main text of the Third Edition. A few other dictionaries followed suit: the Random House unabridged, the *Oxford English Dictionary Supplement,* and the Second Edition of the *Oxford English Dictionary.* Somewhat more surprisingly, Merriam-Webster briefly inserted it in their Collegiate dictionaries; in the Seventh Edition, it overshadowed the next-longest word, *electrocardiographically*, by nearly a factor of two!

The word is a nonce-word that never should have been entered in a dictionary; it has never been used in medical literature, as researchers prefer the simpler *pneumoconiosis*. When Mount St. Helen's erupted in May of 1982, Dr. Sonia Buist, an Oregon University Health Sciences research scientist in the field of public health, was given a grant to study lung irritation in people exposed to volcanic fallout. If ever there was a chance to use the word, this was it; however, Dr. Buist spurned the chance, writing to Edward Wolpow, "I am actually dedicated to using short words whenever possible...I use [the full word] more to amuse and get people's attention rather than a way of getting it into the medical vocabulary."

The word was apparently created by Everett M. Smith, news editor of the *Christian Science Monitor,* and introduced to the world at the February 1935 convention of the National Puzzlers' League in New York City. David Shulman, another NPL member, recalled telling the *New York Herald Tribune* reporter covering the convention about the new "word," possibly coined as a ridiculous illustration of medical word-inflation. The word appears in a subhead in a story in the 23 February 1935 edition with the lead paragraph asserting that it had succeeded *electrophotomicrographically* as the longest English-language word recognized by the National Puzzlers' League.

A slightly mangled version of the word (with *-microsopic-* for *-microscopic-*, and *-volcana-* for *-volcano-*) subsequently appeared in Frank Scully's *Bedside Manna, the Third Fun in Bed Book* (Simon & Schuster, 1936). There it was cited as a word suitable for champion speller Greg Hartswick to spell or pronounce ("might even give <u>him</u> laryngitis").

It is uncertain whether the *Herald Tribune* story or the Scully book prompted the Merriam-Webster editors to include the word in the unabridged dictionary. Perhaps they inserted it as a word of sufficient length to settle all disputes concerning the longest word. However, if a consistent criterion is used to select dictionary words (for example, a citation in at least *n* different sources over a specified time period), a good rule of thumb seems to be the halving one mentioned previously. The Third Edition of the unabridged Merriam-Webster contains one word of twenty-nine letters and four of twenty-seven; by extrapolation, a forty-five-letter word should not appear until the dictionary has expanded by a factor of 100,000.

If the forty-five-letter word is rejected, the next-longest dictionary-sanctioned candidates, both of thirty-four letters, are in the unabridged Random House: *supercalifragilisticexpialidocious* and *diaminopropyltetramethylenediamine.*

In the last three decades the rules have been changed. Just as multiple-birth probabilities have been forever altered by the introduction of fertility drugs, so have word-lengths been vastly expanded by the practice of naming proteins by the sequences of amino acids that characterize them. The first recognition by logologists of such a word occurred in Dmitri Borgmann's *Beyond Language* (Scribner's, 1967), which gives a 1,185-letter word for the protein part of the tobacco mosaic virus strain called dahlemense. Legitimacy for such a word was conferred by *Chemical Abstracts,* which published it in full in Volume 60 (Jan.–June 1964). However, the editors of this journal declined to write out in full the names of longer proteins such as the human pituitary growth hormone (1,385 letters) or Tryptophan Synthetase A (1,913 letters). The latter word was subsequently written out in full in several places, including the *Guinness Book of World Records.*

By 1980, the champion appeared to be the protein Bovine Glutamate Dehydrogenase, a word inferred to have 3,641 letters, the structure of which is summarized in *The Atlas of Protein Sequences and Structure,* (1973), Vol. 5, Supplement 1, published by the National Biomedical Research Foundation. At present this is probably the longest word ever written out in full.

By 1989, Guinness was reporting the record-holder to be a 207,000-word name describing human mitochondrial DNA. Can a longest word that has never been written down in full, let alone used in context in a scientific journal, be regarded as existing?

Writing out the full names of the amino acids, ranging in length from *seryl* to *tryptophanyl,* is exceedingly wasteful. Perhaps these names would be more acceptable if alphabetic letters were substitut-

ed for amino acids. The difficulty is that long consonant strings typically appear no matter what assignment of amino acids to letters is
contemplated. A more workable strategy would be to assign the
twenty consonants to the amino acids, and intercalate vowels as
needed to make the sequence pronounceable.

SOURCES

Chapter One

11 [As a novel, *Gadsby*...] Robert Ian Scott, "The Advantages of Odd Exclusions," Aug. 1977 *Word Ways* (hereafter *WW*), p. 131.

[In general, writing literary...] A. Ross Eckler, "Mary Had a Lipogram," Aug. 1969 *WW*, p. 138.

[The effect of excluding...] Robert Cass Keller (A. Ross Eckler), "On Writing Lipograms," Feb. 1978 *WW*, p. 33.

[One can write text...] Howard Bergerson, "An Interview with 'Ronald Wilson Reagan,'" Aug. 1982 *WW*, p. 160.

[The pinnacle of the...] Cynthia Knight, "Why Couldn't They Say 'I Love You'?" Aug. 1983 *WW*, p. 160; Philip Cohen, "Kickshaws (Splitting the Alphabet)," Nov. 1979 *WW*, p. 234.

12 [In contrast with...] David Silverman, "Kickshaws (Univocalics)" Aug. 1973 *WW*, p. 170; Willard Espy, quoted in "The Poet's Corner," May 1978 *WW*, p. 163, and *An Almanac of Words at Play* (Clarkson Potter, 1980), p. 331.

[Figure 12b is a type-collection...] A. Ross Eckler, "Unsociable Housemaid Discourages Facetious Behaviour," Nov. 1969 *WW*, p. 208; Susan Thorpe, "AEIOU Words in Biology: Part 1," Nov. 1993 *WW*, p. 195, and "Colloquy," Feb. 1994 *WW*, p. 23; David Shulman, "An AEIOU Examination," May 1979 *WW*, p. 122.

[It is possible to...] Dana Richards, "Vowel Structure," Aug. 1987 *WW*, p. 156.

13 [It is conventional knowledge...] Jeff Grant and A. Ross Eckler, "Dctnr Wrds Wtht Vowls," Aug. 1980 *WW*, p. 172; Alan Frank, "On Searching for Vowelless Words," Nov. 1980 *WW*, p. 207.

14 [If the first letter...] Hector Monro, "The Poet's Corner," May 1978 *WW*, p. 164; J. A. Lindon, "Many Happy Hot Cross Buns to Leigh Mercer," Feb. 1969 *WW*, p. 31; Emily K. Schlesinger, "Assorted Avocational Adventures," Nov. 1981 *WW*, p. 195.

[If one knows what...] A. Ross Eckler, "Are Acrostic Messages Real?" Aug. 1985 *WW*, p. 187.

15 [In the preceding sections...] Howard Bergerson, "Automynorcagrams," Aug. 1975 *WW*, p. 157, which contains also the J. A. Lindon reference in the next paragraph.

[Largely unsuccessful efforts...] Richard Rankin, "Beyond Automynorcagrams," Nov. 1989 *WW*, p. 231.

[Homoliteral and heteroliteral texts...] A. Ross Eckler, "The Homoliteral Raven," May 1976 *WW*, p. 96; A. Ross Eckler, "The Heteroliteral Raven," Nov.

1976 *WW*, p. 231; Eric Albert, "Kickshaws (Doubly-Linked Sentences)," May 1983 *WW*, p. 112.

[A special type of...] "Query," Nov. 1970 *WW*, p. 278; Mary J. Youngquist, "A Literary Word Chain," Feb. 1971 *WW*, p. 62.

[In October 1994...] A. Ross Eckler, "Some Men Enjoy Oysters," Nov. 1995 *WW*, p. 195.

16   [A polyphonic substitution cipher...] A. Ross Eckler, "A Readable Polyphonic Cipher," Feb. 1975 *WW*, p. 55.

[If one is willing...] A. Ross Eckler, "Another Polyphonic Cipher," May 1978 *WW*, p. 117.

[Polyphonic ciphers have been...] Donald Knuth, "N-Ciphered Texts," Aug. 1987 *WW*, p. 173.

17   [It is more interesting...] David Silverman, "Kickshaws (Word Dice)," May 1973 *WW*, p. 107.

[Thus far, it has been...] A. Ross Eckler, "Restricted Letter Sets," Aug. 1978 *WW*, p. 159.

[If one is allowed...] Calendar dice are discussed in a note in the Feb. 1978 *WW*, p. 31.

18   [In Figure 18a, a list of...] A. Ross Eckler, "Must You Join the Queue?" May 1976 *WW*, p. 113.

Chapter Two

[Man has been intrigued...] Dmitri Borgmann, "The Rotas Square," Nov. 1979 *WW*, p. 195; "The Rotas Prehistory," Feb. 1980 *WW*, p. 11; "The Ascending Tradition," May 1980 *WW*, p. 90; Harry Partridge, "The Sator Square Revisited," Feb. 1980 *WW*, p. 17.

21   [A palindrome is a word...] Scott Hattie, "Palindrome Pairs," Aug. 1979 *WW*, p. 131.

[If any word or phrase...] Jeff Grant, "A Palindromic Alphabetic Insertion," Nov. 1982 *WW*, p. 208.

[Palindromic phrases and sentences...] A. Ross Eckler, "Leigh Mercer, Palindromist," Aug. 1991 *WW*, p. 131.

[Palindromic phrases can be...] J. A. Lindon, "Ten Logotopian Lingos (Part 1)," Nov. 1970 *WW*, p. 215.

[At least two of...] Lawrence Levine, "Dr. Awkward & Olson in Oslo," Aug. 1986 *WW*, p. 140.

22   [The tautonymic concept...] Edward R. Wolpow, " Triple Tautonyms in Biology," May 1983 *WW*, p. 103.

[A literary version...] Rambo is quoted in Hearst Sill Rogers (A. Ross Eckler), "Charade Sentences," May 1977 *WW*, p. 79; Bonita C. Miller, "The Poet's Corner," May 1974 *WW*, p .90.

23   [Consider the four-armed...] Dmitri Borgmann, "Dudeney's Switch Puzzle," Feb. 1968 *WW*, p. 11.

[Dudeney's problem can be...] A. Ross Eckler, "More About Switch Words," Feb. 1969 *WW*, p. 59.

24 [Place the different letters...] Leonard Gordon and A. Ross Eckler, "A Word Graph Bestiary," Feb. 1995 *WW*, p. 15.

[For some words, no matter...] Gary S. Bloom, et al., "Ensnaring the Elusive Eodermdrome," Aug. 1980 *WW*, p. 131; A. Ross Eckler, "Dictionary Eodermdromes," Aug. 1980 *WW*, p. 141.

[Philip Cohen proved...] "Colloquy," Feb. 1981 *WW*, p. 23.

[Word graphs are closely related...] David Morice, "Kickshaws (Word Molecules)," May 1994 *WW*, p. 112.

[Word molecules and eodermdromes...] David Morice, "Kickshaws (Word Molecules and Eodermdromes)," Aug. 1994 *WW*, p. 172.

25 [Word tiles are a ...] Leonard Gordon, "Introduction to Word Graphing," Feb. 1995 *WW*, p. 3.

[In general, neither...] A. Ross Eckler, "Eodermdromes and Non-Chesswords," Nov. 1981 *WW*, p. 251.

[Finally, one can construct...] Lee Sallows, "Incompatible Strings," May 1994 *WW*, p. 74.

[A related challenge...] Jean C. Sabine, "Word Chess with a Vengeance," Nov. 1968 *WW*, p. 236; Donald Drury, "Word Chess," Aug. 1969 *WW*, p. 165; Jean C. Sabine, "More Word Chess," Feb. 1970 *WW*, p. 40.

[A C-graph...] Leonard Gordon, "A Note on 3-Dimensional Graphs," Aug. 1995 *WW*, p. 142.

[Lee Sallows has proved...] Lee Sallows, "Incompatible Strings," May 1994 *WW*, p. 74.

26 [A word is an isogram...] Edward R. Wolpow, "Subdermatoglyphic: A New Isogram," Feb. 1991 *WW*, p. 18; Dmitri Borgmann, "Long Isograms (Part 1)," May 1985 *WW*, p. 67; Dmitri Borgmann, "Long Isograms (Part 3)," Nov. 1985 *WW*, p. 243; Dmitri Borgmann, "An Overview of Isograms," Feb. 1974 *WW*, p. 33.

[The word *isogram*...] Ted Clarke, "The Coining of Words," Feb. 1995 *WordsWorth* (volume 1, no. 5) p. 8 (privately published by the author at Newquay, Cornwall, England).

[The advent of national...] A. Ross Eckler, "Naming the Schwarzkopf Baby," Aug. 1991 *WW*, p. 144.

[Literary isograms can...] A. Ross Eckler, "Linguistic Thoughts at Random," Feb. 1995 *WW*, p. 22.

27 [A pangram can be ...] Maxey Brooke, "Pangrams," May 1987 *WW*, p. 90; the Morse pangram is cited therein.

[If abbreviations are allowed...] Philip Cohen, "Kickshaws (Using Up the Alphabet)," Nov. 1979 *WW*, p. 237; "Colloquy," May 1992 *WW*, p. 83.

[If one regards...] A. Ross Eckler, "3,330 Pangrams," Nov. 1983 *WW*, p. 234.

[A one-word pangram...] A. Ross Eckler, "The Syndrome," May 1987 *WW*, p. 120.

[The concepts of pangram...] A. Ross Eckler, "Pangram Variations," Feb. 1977 *WW*, p. 41.

[If all words must...] A. Ross Eckler, "Pangram Variations," Feb. 1977 *WW*, p. 41; "Colloquy," Feb. 1991 *WW*, p. 24, and Feb. 1994 *WW*, p. 23.

[Pangrams can be embedded...] "Query," Feb. 1970 *WW*, p. 53; A. Ross Eckler, "Pangram Variations," Feb. 1977 *WW*, p. 41

28   [The pangrammatic window...] "Colloquy," Feb. 1988 *WW*, p. 26; "Colloquy," Feb. 1984 *WW*, p. 30.

[The probability that...] Ralph Beaman, "The Pangrammatic Window," Aug. 1972 *WW*, p. 160; David Silverman, "Kickshaws (More on the Pangrammatic Window)," Feb. 1974 *WW*, p. 50.

29   [Words can be classified...] Dmitri Borgmann, "An Overview of Isograms," Feb. 1974 *WW*, p. 33; Jeff Grant, "Pair and Trio Isograms," Aug. 1982 *WW*, p. 136; "Colloquy," Aug. 1973 *WW*, p. 156; Darryl Francis, "A Fourteen-Letter Pair Isogram," Aug. 1971 *WW*, p. 136; Dmitri Borgmann, "Long Isograms (Part 2)," Aug. 1985 *WW*, p. 140.

[Pyramid words contain...] A. Ross Eckler, "Tennessee's Sleeveless Pepperette," May 1982 *WW*, p. 125; Howard Bergerson, "Kickshaws (The Pangrammatic Pyramid)," Aug. 1980 *WW*, p. 176.

[To give an idea...] A. Ross Eckler, "Letter-Distributions of Words," Nov. 1974 *WW*, p. 205.

Chapter Three

31   [A logologist, like a...] Edgar N. Gilbert, "The Digrams of Webster's Unabridged Dictionary," Nov. 1969 *WW*, p. 215; A. Ross Eckler, "676 Bigrams," Nov. 1982 *WW*, p. 215; "Colloquy," Aug. 1993 *WW*, p. 154, and Feb. 1994 *WW*, p. 24.

[For trigrams or tetragrams...] A. Ross Eckler, "Complete Tetragram Permutations," May 1984 *WW*, p. 125; Tom Pulliam, "More Tetragram Permutations," Aug. 1984 *WW*, p. 176; for a trigram collection, A. Ross Eckler, "A Dictionary of Common English Trigrams," Aug. 1969 *WW*, p. 166, Nov. 1969 *WW*, p. 245, Nov. 1970 *WW*, p. 253.

[Perhaps the best-known...] George H. Scheetz, "In Goodly Gree: With Goodwill," Nov. 1989 *WW*, p. 195; Murray Pearce, "Who's Flaithbhertach MacLoingry?" Feb. 1990 *WW*, p. 6; Harry Partridge, "Gypsy Hobby Gry," Feb. 1990 *WW*, p. 9; A. Ross Eckler, "-Gry Words in the *OED*," Nov. 1992 *WW*, p. 253; "Colloquy," May 1995 *WW*, p. 83; for *ulgry*, Harry Partridge, "Ad Memoriam Demetrii," Aug. 1986 *WW*, p. 131; George H. Scheetz, "Captain Smith's Vlgrie," May 1987 *WW*, p. 84.

32   [There are only a handful...] Faith W. Eckler, "On Searching for Three-L Lamas," Nov. 1969 *WW*, p. 203; "Colloquy," Feb. 1970 *WW*, p. 17.

[What about letters...] Jeff Grant, "Consecutive Identical Letters," Aug. 1981 *WW*, p. 154.

[Figure 32a presents a collection...] A (Nyr Indictor), "Kickshaws," Feb. 1994 *WW*, p. 46; B, C (Joan Griscom), "Kickshaws," Feb. 1978 *WW*, p. 44; D (David Norman), *Logophile* (vol. 3, no. 1), reprinted in "Colloquy," Nov. 1979 *WW*, p. 214; E, F (Joan Griscom), "Kickshaws," Feb. 1978 *WW*, p. 44; I, J, K (Alan Frank), "Colloquy," Aug. 1980 *WW*, p. 152; L (David Morice), "Kickshaws," Aug. 1986 *WW*, p. 168; O (Alan Frank), "Colloquy," Aug. 1980 *WW*, p. 152; P (Joan Griscom), "Kickshaws," Feb. 1978 *WW*, p. 44; S (Dave Glew) *Logophile* (vol. 2, no. 5) reprinted in "Colloquy," May 1979 *WW*, p. 91.

33   [It is difficult to...] A. Ross Eckler, "The Mathematics of Words," Nov. 1983 *WW*, p. 252; "Colloquy," Feb. 1984 *WW*, p. 26; Ralph Beaman, "Alternating Monotonies," May 1971 *WW*, p. 77.

34 [There are 3276 ways...] Leslie Card and A. Ross Eckler, "Words Having Three Rare Letters," Aug. 1972 *WW*, p. 162; "Colloquy," May 1982 *WW*, p. 84.

[Logologists have also collected...] Dmitri Borgmann, "The Multiple-Letter Word Hunt," Feb. 1969 *WW*, 53; Darryl Francis, "More Multiple-Letter Words," Nov. 1970 *WW*, p. 252; Chris Cole and A. Ross Eckler, "Letter Repetition in Web 3," Feb. 1995 *WW*, p. 35.

[It is possible to...] A. Ross Eckler, "All Letter-Orders in a Word," Nov. 1984 *WW*, p. 252.

[There are a handful...] Dmitri Borgmann, "Three Miraculous Solutions," Feb. 1985 *WW*, p. 40.

35 [In the preceding sections...] A. Ross Eckler, "Must You Join the Queue?" May 1976 *WW*, p. 113; Dan Tilque, "The End of the Word: J," Nov. 1992 *WW*, p. 249.

[Acrostic dictionaries were compiled...] Darryl Francis, "Beginnings and Endings," Nov. 1971 *WW*, p. 195; Leslie Card, "More Beginnings and Endings," Feb. 1972 *WW*, p. 40.

[The acrostic type-collection...] Darryl Francis, "Word Chains," Feb. 1970 *WW*, p. 32.

36 [Palindromes and tautonyms...] Leslie Card and A. Ross Eckler, "Palindromic Letter-Sequences," Feb. 1974 *WW*, p. 24; A. Ross Eckler, "Internal Tautonyms," Feb. 1980 *WW*, p. 39.

[One can extend the...] Edward R. Wolpow, "Falalalala-lala-la-la," Feb. 1982 *WW*, p. 13; "Colloquy," May 1980 *WW*, p. 88, Aug. 1981 *WW*, p. 152.

[The book *Combinatorics on Words*...] A. Ross Eckler, "The Mathematics of Words," Nov. 1983 *WW*, p. 252.

Chapter Four

41 [The longest chain...] Dmitri Borgmann, "The Letter Subtraction Championship," Nov. 1973 *WW*, p. 210; "*Games* Magazine Logological Competitions," Aug. 1980 *WW*, p. 159; Chris Cole, "Word Records from Webster's Third," May 1990 *WW*, p. 81; other articles on beheadments and curtailments include Ralph Beaman, "Beheadments," Nov. 1973 *WW*, p. 198, and "Curtailed Curtailments," Feb. 1976 *WW*, p. 62.

[David Silverman introduced...] David Silverman, "Kickshaws (More Contributions)," Aug. 1971 *WW*, p. 169; David Silverman, "Kickshaws (Charitable and Hospitable Words)," Feb. 1972 *WW*, p. 53.

[Successive deletions and insertions...] A. Ross Eckler, "Insertion-Deletion Networks," Aug. 1987 *WW*, p. 168.

[The calculation of the...] Leonard Gordon, "More Insertion-Deletion Networks," Feb. 1991 *WW*, p. 19.

42 [If one considers words...] *mates*, "Colloquy," Aug. 1979 *WW*, p. 153.

[Many words, of course...] *tprw*, "Colloquy," Aug. 1979 *WW*, p. 153.

[David Silverman called...] A. Ross Eckler, "Word Networks (Part 2)," Aug. 1973 *WW*, p. 156; David Silverman, "Kickshaws (A Seven-Letter Onalosi)," Feb. 1972 *WW*, p. 54.

[David Morice rechristened...] David Morice, "Kickshaws (Friendly, Friendlier and Friendliest Words)," Feb. 1992 *WW*, p. 47; David Morice,

"Kickshaws (Friendlier Words)," Aug. 1992, *WW*, p. 173; David Morice, "Kickshaws (Friendlier, Friendliest)," Nov. 1992 *WW*, p. 239; David Morice, "Kickshaws (Friendlier Words Than Ever)," May 1993 *WW*, p. 113.

[By successively changing each...] A. Ross Eckler, "Word Networks (Part 2)," Aug. 1973 *WW*, p. 156; Kyle Corbin, "Minimal Word Ladders," May 1988 *WW*, p. 103; "Colloquy," Aug. 1988 *WW*, p. 148.

[Two words that can be...] A. Ross Eckler, "Word Networks (Part 1)," May 1973 *WW*, p. 67, and "Word Networks (Part 2)," Aug. 1973 *WW*, p. 156.

[As the word length...] Leonard Gordon, "Word Network Spans in the *OSPD*," Feb. 1989 *WW*, p. 28.

[Dmitri Borgmann once asserted...] A. Ross Eckler, "Word-Pairs Differing in a Single Letter," May 1969 *WW*, p. 70.

[A minimum-length pangrammatic...] Leonard Gordon, "Minimum-Length Pangrammatic Ladders," May 1990 *WW*, p. 125; "Colloquy," Nov. 1990 *WW*, p. 215.

43　[How does a network...] Leonard Gordon and A. Ross Eckler, "The Growth of a Word Network," May 1989 *WW*, p. 76.

[The span of the...] Leonard Gordon, "Word Network Spans in the *OSPD*," Feb. 1989 *WW*, p. 28; Leonard Gordon, "Four-Letter Word Network Update," May 1991 *WW*, p. 81.

[In constructing word ladders...] A. Ross Eckler and Leonard Gordon, "The Structure of a Word Network," Aug. 1989 *WW*, p. 141; Leonard Gordon, "Four-Letter Word Network Update," May 1991 *WW*, p. 81.

[The study of subnetworks...] A. Ross Eckler, "A Maximal Spanning Tree," Aug. 1994 *WW*, p. 166; "Colloquy," Feb. 1995 *WW*, p. 23.

44　[The longest word strings...] Roger Hannahs, "A Word Stair Contest," Feb. 1979 *WW*, p. 36; Tom Pulliam, "Word Strings," May 1979 *WW*, p. 119.

[The easiest way to...] Tom Pulliam, "Word Strings," May 1979 *WW*, p. 119; "Colloquy," Aug. 1979 *WW*, p. 152.

[Word strings can be generalized...] Christopher McManus, "Ana-Gram-Mar Chains," Nov. 1990 *WW*, p. 248; Leonard Gordon, "Roller-Coaster Word Chains," Nov. 1992 *WW*, p. 231.

[Word strings and word rings...] A. Ross Eckler, "Directed Word Chains (Part 1)," Aug. 1991 *WW*, p. 154; Leonard Gordon, "Directed Word Chains (Part 2)," Aug. 1991 *WW*, p. 159; Leonard Gordon, "Directed Word Chains (Part 3)," Nov. 1991 *WW*, p. 228; Leonard Gordon, "A Survey of Directed Word Chains," Feb. 1993 *WW*, p. 40.

[This terminology can be confusing...] A. Ross Eckler, "A Word String Network," May 1991 *WW*, p. 76.

45　[Networks in which each...] A. Ross Eckler, "Directed Word Chains (Part 1)," Aug. 1991 *WW*, p. 154; Leonard Gordon, "Directed Word Chains (Part 2)," Aug. 1991 *WW*, p. 159; Leonard Gordon, "Directed Word Chains (Part 3)," Nov. 1991 *WW*, p. 228.

46　[The number of different...] David Silverman, "Kickshaws (Anagram Classification)," Feb. 1971 *WW*, p. 54; David Silverman, "Kickshaws (Anagram Classification II)," Aug. 1971 *WW*, p. 169; A. Ross Eckler, "Six-Letter Transposals," Nov. 1977 *WW*, p. 201; "Colloquy," May 1978 *WW*, p. 88; five-letter anagrams are covered in A. Ross Eckler, "An Anagram Classification System," May 1970 *WW*, p. 24.

[If a transformation is...] A. Ross Eckler, "Transposition Rings," Aug. 1982 *WW*, p. 147; J. A. Lindon, "Note on Repeated Letter-Shuffling," Aug. 1971 *WW*, p. 161.

[The subject of multiple...] John McClellan, "Multiple Anagrams," Feb. 1971 *WW*, p. 3.

[If any English-language dictionary...] Dmitri Borgmann, "The Ultimate Adventure (Part 1)," Aug. 1976 *WW*, p. 131; Dmitri Borgmann, "The Ultimate Adventure (Part 2)," Nov. 1976 *WW*, p. 216; Jeff Grant, "The AEGINRST Transposal (Part 1)," Feb. 1994 *WW*, p. 3; Jeff Grant, "The AEGINRST Transposal (Part 2)," May 1994 *WW*, p. 89; Jeff Grant, "Transposing Rates," Nov. 1987 *WW*, p. 195.

[Long transpositions in the...] "Colloquy," Feb. 1984 *WW*, p. 29; A. Ross Eckler, "Long Well-Mixed Transposals," Feb. 1976 *WW*, p. 20; A. Ross Eckler, "Sixteen-Letter Transposal Pairs," Feb. 1981 *WW*, p. 60.

[There are four well-mixed...] A. Ross Eckler, "Long Well-Mixed Transposals," Feb. 1976 *WW*, p. 20; "Colloquy," May 1976 *WW*, p. 85, and May 1978 *WW*, p. 89.

[Using a slightly more...] Kyle Corbin, "Beyond Long Nontrivial Transposals," May 1989 *WW*, p. 100.

[The transposability of a word...] Darryl Francis and A. Ross Eckler, "Word Transposability," Nov. 1978 *WW*, p. 198.

[Long words often cannot...] "Query," May 1971 *WW*, p. 109.

[If dictionary phrases are...] "Colloquy," Feb. 1981 *WW*, p. 24, and "Colloquy," Aug. 1981 *WW*, p. 151.

47 [There are a handful of...] Ravenscroft J. Cloudesley (Dmitri Borgmann), "Triumphal Transposals," May 1981 *WW*, p. 93; "Colloquy," Feb. 1981 *WW*, p. 23, and Aug. 1981 *WW*, p. 151.

[The advent of national...] A. Ross Eckler, "Gary Gray, Meet Edna Dean," May 1986 *WW*, p. 109; A. Ross Eckler, "Updating Gary Gray and Edna Dean," Nov. 1995 *WW*, p. 250.

[David Silverman called...] David Silverman, "Kickshaws (Challenges)," Aug. 1974 *WW*, p. 176.

48 [Anagrams have been a part...] A. Ross Eckler, "Presidential Anagrams," Feb. 1977 *WW*, p. 3.

[Transpositional poetry...] David Silverman, "Kickshaws (Washington Recrosses the Delaware)," Aug. 1971 *WW*, p. 172; David Shulman, "Anagrams, Anyone?" May 1987 *WW*, p. 69.

[Letter-by-letter transpositions...] Howard Bergerson, "A Whitman Echo," May 1971 *WW*, p. 83; Martin Gardner, "Pied Poetry," May 1973 *WW*, p. 98; Ben Rogers (Howard Bergerson) and J. A. Lindon, "Some Neglected Ways of Words," Feb. 1969 *WW*, p. 14; J. A. Lindon, "The Vocabularyclept Poem, No. 1," Aug. 1969 *WW*, p. 85; Howard Bergerson and A. Ross Eckler, "Three Poems from One Fountain," Aug. 1970 *WW*, p. 139; A. Ross Eckler, "Crazy California," May 1975 *WW*, p. 126.

49 [What is the longest...] "Colloquy," Aug. 1982 *WW*, p. 153; A. Ross Eckler, "Word Roots and Branches," Aug. 1979 *WW*, p. 141; Kyle Corbin, "Two New Transdeletion Pyramids," May 1988 *WW*, p. 75.

[Will Shortz cited a...] Will Shortz, "Kickshaws (German Word-Building)," May 1986 *WW*, p. 113.

[Long transdeletions often involve...] A. Ross Eckler, "Word Roots and Branches," Aug. 1979 *WW*, p. 141; Kyle Corbin, "Beyond Long Nontrivial Transposals," May 1987 *WW*, p. 100.

[In general, there are many...] A. Ross Eckler, "Olympic Roots and Branches," Aug. 1984 *WW*, p. 142.

[Among all words of...] A. Ross Eckler, "Is a Picture Worth 1000 Words?" Nov. 1980 *WW*, p. 236.

[It has been said ...] A. Ross Eckler, "Is a Picture Worth 1000 Words?" Nov. 1980 *WW*, p. 236; Jeff Grant, "Piaster Resistance," May 1981 *WW*, p. 103.

[To perform an alphabetic...] Jeff Grant, "Alphabetic Transadditions," May 1980 *WW*, p. 102; Alan Frank, "Transaddable Letter Groups," Feb. 1984 *WW*, p. 37.

[Substitute-letter transpositions...] Kyle Corbin, "Beyond Long Nontrivial Transposals," May 1989 *WW*, p. 100.

[The December 1984/January 1985 *Games*...] Rod P. Selden (Dmitri Borgmann), "In Search of Perfection," Nov. 1984 *WW*, p. 195; Kyle Corbin, "Subtransposals from A to Z," Nov. 1985 *WW*, p. 220.

Chapter Five

51 [The two-Z barrier...] Philip Cohen, "What's the Good Word?," Nov. 1978 *WW*, p. 195.

[Names have always...] A. Ross Eckler, "The Terminal Man," Aug. 1974 *WW*, p. 180.

52 [This problem has been...] A. Ross Eckler, "Undominated Alphabetic Sequences," May 1982 *WW*, p. 77.

[Figure 52d is an amusing...] George J. Levenbach, "Who Says *A* Must Say *B*," Aug. 1985 *WW*, p. 135.

53 [This topic of alphabetic...] "Colloquy," Nov. 1979 *WW*, p. 218; Howard Bergerson, "Kickshaws (The Panalphabetic Window)," Aug. 1980 *WW*, p. 177.

[Language purists...] A. Ross Eckler, "Scrambled Alphabets in Word-Lists," Aug. 1988 *WW*, p. 145; "Query," Nov. 1984 *WW*, p. 209.

54 [Many of the letters...] A. Ross Eckler, "Nixon and the Bee," Aug. 1976 *WW*, p. 143.

[If near-homonyms...] A. Ross Eckler, "Alphabet Stories," May 1981 *WW*, p. 85; "Colloquy," Aug. 1981 *WW*, p. 153.

55 [There are a handful...] A. Ross Eckler, "Can You Dig For The Nub?," Nov. 1978 *WW*, p. 246; "Colloquy," Feb. 1979 *WW*, p. 22.

[Six-letter words...] A. Ross Eckler, "Can You Dig For The Nub?," Nov. 1978 *WW*, p. 246.

[Eugene Ulrich sorts...] Eugene Ulrich, "Vicinals and Non-Vicinals," Aug. 1983 *WW*, p. 175.

[What is the longest...] "Colloquy," Feb. 1984 *WW*, p. 28.

[Philip Cohen has...] Philip Cohen, "Kickshaws (Joining the Alphabet)," Nov. 1979 *WW*, p. 236.

[A related word classification...] A. Ross Eckler, "Alphabetical Patterns," Feb. 1993 *WW*, p. 9.

56 [It has been known...] A. Ross Eckler, "Alphabetic Letter-Shifts," Nov. 1979 *WW*, p. 243; Leonard Gordon, "Letter-Shift Words in the *OSPD*," Feb. 1990 *WW*, p. 59.

[Contrarily, one can...] David Morice, "Kickshaws (Non-Lettershift Pairs)," May 1990 *WW*, p. 110.

[How many of the...] Charles Bostick, "Kickshaws (Collinear Words)," Nov. 1984 *WW*, p. 233; Leonard Gordon, "Collinear Words," Aug. 1992 *WW*, p. 142.

[*Halfway words,* so...] Christopher McManus, "Halfway Words," Feb. 1992 *WW*, p. 13.

[The related concept of...] Alice Gorki and Dimitri Miller (Howard Bergerson), "Sea-changed Words," Feb. 1969 *WW*, p. 24; Tom Pulliam, "Shiftgrams," Feb. 1980 *WW*, p. 22; "Colloquy," May 1980 *WW*, p. 88.

57 [To illustrate this game...] J. Q. Xixx (Dimitri Borgmann), "Four-Letter Words," May 1974 *WW*, p. 73; "Colloquy," May 1975 *WW*, p. 86.

[In contrast, it is easy...] David Silverman, "Kickshaws (More Contributions)," Aug. 1971 *WW*, p. 170.

[Another reason for...] A. Ross Eckler, "Alphabet Rings of Trigrams," Aug. 1977 *WW*, p. 189.

[The inverse problem...] "Colloquy," Nov. 1978 *WW*, p. 215.

[Alan Frank used...] Alan Frank, "A Friendly Alphabet," May 1982 *WW*, p. 93.

[David Silverman issued...] David Silverman, "Kickshaws (Challenge)," May 1973 *WW*, p. 111; David Silverman, "Kickshaws (The Challenge of the Permuted Alphabet)," Aug. 1973 *WW*, p. 172.

[For what letter-arrangement...] A. Ross Eckler, "Scrambled Alphabets in Word-Lists," Aug. 1988 *WW*, p. 145.

58 [Words having the same product...] Alice Gorki and Dimitri Miller (Howard Bergerson), "Sea-changed Words," Feb. 1969 *WW*, p. 24; "Colloquy," Feb. 1988 *WW*, p. 18.

[Obviously, there are...] Faith W. Eckler, "Lucky Nines," May 1979 *WW*, p. 98.

[If words are classified...] Anonymous, "Extending Francis," Aug. 1995 *WW*, p. 154; Darryl Francis, "Lightweights and Heavyweights," Nov. 1972 *WW*, p. 226; Susan Thorpe, "New Lightweights and Heavyweights," Nov. 1995 *WW*, p. 253.

[*Gematria* is the study...] Barry Chamish, "Is English Gematria?," Nov. 1989 *WW*, p. 228.

[In *Beyond Language*...] "Query," Nov. 1970 *WW*, p. 231; A. Ross Eckler, "Difference Words," Aug. 1971 *WW*, p. 139; Tom Pulliam, "Difference Words Ride Again," Aug. 1975 *WW*, p. 163; "Colloquy," Nov. 1979 *WW*, p. 216.

[Charles Bostick proposed...] Charles Bostick, "Kickshaws (Can Do Words)," Feb. 1977 *WW*, p. 47; "Colloquy," Nov. 1979 *WW*, p. 216.

59 [A balanced word...] Susan Thorpe, "Balanced Words," Nov. 1994 *WW*, p. 206.

[The centrally balanced beam word...] J. A. Lindon, "CBB Words," Feb. 1969 *WW*, p. 37.

[A different type of...] Darryl Francis, "Numerical Tautonyms," Feb. 1970 *WW*, p. 10; Leslie Card, "Six-Letter Numerical Tautonyms," Nov. 1970 *WW*, p. 244.

Chapter Six

61 [It can be argued...] Dmitri Borgmann, "Palindromes: The Rotas Square," Nov. 1979 *WW*, p. 195; Dmitri Borgmann, "Palindromes: The Rotas Prehistory," Feb. 1980 *WW*, p. 11; Harry Partridge, "The Sator Square Revisited," Feb. 1980 *WW*, p. 17.

[Because of the immense...] Douglas McIlroy, "7×7 Computer-Generated Word Squares," Nov. 1975 *WW*, p. 195; Douglas McIlroy, "6-by-6 Double Word Squares," May 1976 *WW*, p. 80.

[Dmitri Borgmann presented...] Dmitri Borgmann, "100 Quality 6-by-6 Word Squares," Feb. 1987 *WW*, p. 5; Dmitri Borgmann, "More Quality Word Squares," Feb. 1988 *WW*, p. 15.

[Only one single-dictionary eight-square...] Eric Albert and Chris Long, "Eight-Squares in Webster's Second," Aug. 1992 *WW*, p. 147; Murray Pearce, "Kickshaws (Word Squares)," Nov. 1986 *WW*, p. 234; Jeff Grant, "Two Hundred Eight-Squares?" May 1988 *WW*, p. 80.

[The first nine-square...] Eric Albert, "The Best 9×9 Square Yet," Nov. 1991 *WW*, p. 195.

[Relatively few double eight-squares...] Jeff Grant, "Double Word Squares," Feb. 1992 *WW*, p. 9.

[The search for a ten-square...] Dmitri Borgmann, "A 100-Letter Word Square," Aug. 1973 *WW*, p. 151; Dmitri Borgmann, "A New 100-Letter Word Square," Nov. 1973 *WW*, p. 248; Darryl Francis, "A Ten-Letter Tautonym List," Nov. 1982 *WW*, p. 241.

[Can a nontautonymic ten-square...] Jeff Grant, "Ars Magna: The Ten-Square," Nov. 1985 *WW*, p. 195; Jeff Grant, "In Search of the Ten-Square," Nov. 1990 *WW*, p. 195; a coined eleven-square is given in Jeff Grant, "Quasi Eleven-Squares," May 1987 *WW*, p. 67; a humorous example of a fifteen-square is given in Edward R. Wolpow, "A Ziticorumbatous 15-Square," May 1981 *WW*, p. 91.

[Douglas McIlroy used the computer...] Douglas McIlroy, "7×7 Computer-Generated Word Squares," Nov. 1975 *WW*, p. 195; Chris Long, "Mathematics of Square Construction," Feb. 1993 *WW*, p. 5.

[The real usefulness of...] A. Ross Eckler, "How Many Words Support a Square?" May 1992 *WW*, p. 67; "Colloquy," Aug. 1992 *WW*, p. 157.

[Chris Long developed...] Chris Long, "Mathematics of Square Construction," Feb. 1993 *WW*, p. 5.

[The experimental support...] Chris Long, "Mathematics of Square Construction," Feb. 1993 *WW*, p. 5; Leonard Gordon, "Word-Square Support: Part 1," Aug. 1993 *WW*, p. 183.

[On the other hand...] Leonard Gordon, "Word-Square Support: Part 2," Nov. 1993 *WW*, p. 245.

[A surprising prediction...] "Colloquy," May 1993 *WW*, p. 82.

62 [An early, but imperfect...] Jeff Grant, "Cubism Revisited," Aug. 1978 *WW*, p. 156; Jeff Grant, "More Word Cubes," May 1979 *WW*, p. 76.

[One can define "cubes"...] Darryl Francis, "From Square to Hyperhypercube," Aug. 1971 *WW*, p. 147.

[A second variation...] Jeff Grant, "Word Squares Using More Letters," Feb. 1980 *WW*, p. 30; "Engineers at Play," Nov. 1974 *WW*, p. 227.

[It is theoretically possible...] Jeff Grant, "More Word Cubes," May 1979 *WW*, p. 76.

[A square that uses...] Jeff Grant, "Word Squares Using Many Letters," Feb.

1980 *WW*, p. 30; for a humorous example, Jeff Grant, "A Pangrammatic Six-Square?" May 1993 *WW*, p. 86.

[A cyclic square...] Leonard Gordon, "A (5,4) Word Chain Network," May 1994 *WW*, p. 119.

[A transposition square...] Philip Cohen, "Kickshaws (Transforming the Form)," Nov. 1979 *WW*, p. 240; A. Ross Eckler, "Single and Double Transposal Squares," May 1980 *WW*, p. 72.

[The compound word square...] Harry Partridge, "Word-Crossed Characters," May 1981 *WW*, p. 67; A. Ross Eckler, "Compound Word Squares," May 1981 *WW*, p. 74.

63 [These word groups...] Robert Cass Keller (A. Ross Eckler), "The Thirteen Words," May 1972 *WW*, p. 78; "Colloquy," Aug. 1972 *WW*, p. 143; A. Ross Eckler, "The Twenty-One Words," Nov. 1975 *WW*, p. 250.

[Further word groups...] A. Ross Eckler, "Word Groups with Mathematical Structure," Nov. 1968 *WW*, p. 212; A. Ross Eckler, "Word Groups," May 1977 *WW*, p. 85; the largest Baltimore transdeletion in Webster's Third is given in Chris Cole, "Word Records from Webster's Third," May 1990 *WW*, p. 85; see also John Holgate, "Transdeletion Nests in Chambers," Feb. 1989 *WW*, p. 58.

[The first four word groups...] J. A. Lindon, "The Seven Sixes Problem," May 1972 *WW*, p. 67; "Colloquy," May 1972 *WW*, p. 81.

[These four groups are...] A. Ross Eckler, "Word Groups with Mathematical Structure," Nov. 1968 *WW*, p. 212; A. Ross Eckler, "Levine's Isomorph Dictionary," Feb. 1972 *WW*, p. 3.

[This trick can be expanded...] Christopher McManus, "Goose Thighs Rehashed," May 1994 *WW*, p. 97.

[There are other ways...] A. Ross Eckler, "A Card Trick Mnemonic Revisited," Aug. 1994 *WW*, p. 185.

[Ted Clarke devised yet another...] "Colloquy," Nov. 1994 *WW*, p. 221.

64 [If two words of the same...] David Silverman, "Kickshaws (Crash)," Aug. 1969 *WW*, p. 185.

[How large a list...] David Silverman, "Kickshaws (Non-Crashing Word Lists)," May 1972 *WW*, p. 107; A. Ross Eckler, "Word Networks (Part 1)," May 1973 *WW*, p. 67; A. Ross Eckler, "Word Networks (Part 2)," Aug. 1973 *WW*, p. 156.

[Noncrashing word lists...] Jeff Grant, "Non-Crashing Word Sets," May 1982 *WW*, p. 95.

[The four three-letter words...] A. Ross Eckler, "Symmetric Crash Groups," Nov. 1978 *WW*, p. 230.

65 [Various word groups can be...] A. Ross Eckler, "Platonic Relationships," Feb. 1980 *WW*, p. 9.

66 [Three symmetric patterns...] A. Ross Eckler, "Three-Letter Hex-Words," May 1980 *WW*, p. 124.

[Similarly, triangles can be...] A. Ross Eckler, "Words on Triangular Pavements," Feb. 1983 *WW*, p. 32.

[Squares represent the third...] "Colloquy," Aug. 1980 *WW*, p. 151.

67 [In the Pocket Merriam-Webster...] A. Ross Eckler, "Dudeney's Lost Word-Puzzle," Aug. 1986 *WW*, p. 146.

68 [The Thirty-seven different presidential...] Leonard Gordon, "The

Ultimate Presidential Rectangle?" Feb. 1994 *WW*, p. 63; the earliest *WW* example is Sam Harlan, "A Presidential Rectangle," May 1976 *WW*, p. 77.

[For a word-search grid…] A. Ross Eckler, "Word-Search Packing," Aug. 1994 *WW*, p. 147.

[However, this is so far…] Leonard Gordon, "A Challenge Answered," Nov. 1994 *WW*, p. 252.

[One can create an even denser…] A. Ross Eckler, "King's-Move Word Packing," May 1994 *WW*, p. 124.

[If one is restricted to…] Leonard Gordon, "Packing Words," May 1994 *WW*, p. 67.

Chapter Seven

[This chapter considers…] A. Ross Eckler, "One Million English Words," Aug. 1978 *WW*, p. 179.

71   [Robert Kurosaka combined…] David Silverman, "Kickshaws (The Barber in Disguise)," Aug. 1972 *WW*, p. 171; David Silverman, "Kickshaws (Autologicians at Play)," Nov. 1971 *WW*, p. 240.

[Lee Sallows is the author…] Lee Sallows, "In Quest of a Pangram (Part 1)," Feb. 1992 *WW*, p. 3; Lee Sallows, "In Quest of a Pangram (Part 2)," May 1992 *WW*, p. 74.

[Later, Sallows succeeded…] Lee Sallows, "Reflexicons," Aug. 1992 *WW*, p. 131.

[These are the only two…] Ibid.

72   [The number *four*…] "Colloquy," May 1972 *WW*, p. 80.

[Other languages have more…] "Multilingual Convergence," Feb. 1975 *WW*, p. 37.

73   [The number names *thousand*…] A. Ross Eckler, "Alphabetizing the Integers," Feb. 1981 *WW*, p. 18.

[As Figure 73a indicates…] "Colloquy," May 1981 *WW*, p. 87.

[If *eight* is the first…] Edward R. Wolpow, "Alphabetizing the Integers," Feb. 1980 *WW*, p. 55; "Colloquy," Aug. 1980 *WW*, p. 152; Edward R. Wolpow, "More About Number-Names," Aug. 1981 *WW*, p. 166.

74   [The longest number-name…] Edward R. Wolpow, "More About Number-Names," Aug. 1981 *WW*, p. 166.

[If the number-names are…] "Colloquy," Nov. 1981 *WW*, p. 215.

[The number-names from *one*…] Eugene Ulrich, "Kickshaws (Number-Names)," Aug. 1983 *WW*, p. 178; "Colloquy," Nov. 1983 *WW*, p. 218; Willard Espy, "Kickshaws (A Sequence of Pentagrams)," May 1987 *WW*, pp. 111, 128.

[The letters of *one*…] David Morice, "Kickshaws (Panoramic Number-Names)," Nov. 1994 *WW*, p. 243.

[Some number-names…] Darryl Francis, "Words into Numbers," Feb. 1977 *WW*, p. 37; "Colloquy," May 1987 *WW*, p. 82, and Aug. 1987 *WW*, p. 153.

[There is a small…] "Colloquy," May 1987 *WW*, p. 82.

[Figure 74d depicts an insertion-deletion…] A. Ross Eckler, "Insertion-Deletion Networks," Aug. 1987 *WW*, p. 168.

75   [A square of numbers…] Lee Sallows, "Alphamagic Squares," May 1991 *WW*, p. 70.

76 [If one sets *A*=1...] Edward R. Wolpow, "More About Number-Names," Aug. 1981 *WW*, p. 166; David Morice, "Kickshaws (Perfect Number Names in Neo-Alphabets)," Nov. 1989 *WW*, p. 238.

[Experimentation suggested that...] A. Ross Eckler, "38 Self-Descriptive Number Names," Feb. 1990 *WW*, p. 20.

[Lee Sallows generalized the...] Lee Sallows, "The New Merology," Feb. 1990 *WW*, p. 12; Lee Sallows, "Einschwein's Magic Numbers," Aug. 1991 *WW*, p. 165.

[In French, the number names...] Lee Sallows, "The New Merology," Feb. 1990 *WW*, p. 12; Lee Sallows, "Spanagrams," Feb. 1992 *WW*, p. 59; Lee Sallows, "Rare Maps for Collectors," Nov. 1993 *WW*, p. 204; Lee Sallows, "Rare Maps for Correctors," May 1994 *WW*, p. 126.

[How many number-names...] Leonard Gordon and A. Ross Eckler, "Answering the Sallows Challenge," May 1990 *WW*, p. 93.

77 [The number-system...] Philip Cohen, "Base 26," Feb. 1977 *WW*, p. 30; Lee Sallows, "Base 27: The Key to a New Gematria," May 1993 *WW*, p. 67.

Chapter Eight

81 [Two-letter words can...] David Morice, "The Alphabet Cube," May 1990 *WW*, p. 96.

82 [How should letters be...] A. Ross Eckler, "Word Worms," Aug. 1993 *WW*, p. 131.

83 [The word is a nonce-word...] Edward R. Wolpow, "Kickshaws (Volcanic Bulletin!)," Nov. 1982 *WW*, p. 234; "Colloquy," May 1983 *WW*, p. 93.

[The word was apparently created...] Chris Cole, "The Biggest Hoax," Nov. 1989 *WW*, p. 205.

[A slightly mangled version...] Edward R. Wolpow, "Pneumonoultramicrostuff," Nov. 1986 *WW*, p. 205; Chris Cole, "The Biggest Hoax," Nov. 1989 *WW*, p. 205.

[In the last three decades...] Dmitri Borgmann, "The Longest Word," Feb. 1968 *WW*, p. 33.

[By 1980, the champion...] A. Ross Eckler, "Superultramegalosesquipedalia," May 1980 *WW*, p. 117.

WORD WAYS

Word Ways was founded in 1968 at the suggestion of Martin Gardner and published for two years by Greenwood Periodicals; its first two editors were Dmitri Borgmann and Howard Bergerson. Finding it financially unprofitable, Greenwood sold the magazine in 1970 to the author, who since then has acted as editor and publisher with the aid of his wife as business and subscriptions manager. The journal appears four times a year in a 7×10-inch format with 64 pages per issue. It is available only from Spring Valley Road, Morristown, NJ 07960, for a subscription price of $20 per year (all back issues are still in print).

INDEX

ABOUT THE AUTHOR

A. Ross Eckler, born in Boston in 1927, received a B.A. from Swarthmore College and a Ph.D. in mathematics from Princeton University. For the next thirty years he worked as a statistician at Bell Telephone Laboratories. Besides wordplay, he has been a devotee of genealogy, hiking, caving, ballet, and human longevity (the evaluation of the truth of extreme age claims). He played a 47-bell church carillon for two decades of Sunday services, has led hikes to pre-Revolutionary mileposts along the New Jersey–New York boundary, and since retirement screened eyes for glaucoma using an air-puff tonometer, assisted elderly citizens with their tax returns, and helped maintain hiking trails in northern New Jersey.

Eckler first collected words as a lepidopterist collects butterflies. In college, he and his wife-to-be spent numerous evenings identifying three-way homonyms (*idol, idle, idyll*). In 1964, challenged by a list of 2,510 trigrams tabulated from 28,834 words by Fletcher Pratt in *Secret and Urgent,* he amassed a type-collection of six thousand different trigrams in words from Webster's Collegiate (*hAAF, lAAGer, ..., buZZWig, fuZZY*). Later that year, he responded to *Bible atlas goose thigh* in Martin Gardner's "Mathematical Games" column in *Scientific American,* generalizing this card-trick mnemonic to *lively rhythm muffin supper savant.* But it was not until he received his first copy of *Word Ways* in 1968 that he realized how wordplay, like mathematics or geology, could be made a legitimate subject for research and discovery. He sent in so many articles to the infant publication that Howard Bergerson, the editor when Greenwood decided to divest itself, suggested that he edit and publish *Word Ways* privately. The idea appealed as a retirement project, then twenty years away—but would he ever get another chance to take over an up-and-running logological journal?